GLOBALIZATION AND TERRITORIAL IDENTITIES

Globalization and Territorial Identities

Edited by

ZDRAVKO MLINAR
Professor of Sociology
Faculty of Social Sciences
University of Ljubljana

Avebury
Aldershot · Brookfield USA · Hong Kong · Singapore · Sydney

Published by
Avebury
Ashgate Publishing Limited
Gower House
Croft Road
Aldershot
Hants GU11 3HR
England

Ashgate Publishing Company
Old Post Road
Brookfield
Vermont 05036
USA

A CIP catalogue record for this book is available from the British Library and the US Library of Congress.

ISBN 1 85628 426 3

Printed in Great Britain by
Athenaeum Press Ltd, Newcastle upon Tyne.

Contents

Preface

The theme of this book was conceived before the most dramatic changes in Europe took place. Our main preoccupation however is to trace the long-term processes rather than to describe particular events. Nevertheless, two events which occurred in the course of the preparation of this volume should be mentioned: War in the Balkans and the Maastricht Treaty. They symbolize both the contradictory tendencies in the transformation of territorial social organization as well as the immediate relevance of our subject.

This book was begun in a country which had one identity, it was completed in another. Slovenia.

It is only very recently that sociology, following several other social science disciplines, has started to respond decisively to the radical changes in society which were conceptualized as the process of globalization. Thus we see a delayed response to what Wilbert Moore, as early as 1965, expressed as a call for a "global sociology" and as a consideration of "the world as a singular system". The most visible recent indication of this awakening interest was the general theme of the International Sociological Association's 12th World Congress of Sociology: "Sociology for One World: Unity and Diversity" (Madrid, 9-13 July, 1990). In spite of some warnings about the acceptability of the theme and the danger of following the practice of some international organizations - falling into the trap of nebulosity and becoming removed from empirical reality - the issue of globalization was readily accepted. However, at that time, further challenging questions were raised such as: "sociology for one world" - yes, but for which one - the first, the second or the third? The symptomatic response was: "unity and diversity".

Thus a framework was also established for researchers dealing with socio-spatial development and territorial political organization to hold a session on "Globalization, Technology and Territorial Identities" which took place within the Research Committee for Social Ecology of ISA. The complexity of the subject required a wide, multidisciplinary, contribution. In addition to sociologists dealing with "territorial communities", the participants also included geographers and political scientists dealing with local and world politics, and with international relations. Most of their contributions were widely open to relevant findings from other disciplines, even those outside the "main-stream" of social science. Thus they were trying to avoid the common practice of dealing with global processes within narrow, segmental cognitive frameworks.

This volume includes not only the selected papers from this session but also further contributions (paper by DiMuccio and Rosenau, and texts by Mlinar). The authors reflect the diversity of theoretical and conceptual approaches and also of the empirical references to countries such as the US, Canada, Great Britain, France, Italy and former Yugoslavia. However, they share a commonality of approach in interpreting certain basic dimensions of the subject. Both diversities and commonalities are more explicitly reviewed in the Introduction.

Several people took part in the preparation of this book to whom I owe my acknowledgements. I would like to thank all the contributing authors, and particularly Henry Teune, Raimondo Strassoldo and Chadwick Alger who aided greatly in the editing. My thanks to Adolf Bibič who commented my introductory chapter. I am especially grateful to Alan Duff, who not only contributed as an English language expert but shared with me his editorial experience as well.

I would also like to thank my own institutions, the Faculty of Social Sciences at the University of Ljubljana, the Institute of Social Sciences and the Center for Spatial Sociology which provided me the operational base and the requisite infrastructure. The administrative burden from the beginning to the end was patiently borne by Janja Zvonar, who deserves my special thanks. The Central Social Science Library Jože Goričar offered me much useful background support. Daniel Černe, a student of sociology, was helpful as well.

Ljubljana, June 1992 Editor

1 Introduction

Zdravko Mlinar

General points of departure

This volume focuses on the changes in the territorial organization of societies within the context of an emerging global civilization. It addresses one of the most puzzling and controversial subjects, both in social theory and in relation to policy alternatives, at the time of transition from modern to postmodern society. The issue concerns the changes which are decisively marked by the "communication revolution", and which have been variously described as "shrinking space", "time-space compression", or as a shift from the "space of places" to the "space of flows".[1] Within such a context, and thus considering "the process of shrinking the cushion of space and time that previously separated cultures and societies" (Ploman, 1984), we will try to identify the implications for the territorial, social and political organization which we inherited from the (pre-)industrial period.

From such a perspective we may find in social science that some authors are optimistically tracing the future with the notion of the "*world without borders*"[2] (Brown, 1973), pointing out the advance in the overcoming of space as a barrier. With the increasing flow of people, goods and ideas, however, it is becoming apparent that this emancipatory perspective is only one side of the coin. These flows, particularly if unbalanced and unidirectional, also appear as *intrusions* (see Alger in chapter 5), which may become threatening to the autonomy and identity of the territorial units affected.

Barriers and borders thus reveal their contradictory nature: eliminating the barrier means at the same time eliminating protection and thus increasing a group's or an individual's own vulnerability. Hence another perspective enters into social science and into policy considerations: "We are moving toward a *unified* world system with almost *frightening rapidity*, and it may be that one of the most important questions the human race will face in the next 100 years ... is how to preserve variety..." (Boulding, 1985).

The traditional territorial identities based on *contiguity, homogeneity*, and clearly (physically and socially) identifiable *borders* are now being threatened. Does this mean that we are approaching the end of territorial identities as such or is it more a question of their transformation and (re)construction?

With the decline of the exclusionary nature of the territorial units, and with the trend towards *ubiquity*, there is a transformation under way - which could be methaphorically designated as the transition from *identity as an island* to *identity as a cross-road*[3]. It is increasingly unlikely that a territorial unit can continue to *preserve* its distinctiveness on the basis of frontal insulation ("dissociation" or "de-linking"), while there is an increasing probability that distinctive identity may be *formed* as a unique crossroad in the flow of people, goods and ideas.

Identity, as an island, becomes all the more distinctive the more it is separated from the rest of the world (thus it is said that there would be no Italians without the Alps). The future of (territorial) distinctiveness however is - at least primarily - not in frontal separation but rather in selective association. It is only in this sense that we can understand the trend toward the increasingly flexible, diversified, individualized and (re)constructed territorial identities in the context of the readily accessible variety of the whole world. The greater the variety of characteristics which the unit (an individual or territorial community) acquires, the higher is the probability that it (he) will combine these characteristics in a unique way. Thus the units - in terms of their individual components - become more similar to an increasing number of other units. But the combination of these characteristics makes them different from others.

It is within the contours of this general interpretation that we shall try to search for a resolution of the controversy concerning globalization as homogenization and/or diversification. On the one hand, we see many interpretations of the present changes as a general trend towards world homogeneity, which implies that there is no place left for territorial distinctiveness and identity. On the other hand there is much "evidence" supporting the counter-arguments. The first is well expressed by Levitt and by Smith. Levitt (1983) maintains: "Now in all respects the world levels up in all places to world-standard commonality".[4] Smith (1990) similarly argues that the present "emerging global culture is tied to no place or period. It is contextless, a true melange of disparate components drawn from everywhere and nowhere, borne upon the modern chariots of global telecommunications systems."

Several other authors, argue for the continuing importance of local, regional or national differences and point to the resurgence of the assertion of territorial identities. Agnew (1987) disputes the theories of modernization which interpret the process as moving from diversity and particularity ("not to say barbarity") toward homogeneity. According to him: "Even in a world dominated by global division of labor, place maintains its significance... Common experiences engendered by the forces of 'nationalization' and 'globalization' are still mediated by local ones" (ibidem).

In a similar way a large number of diverging interpretations of the present changes at the local, regional and national level could be reviewed. Most often we find them in "peaceful coexistence", e.g. the ones concerning "community decline" and "renewed localism"; or "the destruction of regional cultures" and "revival of regionalism"; the "loss (obsoleteness) of the national autonomy" and its continuing importance or renewed assertion. Such "state of the art" clearly indicates of a need for a more comprehensive theoretical interpretation, enabling one to account for the contradictory nature of the underlying dynamics of restructuring and destructuring of territorial social organization. This volume is intended to take a further step in this direction.

In spite of the great complexity of the issues dealt with by the contributors to this book, we can nevertheless distinguish some major points. These will be briefly reviewed in this introduction under *the following topics*:

1) Firstly, the conceptualizations of the broadest theoretical framework are indicated as: the unity of opposites - of individuation and globalization (Mlinar), as tension between interdependence and sovereignty and "multidirectional shifts" (DiMuccio and Rosenau), as the relationship between globalism and localism (Strassoldo) or in terms of universalism and particularism (Larochelle).
2) Changes concerning the territorial basis of identity: This involves the process of deterritorialization (Mlinar), the changing functions of territory (Larochelle and others) or cases of emergence (Strassoldo) or erosion (Williams) of regional identities.
3) The third topic concerns the cross-level relationships, with emphasis on "local responses to global intrusions" (Alger) as well as on some more general questions of the - "zero sum" or "positive sum" - nature of these relationships (Teune), erosion of the territorial hierarchy (Mlinar, etc.).
4) Two of the contributors (Poche, Larochelle) draw attention to the different nature of politico-economic integration and of social identification. This represents a critique of the "mechanistic conception" of globality.
5) The fifth complex outlined in our introductory review concerns the transformation from given to (re-)constructed identities and some empirical manifestations of this, such as the "new localism" (Teune, Strassoldo and others).

1. The unity of opposites: inward and outward shifts

One of the common concerns of the contributors to this volume is, as already indicated, an understanding of the basic transformation of territorial social organization. This is not viewed as an unidirectional process of globalization (integration, homogenization or universalization), nor is this transformation taken simply as some form of cross-level "zero-sum" relationship, in the sense that the more power the larger territorial unit gains, the more the smaller units lose.[5] Although the contributors use different terminologies, they all avoid such a one-sided interpretation.

Mlinar[6] interprets the subject in the context of his paradigm of socio-spatial development. This refers to the unity of the opposing tendencies of change toward globalization (societalization) and individuation (increasing autonomy and distinctiveness) of groups and individuals within the emerging world society. The incompatibility of the two processes - in the sense that a step forward in one direction leads to retreat in the other - tends to diminish with decreasing amplitudes of zig-zag advances over time until they reach a point of qualitative transformation from incompatibility to mutuality. Thus the relationship between individuation and globalisation changes from one which can be understood in terms of a "zero-sum game" to one of "positive sum". Higher (global) interconnectedness increases the possibilities for higher individuation, and vice versa. And within such a transformation we can see some long term trends toward a (re-) constructed territorial as well as de-territorialized identities. The process of individuation multiplies and diversifies a number of autonomous, territorial and nonterritorial actors who gain more and more direct access to - and a possibility of authentic assertion of - their particular identity within the global (world) society.

Strassoldo argues that "post-modern man/woman, just because he /she is so deeply embedded in global information flows, may feel the need to revive small enclaves of familiarity, intimacy, security, intelligibility, organic-sensory interaction in which to mirror him/herself... The possibility of being exposed, through modern communication technology to a near infinity of places, persons, things, ideas, makes it all the more necessary to have a center in which to cultivate one's self. The easy access of the whole world, with just a little time and money, gives new meaning to a need for a subjective center - a home, a community, a locale - from which to move and to which to return and rest."

Following this interpretation of the bifurcation and contradictory polarization, Strassoldo approaches the problem of understanding why there are still some basic changes under way in evaluating localism and rootedness. While history may seem to have unfolded unilinearly and unidirectionally towards cosmopolitanism, universalism, and mobility, the traits of localism and rootedness have been considered backward or even reactionary. However, the more the countervailing forces have emerged, the more it has become clear that these were not simply phenomena of the past, and that there was a need for their re-evaluation.

DiMuccio and Rosenau focus on the somewhat more specific issue of the "loyalty shifts", but their main preoccupation is to interpret these as *multidirectional phenomena* - particularly as "*inward shifts*" - when loyalties are redirected toward subnational groups and institutions, and as "*outward shifts*" when loyalties are redirected toward supranational or transnational entities. They discuss this subject in the broader context of integrational and disintegrational changes in world politics and reflect upon the tension between the *interdependence and the sovereignty* of the state. The limitations of identification theory and neofunctionalist theory of loyalty shifts should be overcome by "turbulence theory" (Rosenau, 1990) which suggests multidirectional shifts. The argument of this theory is: "that instances of supranationalism and subgroupism are *outgrowths of the same global dynamics* that have led to the bifurcation of the system and the onset of pervasive authority crises". The aim of the authors is to explain the redirection of legitimacy sentiments in terms of the intersection of *interdependence* and the increasing *skills of individuals*. According to the authors "turbulence theory sees the *simultaneity* of integration and disintegration, fragmentation and aggregation, centralization and decentralization, not as a paradox but an expectation". [7]

Larochelle refers first to the disputed direction of the evolution of the world in terms of the integration or the incessant extreme differentiation of its components. He maintains that the recent appeasement of this dispute is less attributable to the victory of one school of argument over the other than "to their common inability to have *simultaneously* considered the *contradictory tendencies* that coexist synchronously...". Thus world-centred universalization, according to him, does not eliminate conflict but even gives rise to it, particularly in the sense of resistance to the threat of the leveling of characteristics on the basis of territorial belongingness. And thus "diversity reveals itself as a moment of unity". Here he also refers to Debray (1986): "The end of the universal bursts in the universal explosion of particularism". And thus our contributor argues that the idea of postmodernity may present the "process of recuperation and reinstatement of the value of *minority cultures* that modern imperialists sought rather to reject for the gain of the goal of global homogeneity".

The historical dimension, introduced by Strassoldo, complements this discussion by broadening the understanding of globality. He reminds us that just as the primitive societies tended to identify themselves with Mankind and the World, so too we find, at a later stage, an analogous tendency in Europe and the West to absolutize one of the particularities and assign to it the status of globality (universality).[8] This at the same time implies a change in the conception of globality from exclusionary homogeneity toward inclusiveness, encompassing the total diversity of world society. But this still raises many more questions, such as whether "one can be civilized in more than one way", whether shared core values are necessary, the question of tolerance of diversity.

2. The territorial basis of identity

Two defining criteria of any identity are: differentiation and continuity. These criteria have been extensively studied in terms of the identity of the individual. For example Baumeister (1986) has pointed out that "whatever differentiates one from others and makes one the same across time creates identity". In this volume more attention is paid to territorial bases of collective - cultural, ethnic, political and other - identities at the local, regional and national level.

Territorial identity has no meaning unless it is confronted and associated with dissimilarities in the present and the future (Bassand, 1990). It does not exist by itself, in isolation, but only through its distinction from and/or opposition to other territorial identities. "Like individuals, cities get to know what they are and what is distinctive about them from the unified observation of others" (Suttles, 1984). It is confrontation rather than sheer coexistence in space which contributes to the constitution of a particular identity. In other words: "The territorialization of the collectivities accompanies the synchronous construction of relations with others" (Sack, 1986). And Larochelle continues: "For that which unites contains also that which excludes". Existence of a barrier "simultaneously expresses the *interdependence of identity and of alternity*". Extended accessibility from new information, communication and transportation technology tends to intensify such confrontations at all the levels of territorial social organization.

Strassoldo, in his chapter, presents a typical basis for the formation of regional identity in the Italian context. The case of "Lega Lombarda", where regional identity feelings were converted into a political movement, could, at least partially, be explained, first in terms of the mounting hostility toward Southerners whose particularities had become increasingly more visible and who were therefore perceived as more directly threatening and, second, in terms of the confrontation with and hostility towards the oppressive Central state, for example parasitic bureaucracy, the Byzantine practices of the "Roman Parties", both of which are equally relevant to the explanation of the present war in Yugoslavia. The decline of the East - West confrontation in Europe led to a split in "the internal regimentation of the Italian masses into the two main parties", and thus, according to Strassoldo, "other basic divergences were free to emerge".

More generally territorial differentiation could be restated in terms of Peter Blau's (1977) "decomposition question": "how much of the society's differentiation occurs among and how much within substructures"? In his terminology, the above trend could be designated as "penetration of differentiation into substructures", and this implies that the criterion of differentiation between (wider) territorial units less and less defines their distinctive identity.

Williams shows how "the territorial basis of the Celtic cultures has been severely eroded during the present century". In Wales he notes that instead of the earlier clear linguistic divisions, today there are *many gradations* of Welshness. The transition is a movement from the "Welsh-speaking community" to "Welsh-speakers in the community", even within many parts of the former Welsh heartland. Theoretically, it is symptomatic to observe that "individuals are now *more autonomous*, seeking language contiguity *without* necessarily expecting that interaction to take place within *geographic contiguity*". We could (re)interpret this as a case of "disembedding" (Giddens, 1991), accompanying processes of individuation.

For Williams, the "land has become a new battle-ground wherein the conflict between the local and the universal, the indigenous and the exogenous interest groups becomes mediated". He points out that *territory* "is not only contextual, it is not only a scene for the playing out of socio-economic factors, it is itself a significant source of *symbolic and resource power*. Its possession and control is often deemed vital to the very survival of specific cultural groups". He shows how "territorially-rooted group identities are facing extreme pressures which serve to devalue place at many levels of spatial hierarchy"; he also warns against the possibility of abandoning the role of place and territory too readily in our analyses, rather than seeking to reformulate their influence.

Williams' focus is the analysis of ethno-territorial identity in an increasingly open and fluid environment. He addresses the question: "If the *territorial base* of Europe's lesser-used language communities *is being eroded*, does this necessarily presage their death?"[9] And this is part of the wider issue of the relationship between land, language and social context which he aims to clarify from the point of view of a transition from "place-centred geography" to a "transactional flow geography".

These questions are elaborated by Larochelle. He refers to the changing importance of the territorial dimensions of identity in the field of international relations and particularly in connection with the concept of interdependence. First, he offers the argument that: "spatial proximity constitutes the causa prima from which point the occurrence of multilateral ties have been able historically to rise in the interstices that separate human communities". Historically, the appropriation of a locality by a group creates the favorable conditions for social adherence which, through geographical demarcation, acquires the first symbol of its justification (Duchacek, 1986).

Larochelle points out that universal fraternities (Communism, Islamism or Christianism) "have been incapable of declassing the attachment of men to their piece of earth, certainly more and more fragmented, but no less effective symbolically". According to him, even some of the recent attempts to plead in favor of a world society have "proved themselves unable to transcend the territorial enclosures and the identifications that are being conducted on this basis". He concludes that the image of the "global village" is "only valid insofar that the global does not erase the village".

What here may be left as an open, issue is that even the "village" cannot be treated as a constant. Its transformation in the context of postmodernity and global civilization has to be explained. Even the "world civil society" conceived as a mosaic, rather then as a (single) unit, cannot be based on local cultures as homogeneous and *irreducible* fragments.

Despite the fact that many authors, such as John Bennett (cited by Alger in chapter 5), focus on "the incorporation of communities into larger and larger systems", it is now less and less a question of incorporating undifferentiated wholes, and increasingly a matter of incorporating the variety of their constituent parts which assume the character of autonomous actors in an expanded global context. Those who merely point out that local communities should not be treated as tribal isolates are sitting on the fence if they ignore the internal transformations of these units as well. Agnew (1987) has noted that space: "is increasingly divided into enclaves in which distinctive social groups carry on parts of their everyday lives in isolation". This is not however an absolute isolation but rather a disembedding of the group from its local environment, which at the same time implies involvement in wider or even global networks, which Teune and Strassoldo consider as one of the constitutive dimensions of the new localism.

3. Cross-level interpenetration: small communities and global issues

Another common concern shared by the contributors to this volume is reflected in the questions of multilevel analysis and cross-level relationships. Globalization, ipso facto places these questions in the forefront. Instead of the perspective in world systems theory that one level of analysis, of countries or states, is being *replaced* by another level (the world-economy) the current reality seems to be a changing range of levels of territorial organization.

Alger focuses on cross-level relationships; he does not follow mainstream social science, which has been very slow to recognize linkages between "*local places and world systems*". Instead he critically points out the tendency of research to deal with "societies", understood as synonymous with states. This implied that world relations were limited to relations between states/societies, excluding relationships among "local places". Even the recent interest in the impact of worldwide linkages among local places is still, he maintains, characterized by a one-way perspective: the influence of global on local levels.

Alger attempts to readjust this perspective by focusing on local involvement in global issues, on "the human being or small communities of human beings" as the "*ultimate actors*". He does not deny that global intrusions are more powerful than any possibility of local resistance. In addition, he demonstrates the implications of the bias of the uni-directional influence, which *ignores or underestimates* the potentials of active local response to global intrusions.

Alger also discusses examples of *local involvements* in *global issues*. He finds, for instance, that "dramatic changes are now taking place in the willingness of local people to become involved in foreign policy issues". Citizens have created a diversity of strategies for coping with global intrusions. They strive to implement universal human rights in their own communities as well as in remote places. Alger further reviews the "growth in efforts to put international issues on the agendas of city government and to put foreign policy questions before the electorate in local referenda". Thus we arrive at symptomatic *cross-level mixing*, such as may be seen in "municipal foreign policies" when local level governments deal with international issues.

In his comprehensive review of new forms of local activism Alger has demonstrated how "local people", instead of merely appealing to the higher level officials for changes in relationships with other countries, "have established their *own relationships* with people in cities abroad. In so doing they are significantly challenging traditional norms for the participation of local people in world affairs both by making the local community an arena of foreign policy action and by direct involvement abroad".[10]

Instead of the practice which was known in (former) Yugoslavia as "local autonomy concerning local issues", i.e. autonomy with marginalization, we now see a tendency toward local involvement in global issues. This is a manifestation of a general trend towards the *rapprochement* of levels of territorial organization, toward *local-global convergence* or even merger. Political movements could thus be seen, for example, from the Green perspective, as including both a worldwide movement and at the same time one which is responsive to "the human being or small communities of human beings ... (as) *the ultimate actors*" (Friberg and Hettne, 1982).

While Alger, in his overview of the relevant research, demonstrates the expanding range of cross-level linkages and interdependences, DiMuccio and Rosenau examine a particular case of narrow conceptualization. They point out the limitation of the theories of regional integration which ignore global developments and inward shifts.

They also argue that the "turbulence theory" has a "*multi-level quality*" because it demonstrates the interrelationships between "micro-" and "macro-level" factors in world politics and posits a "continuing process of dis-aggregation of whole systems and the aggregation of diverse sub-systems either within whole systems, around certain issues, or between whole systems".

This parallels Mlinar's presentation on the *erosion* of a rigid, multilevel *territorial hierarchy*, i.e. skipping over intermediate levels and the general trend toward local, individual, and global convergence. In spite of the predominance of one-way, global-local flows, this perspective provides an expanding space for the (re)construction of territorial identities.

The issue of "zero sum" relationships among loyalties related to different levels of territorial social organization is dealt with by Teune. What are the shifts of loyalties accompanying the increasing social and political fragmentation? Can the emergence of overlapping political entities, recently increasing in numbers, attract individual loyalties without diminishing previous ones or creating divided loyalties?

He argues that "individuals can have *multiple loyalties* and that these loyalties are being continuously reshaped". They are fluid and not necessarily hierarchically arranged. It has been established that claims for loyalty do not have to be exclusive. Limited claims may be a sufficient base upon which to begin building components of viable political units.

In addition to the fragmentation observed in the richest countries (new localism), Teune also observes that the present economic decline (Eastern Europe, Africa) leads to withdrawal and closure of the primordial niches of family, ethnicity and religion. "With decline, external intrusions are responded to as threatening. The consequence might be the breakup of larger political communities which have based their legitimacy on growth". If, however, the world is to experience long term growth into the next century, then the loyalties of the people can be distributed among the new entities *without loss* of the older ones.

4. Political-economic integration and social identification

While some contributing authors (DiMuccio and Rosenau, Strassoldo, Mlinar) point out that *the same dynamics* represents the ground for opposing processes, Poche argues that "territorial identity, following its own logic, develops along lines other than those of globalization". The archetypal models of globalization "are generally borrowed from phenomena connected with technology, communication and world markets" and this implies the unification of cultural phenomena and "the supremacy of attachment models which are *not* necessarily *territorial*". However, according to Poche, the problem with globalisation is not the disappearance of identificatory signs and contents. The material/functional process of globalisation and the interpretive processes, by which these are appropriated by individuals and groups "are of a different order..." He is rejecting the "neo-scientistic" thinking according to which globalization corresponds to the dissolution of social control in organizational management, and thus attempting to free us from the blindness of a "*mechanistic conception* of globality" and from a "millenarian" fear of the end of territorial identities. He sees no reason why "the territory of politico-economic integration and the territory of social identification" should coincide... They are not of *the same order*".

The fluctuations in territorial identification are much slower in their drift, satisfying quite different anthropological laws, than fluctuations in the spatial organization of political control. Poche's argument is supported by the "experiments" in Eastern Europe, showing that even 45 or 70 years of a new political organization were not enough to produce the change of some basic territorial identifications and the expected loyalty shifts. There is no trace of the new "Soviet man".

Poche challenges contributors who stress that globalization and individuation (autonomy, sovereignty, identity...) represent two sides of the same basic and contradictory dynamics of developmental change.

Even within the theory of economic rationality there are differences between the advocates of world (segmental) homogenization on the basis of the economies of scale (Levitt, 1983) and those arguing for increasing sensitivity towards the local differences - "When in Rome do as the Romans do ..." (Rosow, 1988). Larochelle, like Poche, argues that the awakening of different forms of political identification is by no means subordinated to the *determination* of "*the economic variable*".

The present changes in the Balkans, the former Soviet Union and elsewhere seem to support Larochelle's interpretation. The achievement of political independence turns out to be, at least in the short run, more important than any economic considerations, such as the losses of economies of scale, territorial division of labor, decline of tourism. The use of the Cyrillic script in Serbia (although not very consistent, in recent decades) has become an important symbol of allegiance to Serbian identity despite the technical inconvenience involved and the difficulty of communicating with the West.

What is not clear, however, are the ways in which the relationship between political identifications and economic determinants varies at different times and contexts. Descriptive exemplification, clearly, is not enough. We can easily enumerate cases to show, that the economic strength of an ethnic or cultural minority was decisive for its political affirmation. Compare the differences between the economically powerful German-speaking minority in the South Tyrol (Italy) and the economically weak Slovenian minority in Carinthia (Austria).[11]

5. The given and (re-)constructed identities

While a lot of attention has been paid to the *threats towards and the decline of* territorial identities, much less is given to the (re-)construction and *changing nature* of those identities. While sociology does distinguish between the ascribed and achieved status of individuals, this distinction has been largely neglected in the case of territorially-based collective identities. A territorial identity is considered as historically and contextually given, and hence stable and passive. Nonetheless, increasing competition within the emerging world market and "time-space compression" have exerted strong pressure on the need to *identify and redefine* a unit's own comparative advantages and correspondingly to build an image as well as the socioeconomic and cultural basis of a new identity. An important part of this puzzle - what will happen to the existing territorial identities? - can thus be clarified. While in the past the concrete territorial identity was largely pre-determined, now identities are increasingly shaped by the particular individual and collective actors.

A given locality - both at the collective and at the individual level of analysis - confronts an extended range of choices, which become decisive in determining how much its distinctive features will be promoted, preserved or eroded. This further implies that we *cannot expect an uniform answer* to the question of what will happen to territorial identities. There are very different outcomes concerning the preservation of ethnic identities, e.g. language shifts, language decline and/or language death. As Strassoldo points out, individuals are - on the basis of expanded access to others, resulting from the communication revolution - "free to build relations and communities across space, throwing into disarray the old hierarchical order of local communities". They can belong to a growing number of social circles and they "are free (with all the necessary qualifications) to choose among a wide range of information sources, and can structure their own information environment."

From an economic point of view, Harvey (1989) has called attention to increasing sensitivity towards differences in space and thus to the increasingly mobile capital as well as to the response of the various localities in their competitive efforts to attract capital. At least this is a response to external threat to the position of individuals, enterprises or of communities, which are perceived as introducing certain elements of change.

Baumeister (1986) discussed how "people gradually ceased to feel that their identities and lives were essentially or irrevocably determined by their family descent." The same could be said concerning the role of "permanent residence" or place of birth. Once the place of birth or living is no longer taken for granted, it becomes one of the alternative choices, increasingly evaluated in comparison with other alternatives. An expanded range of accessible places reduces dependency on a given locality and contributes to the process of individuation of sub-groups and individuals which further increases the diversity of behavior of these, more autonomous, actors.

Williams, drawing on his experience of Wales, has pointed out that the *erosion* of ethno-regional identity may be taking place while, at the same time, an intensification and organization of regional movements is also under way. Here it is important to distinguish between the traditional territorial identities and the "new localism" or regionalism. This distinction is spelled out by Strassoldo and Teune in their characterization of the old and new localism.

While the old localism is referred to by Strassoldo as "primordial and unthinking", the new one is the outcome of free will, conscious choice; the first is "necessary and natural", the second, voluntary and intentional. The old localism tended to minimize contacts with the foreign world, to maintain a strong, closed boundary, while the new localism is fully aware of the rest of the world, and is open to contact. The old localism was based on the principle of insulation; the new localism advances association in a broader space. The first was a exclusive; the new is selective in establishing supra-local linkages.

The question remains: is this still localism? With increasing openness towards the rest of the world we have come to the point of the transformation of local identities. The "local" - at least segmentally - converges with the "global". The same phenomena assume *both a "local" and a "global"* character. Thus localism could become indistinguishable from globalism. The local and global levels of society tend to converge. However, considering the paradigm of socio-spatial development (Mlinar), this interpretation has to be extended. The transformation at the local, as at the regional or national, level cannot be understood only in relationship to globalization. It has also to take into account the increasing diversification and autonomy of the actors (their individuation) who are shaping the "new localism". Thus the assertion of individuality also increasingly converges with the *diversified expression of locality*.

Such changes can be seen in the contribution by Teune who observes how the "new localism" is emerging in many parts of wealthy countries. This process involves new forms of urban association for collective activity, thus implying higher political fragmentation. He offers examples: 60% of newely acquired private residences in the US are organized into residential associations; industrial parks create political entities which provide services on a semi-volunteer basis; computer-based printing of community newspapers is carried out by part-time helpers etc. But Teune like other authors, points to two sides of the process. The new localism divides, and yet can still be tied together through global communications by satellite, ship, and plane. The nation-state is no longer the gate-keeper it once was.

We can conclude by saying that the above represents a building block of a general developmental paradigm of individuation and globalization. Within such a context we have become attentive to the transformation from a local unit "*an sich*", as an "unwilled phenomenon" (Peachey 1984) to the unit "*für sich*", i.e. an intentionally chosen or constructed territorial unit. While the first provides no space for individual will and differences, the second represents an expression and outcome of the two. The new localism or regionalism typically manifests itself as a movement of change rather than a (rigid) structure.

Notes

1 From the perspective of the developmental logic of social systems we could even more generally characterize this changes as a transition from "interaction systems" to "transaction systems" (Teune, Mlinar, 1978).

2 All underlinings, unless otherwise indicated, are by the author.

3 Thomas uses similar terms - "cultural islands" and "cultural cross-roads" in his discussion of the role of the media in the survival of cultures (quoted by Williams, see chapter 7). A similar interpretation is that of Simmel (1964): the individuation within "the web of group-affiliations"("Die Kreuzung sozialer Kreise").

4 He continues: "Everywhere everything gets more like everything else, as the world's preference structure gets pressed into homogenized commonality ... Such differences as remain are vestiges of the hardened inherited past as to cultural preferences, national tastes and standards" (ibidem).

5 Dahl and Tufte, 1973, on the other hand observe how smaller territorial units surrender their autonomy to the next larger units in an ever-ascending series of actions.
6 In order to avoid repetition of the fuller text in chapter 2 here only the outline of the theoretical structure is given.
7 The above indicates that they consider - on the side which I call individuation - both the autonomy (sovereignty) of the groups as well as ("skills") of the individuals. Where they speak about the tension between interdependence and sovereignty, I am using the concept of contradiction or the unity of opposites between globalization (integration) and individuation (autonomy).
8 One of such particularities which tend to assume to represent the globality of the contemporary world is often designated as "americanization", sometimes distinguished from "modernization" as a general developmental proces; but even modernization is criticized for implying "westernization".
9 This is further related to the question (and not only for lesser-used language communities) of how much the final outcome depends on the defensive involvement of the threatened community. Ogan (1988) has already pointed out that the more "interdependent the world becomes, the more cultures blend into one another. What is unknown is the point at which resistance to foreign cultures breaks down and indigenous values are replaced with foreign ones". Sometimes this resistance does not even start. In a long-term perspective there is no guarantee for survival of a distinctive identity even if resistance persists.
10 Friedmann and Wolff (1982) pointed out that many local problems can ultimately have only global solutions, as well as the corollary that local actions may have global consequences. This should enable us - particularly in the "world city" perspective-heuristically to disclose the major structural causes of specific problems.
11 Economic position is not the only important factor. What matters is also the fact that in the first case we have a minority which is aware of being part of one of the main languages and cultures in Europe, while in the second, the minority has much weaker backing by one of the smallest nations in Europe.

References

Agnew, J. (1987) Place and Politics, London, Allen and Unwin.

Allardt, E. (1979) Implication of the Ethnic Revival in Modern Industrialized Society, in Commentationes Scienciarem Socialium, 19, Helsinki, Societas Scientiarum Fennica.

Bassand, M. (1990) Culture et Region d'Europe, Conseil de l'Europe, Lusanne, Presses Polytechniques.

Baumeister, R.F. (1986) Identity: Cultural Change and the Struggle for Self, Oxford, Oxford University Press.

Blau, P. (1977) Inequality and Heterogeneity, New York, Free Press.

Boulding, K. (1985) The World as a Total System, London, Sage Publications.

Brown, L. (1972) World without borders, New York, Vintage Books.

Dahl, R. and Tufte, E. (1973) Size and Democracy, Stanford, Stanford University Press.

Debray, R. (1986) Les Empires contre l'Europe, Paris, Gallimard.

Duchacek, I.D. (1986) The Territorial Dimension of Politics Within, Among and Across Nations, Boulder and London, Westview Press.

Friberg, M. and Hettne, B. (1982) The Greening of the World: Towards a Non-Deterministic Model of Global Processes, University of Gothemburg, Sweden (xerox).

Friedmann, J. and Wolff, G. (1982) World City Formation: an Agenda for Research and Action, International Journal for Urban and Regional Research, Vol. 6, No. 3.

Giddens, A. (1990) The Consequences of Modernity, Cambridge, Polity Press.

Harvey, D. (1989) The Condition of Postmodernity, Oxford, Basil Blackwell.

Hirschman, A. (1970) Exit, Voice and Loyalty, Cambridge, Harvard University Press.

Levitt, T. (1983) The Marketing Imagination, New York, The Free Press.

Moore, W. (1966) Global Sociology: the World as a Singular System, American Journal of Sociology, No. 71.

Ogan, C. (1988) Media Imperialism and the Videocassette Recorder: The Case of Turkey, Journal of Communication, Vol. 38, No. 2.
Ploman, W.E. (1984) Space, Earth and Communication, London, Frances Pinter.
Rosenau, J.N. (ed.), (1990) Turbulence in World Politics, Princeton University Press.
Rosow, J.M. (ed.), (1988) The Global Marketplace, Oxford, Facts on File.
Sack, R.D. (1986) Human Territoriality, Cambridge, Cambridge University Press.
Simmel, G. (1964) Conflict, The Web of Group-Affiliations, New York, Free Press.
Smith, A.D. (1990) Towards a Globe Culture? in Featherstone, M. (ed.) Global Culture, London, Sage Publication.
Suttles, G. (1984) The Cumulative Texture of Local Urban Culture, American Journal of Sociology, Vol. 90, No. 2.
Teune, H. and Mlinar, Z. (1978) Developmental Logic of Social Systems, London, Sage Publications.

2 Individuation and globalization: The transformation of territorial social organization

Zdravko Mlinar

1. Introduction

The points of departure for the present text are: first, today we are faced with basic and far-reaching changes in the territorial organization of societies that we can speak of a radical discontinuity in relation to the traditional "territorial communities"; second, neither sociology nor any of the other social sciences has theoretically incorporated these changes at all levels of territorial social organization and third, in social theory and in urban and regional studies as well we have reached a point of "satiation" with examination of "what the author(s) actually meant".

I will therefore try to take a step forward within the paradigm - already indicated in my introduction - of socio-spatial development as the unity of opposites: individuation and globalization (Mlinar, 1986). It is broad enough to enable one to account for the central dynamics of the changes at both the micro and the macro levels of analysis and of their interrelationships, as well as to observe the interdependencies between the structures and the actors of change. Since the sociological conceptualisation of opposing development processes is still not adequately defined, this will be discussed. Only then will an attempt be made to interpret the transformation of the traditional territorial social organization in the processes of transition from modernity to postmodernity.

2. Sociological conceptualization of the processes of individuation and globalization

2.1. The concept of individuation

The concept of individuation refers to processes of increasing the autonomy and distinctiveness of the actors at both the collective and the individual levels. And since both of these have their own special features, they may be in harmony or opposition. The individuation of a group in relation to others contributes to the individuation of its individuals, but at some point, their paths begin to diverge.

My goal here is not a general theoretical discussion of groups and individuals. The focus will be on the factors relating to the spatial organisation of society. Nonetheless, I will first briefly sketch the possibility of the conceptualisation of this process in terms of the following basic dimensions.

Individuation as the weakening of predetermination on the basis of origin Individuation can best be observed by the degree of predetermination of the individual and the course of his life by origin, or his birth and the characteristics of his previous generations. The higher the degree of this predetermination, and the greater the extent to which the characteristics of the behaviour of the individual are a continuation of the characteristics of ancestors, the lower the level of individuation. This dimension of individuation, can also be understood at the level of collective actors. We cannot speak of individuation when an individual (group) is subjugated by the hereditary inertia of the physical and social environment. The lower the degree of inter-generational, spatial and social mobility, the lower the degree of individuation. Inter-generational changes distinguish between what the individual inherited and what was acquired , thus defining the scope for individuation. If, for example, childrens' permanent place of residence is their place of birth, and the residence of their parents, there has been little inter-generational individuation. When these two places are different this is an indication of individual autonomy. The greater the number of criteria according to which there is a coincidence between two generations, the lower the degree of individuation.

Individuation as a weakening of determination on the basis of territory The autonomy of the individual or of the group increases in counter-proportion to the constraining factors of the environment. The greater the amount of individual variability, which *cannot be explained* on the basis of knowledge of the individual's spatial *environment*, the higher the degree of individuation.

What is the role (autonomy) of the individual or social group in a context of radical time-space compression? There is a rapid increase in access to other subjects. Thus individuals enter into (inter)dependence with an ever increasing number of actors in broader environments. What is important here (Simmel, 1955) is that as the number of actors on whom the individual depends increases, his dependence *on any one of them decreases*. It thus follows that with the extension of space for alternatives, there is a relative decrease in dependence and vulnerability in relation to those in the immediate environment.[1]

Individuation, as a weakening of restraints based on a specific geographic environment, is valid not only for individuals, but also for local communities or regions. King (1990) and others involved in research on "global cities" found that in recent years they tended toward "disembedding" from their nation-states and took on characteristics which increasingly deviated from those of their traditional hinterland.

Individuation as an increase in the diversity of the "time-space paths" In the sociological conceptualisation of individuation, which we are trying *to model for use* in an analysis of spatial organisation and its restructuring, we should not be limited to the role and position of individuals in space at a specific moment in time. We can build on "temporal geography" and, in particular, on Haegerstrand's (1975) research on "life paths in time-space". Although Haegerstrand is basically descriptive, the way in which he presents *daily or life time-space paths* could contribute to a definition of one dimension of the processes of individuation.

Since the goal is comparison not only of single time-space situations but also of comprehensive patterns or profiles of spatial mobility in a defined period, we have a considerably greater discriminatory capability as regards the differences between individuals. In this sense we are concerned with a more comprehensive coverage of the individual characteristics which are increasingly manifest as we move into "postmodernism" or "postfordism". In the framework of socio-spatial restructuring and an increasing flexibility or even "melting" (according to Berman, 1982, "all that is solid melts into air"), individuation thus appears in the form of an increasing variety of patterns of time-space paths. With this the concept of individuation is linked to the wealth of diversity of this new flexibility which at the same time destroys the hitherto established concept of spatial order - for example time-space flexibility in the execution of work, which is increasingly deviating from the erstwhile uniformity.

In the context of the classical industrial or "Fordist" organisation one could predict with a high degree of certainty that almost all workers in a factory or an area would be found in a specific place, for example, from six a.m. to two p.m. inside the enclosed factory complex. But in a postmodern era there is increasing time-space variability, which is already quite significant for individual strata today, for example in the "time-space paths" of the lives of artists or scientists.

There are a number of ways in which this dimension of individuation could be observed and operationalised. The wider the spatial frame over which individuals or groups extend, the greater the likelihood of unique "life paths". In this sense the greatest likelihood for the emergence of unique patterns is when they extend out into global, world space.

Individuation as increasing control and decrease of (random) intrusions from the external environment Every assertion of identity by an individual or a group presupposes that the actors have specific or *unique selection criteria* in relation to the physical and social environment. In this way an actor asserts his control over the impulses from the environment. But this does not mean that we can equate a higher degree of control with a higher degree of isolation. The measure of individuation is *not isolation, but selectivity*. Greater selectivity does not *exclude*, but as a rule is even concomitant with an intensification of communication and association.[2]

In this sense the spatial organisation and the established environment also play an instrumental role. We can assess their adequacy in relation to the measure in which they enable - or do not enable - such selectivity and individuation. As the process of urbanization led to more dense settlement, and as technological change led to greater spatial mobility (of people and goods) and an intensification of communication, so too the identity of the individual and of different groups became increasingly dependent on *protective mechanisms*, which prevent it from being simply flooded by random intrusions.

The combination of the substantive, the temporal and the spatial creates *niches* in which identities of individuals and groups are asserted. Under which of these combinations do these protective mechanisms become increasingly porous, leading to the disintegration and annihilation of such identities?[3] There is thus a wide range of *protective mechanisms*, both at the level of the individual (for example, in the living and working environments) and at the national level when borders and various control mechanisms are abolished and set up again.

A dominant protective mechanism of the collective identity of traditional groups is the preservation or even strengthening of internal homogeneity, by forms of spatial segregation. However, this goes against the trend towards "subgroupism" (see DiMuccio and Rosenau, chapter 3) and individuation of individuals, which will, in the long run, undermine the territorial enclaves of homogeneous populations.

Individuation as increased authenticity of the assertion of identity What is the authenticity of expressions and assertions of identity by individuals and groups? It is linked to the question of direct and indirect incorporation into the system. First, the more indirectly the identity is asserted through *intermediaries and representatives*, the less the likelihood that it will be fully asserted in its undiluted, *authentic* form. Second, the greater the deviation of the individual identity from the average, and the more it differs from its environment, the less likely that it will be represented. To take an extreme case: where there is a unique personality, no one else will be able to represent or replace it adequately. In this sense the individual is irreplaceable.

Wherever individuals are indirectly represented via mediators, there is a tendency to treat them *as categories rather than individuals*. As Roszak (1981) found, there is an inclination towards reducing differences among individuals to a few characteristics, in "*identity boxes*". For territorial groups, as conflicts with the external world increase, internal homogenization tends to grow i.e. individual differences are suppressed or ignored. This serves as a basis for unquestioned and legitimate political representation at the collective level. This runs contrary to the process of individuation, which leads to increasingly direct and authentic expression of the identity of each and every individual. Pressures towards uniformity and *stigmatisation* - which is not only an ideological and political issue - can develop into a kind of general blockade, to which numerous institutions also succumb. This is particularly true of ethnic minorities, which tend to be unnoticed until severe tensions arise; and then - at least in critical situations - they take on a completely new identity almost overnight, which disturbs the hitherto (apparent) homogeneity of the national territory, for example the Gagauzy in Moldavia; the Serbian settlements and areas in

Croatia; the Moslem Sandzhak region in parts of Serbia, Montenegro, and Bosnia-Herzegovina.

2.2. The dimensions of the process of globalization

Globalization has attracted increased interest in recent years. Most of the discussions are not based on definitions of this concept, but rather on a number of narrow, fragmentary approaches to it. We find communication research with titles such as *Global Information and World Communication* (Mowlana, 1986). Researchers studying the social implications of the "information revolution" emphasize themes, such as *Information Technology and Global Interdependence* (Jussawalla et al., 1989). Among the more popular studies in sociology and in social sciences currently are those which discuss the theory of the "world system" (Wallerstein, 1974, 1980, and others). From a theoretical point of view a well known social scientist has presented a study on *The World as a Total System* (Boulding, 1985); another is *Global Culture* (Featherstone, 1990). There have also recently been a number of publications in the field of urban and regional studies with such a global focus: *Cities in a Global Society* (Knight and Gappert, 1989), *Global Restructuring and Territorial Development* (Henderson, 1989); *Globality versus Locality*" (Kuklinski, 1990). Among the latest is the contribution to the "sociology of the global system" which attempts to define the global system from the point of view of the "theory of transnational practices" (Sklair 1991).

Globalization is a process extending the determinative frameworks of social change to the world as a whole. Thus while social change was initially considered within local, regional and national frameworks, the focus is now on internationalization and globalization. Those sociologists who once professionally limited themselves to the study of cities, the rural areas, local communities or regions, find that they can no longer ignore the influences of events at the world level. On the one hand attention is directed away from the narrow to the wider space; on the other, this has been accompanied by growing interest in explaining relationships between individual areas (territorial units) and the world as a whole. The focus is on such questions as the "micro-macro linkage" (Knorr-Cetina and Cicourel, 1981), "local-global nexus" (Alger, 1988) and multi-level analysis.

A basic question remains open: How to approach a *clearer definition* of the concept of globalization with a definition which is sufficiently inclusive, while at the same time permitting its operationalization? In other words, how to *go beyond the merely illustrative* enumeration of different indicators of globalization, such as, for example, the operations of multinational or transnational corporations, satellite communications, world languages, ecological problems of the present-day world, the globalization of questions of security and peace. In an attempt to achieve a more comprehensive conceptualization of the process of globalization, let us consider five of its dimensions.

Globalization as increasing interdependence at the world level This concerns both the extension of the spatial frame of interdependence of events and its intensification on the basis of a complementarity of differences and competitiveness of alternatives. More and more often the behaviour and activities of people in specific areas have repercussions which go beyond local, regional or national borders and - sooner or later - achieve global dimensions. The longer the time frame, the greater, in general, will be the share of individual and collective activities which have global impact. In this process there is a growing sensitivity to differences which are emerging on the world scale. These differences form the basis for both complementary and competitive interaction. Both of these are today becoming more intensive, at a level which goes beyond the framework of the nation-state.

While in the past, and still today, at least the social elites were able to withdraw from other people into a private world of their own - into their private "niches" - technological development has made this increasingly difficult. With increasing "time-space compression", it is becoming impossible to "solve" problems by withdrawing from them spatially - as, for example, the suburbs represented a withdrawal, an escape, from the problems of the urban core. With the increase of interdependence on the world scale and recognition of the fact that there is "only one world", the possibilities are now diminishing for separate, partial solutions, whether for the individual, the local community or the nation state. As already discussed (Mlinar, 1989), the problem of air pollution, for example, is becoming increasingly difficult to escape, irrespective of material and political resources available. Not only individuals, but also individual states are incapable of stopping the growing number of intrusions from beyond their borders. "Acid rain" makes no distinctions as regards private property, local or state borders.

Although we generally tend to see the opening up into a wider area from the point of view of emancipation from ties to the narrower local, provincial or national constraints, the other side of the coin must also be taken into account. The higher the level of globalization, the *narrower the scope for "escape alternatives"*. In this sense globalization is a kind of *totalitarianization* of world space.

Globalization as the expansion of domination and dependence The "world society" (Burton, 1972) or "world system" (Wallerstein, 1974, 1980) is not emerging only on the basis of interdependence and a balanced, mutual linkage of its parts. Theoreticians of dependence (the "dependistas") have pointed out that interdependence is a cover for domination and subjugation on a world scale. This is not proposed here as an alternative, but to emphasize that globalization can advance in both freedom and domination. The latter can be seen in the relations between the world metropolitan core and the world periphery. This is an inter-connectedness on the global scale, in which *radial* rather than *lateral links* predominate. And the basis of the linkage is the logic of a "zero sum game": the greater the benefit (profit) which the world core has from these relationships, the greater the losses and the exploitation of the periphery or semi-periphery.

The dominance and dependence in the extension of international and transnational relationships applies particularly to economics, politics, culture (conceptualized as "cultural imperialism"). A crucial point, however, is that the importance of this way of expanding world relations is not constant. It varies, depending on the ratio between radial and lateral communications.

Globalization as homogenization of the world Universal standards spread, replacing the particular and parochial homogeneity of small territorial units. Instead of differences among territorial units which were mutually exclusive, there is now a *uniformity*, representing an infrastructure of the "space of flows" and unhindered movement of material goods, people and ideas on the international and global scale. This is the aspect of globalization to which critics most often react, because they feel that we are becoming the same all over the world (Luard, 1979). Such trends are seen as negative, especially where standardization and uniformity appear in conjunction with a tendency to one-way domination, indicated by concepts such as "Westernization", "Americanization", "Cocacolization" (Dore, 1984). There is standardization of both the material and non-material culture, for example certain "chains" (networks) of hotels, trade marks, air traffic, or the use of a world language, such as English (De Stefano, 1989).

A similar intense process is in progress on a narrower territorial scale in efforts towards "European integration". Three hundred different measures have been proposed to ensure the *homogenization* of the territory of Europe, a "Europe without borders". Here too we have on the one hand an elimination of *mutual exclusiveness*, which posed few problems as long as there were closed systems coexisting at the level of nation states; and on the other, the introduction of uniform standards and a common culture, either as a process of diffusion or joint participation in creating a new one.

Globalization as diversification within "territorial communities" The level of globalization can be measured by the extent to which narrow territorial units are open and permit access to the wealth of diversity of the world as a whole. There is no globalization where there are closed "territorial communities" at the local, regional or national levels. If such were the case, the world would be a mechanical total, an aggregate of closed and internally homogeneous territorial systems ("billiard balls"). Globalization takes place when there is a territorial redistribution of the diversity of the world as a whole. Thus, the higher the *share of the overall global diversity*, present or accessible within the territorial community, the higher the degree of globalization. This is, as indicated earlier, analogous to what Blau (1977) presented as the "penetration of differentiation into the substructures". Within (former) Yugoslavia, for example, over the past few decades there has been a continuous increase in ethnic diversification within the constituent republics.
Similarly we can observe what proportions of various ethnic groups are to be found among the inhabitants of the big "global cities", such as New York, London, Paris and Tokyo. How high is the proportion of the world-known

diversity of "national cuisines" in the restaurants of these big cities? From the point of view of the spread of information and telecommunication technology the important question is how easily information from wherever and about whatever is available everywhere (at every point in space or within each territorial unit).

The more inclusive the territorial subsystems become in relation to the diversity in the wider environment and on the global scale, the more they resemble the global system as a whole. Total globalization would mean that local features would be the same as global ones. We are approaching a situation in which the whole world will be found in each locality and at the same time each locality, region, nation, will be found all over the world. Every individual *part is becoming* increasingly *like the whole*, while *the whole* is increasingly *manifesting all its parts*. With an increase in diversity, or at least of access to it, particular territorial units lose their former exclusiveness. And the conflicts at the local level are no longer primarily about local questions; increasingly, local disputes are about global social problems.

Globalization as a means of surmounting temporal discontinuities Just as globalization from a spatial point of view leads from a "space of places" to a "space of flows", so there is also a unification of time frames. Globalization can thus be seen as overcoming temporal discontinuities on the basis of:

a) connectedness of the asynchronous rhythms of different activities and
b) temporal inclusiveness resulting from the extension of the functioning of particular services to global space frames.

Just as individuation has increased the asynchrony of life rhythms, so too are the possibilities of *asynchronous communication* increasing with the new information and telecommunications technology. Time discrepancies no longer exclude an area from the global system. This is particularly important now that there are linkages between people in different time zones, for example, the stock exchanges in New York, London and Tokyo (Brotchie et al., 1987). In those services that are most integrated in international and global flows, people can no longer afford daily breaks in accordance with local time. In the world's "global cities" one finds the largest numbers of different activities or institutions which work continuously in "global time", for example, international airports and the hotel industry.

Despite their flexibility, the global flows can be increased only where there is increasingly *exact time synchronization* of the particular phases or operations of production processes which take place at diverse locations. The "*just in time*" concept is becoming increasingly important.

2.3. The interdependence of the two processes

In the previous two sections an attempt was made to conceptualize each of the processes, globalization and individuation, separately and in general terms. What are the relationships between them? Does a higher level of globalization imply a higher level of individuation and vice-versa? Or does a step ahead in the direction of individuation perhaps entail a retrogression in globalization?[4]

The literature is full of one-sided discussions of these changes, but it ignores the changing interrelationships between these processes. Let us look at some of these approaches.

The autonomy of the individual or the group - and each is considered separately - is usually discussed only in a specific time-frame and more rarely as a process of increasing autonomy or individuation. Considerable attention is paid, for example, to human rights, but there is more emphasis on *ad hoc* normative-institutional arrangements than on the developmental logic of individuation. At the collective level, Almond and Powell (1966) saw the essence of the development process in the *strengthening of the autonomy of the sub-systems*, but did not link this to processes of supranational integration. Local autonomy and decentralisation are usually discussed as "internal affairs" of the individual countries and as questions in the sphere of political decision-making (e.g. Smith, 1985) rather than as part of macro development processes.

Similarly, discussions on globalization, especially in frameworks of economic and geographical research, neglect the question of autonomy, or at least of individual autonomy (Scott and Storper, 1986; McKinlay and Little, 1986; Dicken, 1986; and others). "Critical urban sociology", which has a tendency towards economism and structuralism, has been recently extended to questions of global restructuring and territorial development (Henderson and Castells, 1987), or "global restructuring and community politics" (Smith and Feagin, 1987). However these questions have either not been linked, or else are only peripherally so with processes of individuation. In discussing the influence of information technology Castells only marginally and descriptively adds a number of manifestations of individualisation (Castells, 1985).

Adherents of the "dependency theory" see globalization as domination and exploitation and thus direct their attention to the question of how to prevent this. Various concepts have been developed in theory and practice, their common denominator being to seek a solution in withdrawal from a world system of capitalist domination. As counter-forces to imperialism in the economic and cultural spheres and in particular in telecommunications, are "*dissociation*" or "*delinking*", "*endogenous development*" and "*self-reliance*".

Dahl and Tufte's explanation (1973) of how, in the processes of development, narrow territorial units lose autonomy to increasingly larger units, is one-sided. The premise is a historical developmental logic in which the power and authority of smaller systems - villages, smaller towns, cities, municipalities, provinces and regions - become *de facto* and *de jure* subordinated to the power and authority of the nation state. Today nation states too are beginning to experience limitations on their sovereignty as a concomitant of their integration into supranational organizations. This is a sign that the nation state is becoming a kind of local authority.

If such an explanation were correct, we would end up with a world system whose parts (at least as regards territorial units) would lack all autonomy. Behind this is the premise of cross-level exclusion in that the more the wider territorial units gain, the more the smaller ones lose (see also Teune, in chapter 6).

The focus of attention, particularly in the field of international relations, is on *bifurcation* at the level of the nation-state. The nation-state is on the one hand considered to be too far removed and rigid to be able to respond to an increasing heterogeneity of the vital problems of the people within its own territory, while at the same time it is too small and confined to deal with the more important external determinants of the events taking place within its borders. It is therefore understandable that on the one hand there are processes of *decentralization* and at the same time processes of supranational *integration*. Cameron (1981) says that we are faced with changes which are characterized by forces which exert simultaneous pressure in two *opposite directions*: towards the smaller, more decentralized structures and towards larger, more integrative ones. He calls the former "regionalism" and the latter "supranationalism". The demands of economic development and greater security are seen as the basis of the pressures towards integration into wider areas, while the trend towards smaller territorial and political units is in essence a greater responsiveness to the wishes of the population, giving greater scope for the expression of specific local peculiarities (Watts in Cameron, 1981).

There is no one single answer valid for all situations to the question of the relationship, or the interdependence of the processes of individuation and globalization. A step in the direction of greater autonomy generally involves a certain narrowing of the circle of interconnectedness. Thus for example the disintegration of the Austro-Hungarian empire in 1918 led to greater independence and autonomy for the individual nations, but at the same time there was also a narrowing of the spatial framework of social mobility and association. Today's processes of European integration call for a certain limitation of the sovereignty of the nation states (Mlinar, 1990).

A hypothetical, general, formulation of these processes is that individuation and globalization are interdependent, but in such a way that at the initial stages there is a stronger oscillation, as alternately one is asserted at the expense of the other. This oscillation gradually converges and the relationship changes from exclusion to mutuality.

3. Restructuring or destructuring of territorial social organization?

Considering the presented conception of individuation and globalization as the core of the dynamics of socio-spatial changes, let us turn to an overview of the most characteristic dimensions of restructuring or even of the breakdown of the traditional territorial organization of society.

3.1. The process of deterritorialization

Both individuation and globalization undermine the traditional territorial organization of society. "Territorial communities" are *losing their traditional identity* due to both growing internal differentiation and individuation of their components (groups, individuals), as well as to an increase of mutual interdependence in the space across their borders. In developed societies, belongingness to a specific territorial unit is generally diminishing in importance as an explanatory factor of the characteristics of the individual or the group. The number of *non-territorial actors* is increasing. Their activity can best be understood in a framework of systems which are not primarily territorially defined. Territorial proximity is becoming less important for the definition and explanation of "social proximity" or "social distance". Just as on the one hand individuation separates the individual or group from the environment (Giddens, 1990, uses a very suitable expression - "disembedding"), so on the other hand globalization is becoming so inclusive that it tends to encompass the whole world rather than certain territorial units.

To ensure that such generalizations do not become a simplification, we should note that the increase in *sensitivity to differences* in space can also lead to a "reterritorialization", which could be connected to specific features of the geographical environment, or of people - the workforce - in individual locations. But such socio-spatial differentiation will no longer have the same character as it had in the past: instead of an inflexible, lasting and comprehensive encompassment of closed areas, there will be a flexible, temporary and more segmented coverage of territories distinct from the broader hinterland.

In the context of the traditional, static society, territoriality was very clearly expressed in terms of exclusiveness of locations or "communities" in space. With the intensification of social dynamics, away from the space of places to the space of flows, exclusiveness of this kind is becoming increasingly transcended. In the context of flows, certain ideas, can be present everywhere, without their presence or use in one location precluding that in all others. As accessibility increases, the importance of the location is thus both relativized and diminished. With "perfect" accessibility - everywhere, at any moment and at no cost - location would be irrelevant. Changes in this direction are to be expected from the spread of satellite communications and with the general increase in the volume and importance of information in society.

Parallel with the transcendence of the exclusiveness of alternatives in space the threat to the existing *territorial identities* increases, in the context of a "time-space compression".

3.2. The change of frontal territorial boundaries

A boundary is a precondition for the existence of any system, including every territorial community or territorial identity. Today, attention is focused on the boundaries of nation-states, which are in general becoming increasingly permeable.

Globalization implies free movement across all territorial borders, while - as we have seen - the individuation of individual parts at the same time depends on "trans-border" movements and connections. A characteristic bifurcation can be noted here:

a) Firstly, *borders are moving apart* - as exemplified in the history of Europe over the centuries - and there is a consequent reduction in the number of political systems. Clearly, the present borders of the European Community are still not final, and they will not stop at the borders of the European continent.
b) Secondly, there is a reverse tendency towards an *interiorization of the borders* of territorial communities. The more recognition there is of the autonomy of subsystems and individuals, the more understandable it becomes that these also assume authority over their "external affairs" and in the long run the responsibility and control which was previously located in the centre and at the outer edge of the territory of the nation-state. Today their borders are symbolized by customs services at international airports, satellite communications terminals , or - as Alger (1984) says - even the living room of a businessman of a transnational corporation in our neighbourhood.

Border control is becoming relatively less effective over time because in as far as it is based on predefined categories rather than on the process of individuation (diversification), there are more cases which do not fall into any category. In so far as cases defy categorization, they also defy control. As the flow of traffic of border crossings becomes unmanageable, the solution would seem to be that of greater individual autonomy. Only *greater trust in the individual*, who, for example, chooses the "nothing to declare" exit channel at the airport, will permit massive geographical mobility of populations. Thus control, similar to collecting fares in public transport systems in many cities, is receding into the background, and is present only as a periodic check to prevent abuse of the trust given to individuals.

Less obvious are the changes involving internationalization of standards, or "homogenization measures" which *make border controls unnecessary*, (Cecchini, 1988).

3.3. Domestic and external affairs ("at home" and "abroad")

These changes affecting the borders among territorial communities, blurr traditional divisions of "domestic affairs" and "external affairs", "domestic" and "foreign policy", "natives" and "foreigners", "homeland" and "foreign parts". With the growing *spatial mobility* of people across local and national borders, developing into a global flow, it is becoming increasingly difficult to determine whether or not particular individuals belong to a specific local or national unit.

These changes force us to reconsider our concepts, at least in the following areas:

a) Out of sheer inertia researchers tried to explain events within the traditional territorial frameworks and either did not even pose the question, or else marginalised the importance of determinative systems outside given boundaries.
b) For the most part issues have been posed in terms of "internal" and "external" policy. However, as activities inside a territorial unit have consequences beyond its borders, it is evident that decision-making processes can no longer be mechanically separated into internal and external spheres. There is a growing tendency to *"internalise" external affairs*, so that they are no longer exclusively a matter for foreign ministers and diplomacy, but are becoming a component of a growing circle of emancipated, local actors.
c) Similar conclusions can be reached for socio-economic, cultural, ecological and other questions. Thus for example the nuclear power plant at Krško is not only an "internal matter" concerning Slovenia (and previously, Yugoslavia) as it also very directly affects Austria, Italy and other countries. Another dramatic example is Chernobyl.
d) It should be obvious that national borders cannot be *moral borders* (Lichtenberg, 1981). Thus from the point of view of moral obligations to people and groups, the importance of the distinction between the domestic and the external world is diminished.

No matter how we define the concepts of "foreignness" and of "foreign places", it is obvious that the processes of globalization and time-space compression are bringing them ever closer. We could, for example, define and consider foreign places as:

a) a distant and unknown - if not dangerous and inimical - world beyond the borders of our homeland;
b) an area which does not concern us, which does not affect our lives, and to which we have no moral obligations;
c) something different from the domestic environment, which we know and in which we live;
d) a label for the outside world, where we might get lost and in which we cannot count on the support of others.

On the one hand the "foreign world" comes ever closer, on the other hand, the domestic environment, our homeland, becomes increasingly *"foreign"*. Wherever we go we meet foreign products, ideas, companies, food, capital, observers and foreigners. We are exposed to foreign broadcasting stations transmitting programmes via satellites or subject to "remote-sensing" by foreign satellites. As the number of foreign things we have around us in our homeland increases, our homeland is becoming increasingly like those "foreign" countries and to the same extent foreigness is diminishing in significance.[5]

3.4. From the territorial community to the global network

Another aspect of the destructuring and restructuring of the traditionally predominant spatial organization of societies on the threshold of the information age, may be described as transitions from territorial communities (local, regional, national) to *networks*, which take shape on the basis of specific interests and functions and which are independent of a specifically defined territorial base. Territorial communities evolved[6] over longer periods of time and in contiguous areas. They survived as relatively inflexible, permanent and multifunctional formations, which were inclusive within their borders and externally exclusive. Today we see a wide variety of very different networks of transnational linkages of people with specific interests.

Such linkages are selective and flexible and the spatial distance between the various actors is diminishing in importance. The technical basis for the rapid advance of these networks is, of course, the new information and communication technology. In the context of "delocalization" and "deterritorialization" there was first an extraordinary rise in the number of multinational and transnational corporations. These were, of course, characteristic of processes of globalization, but above all globalization with domination. It is symptomatic, however, that representatives of these corporations are today showing a greater sensitivity towards the differences and specific features of individual territorial units. Thus their motto has become: "When in Rome, do as the Romans do" (Rosow, 1988).

The case of "Benetton" is instructive. This company was able to expand considerably in a short period of time because among other reasons it set up a widely dispersed international network, permiting sensitivity and responsiveness to rapidly changing needs in different parts of the world (Belussi, 1989). In the framework of the "model of a network firm" proposed by Belussi we also find an innovation which Benetton introduced: the information system permits the linking of the network of wholesalers and retailers with numerous smaller production units. On the one hand, the range of the network is spread over the whole world market; and, on the other hand, a structured production process spreads spatially over numerous units. Effective information linkages enable this kind of network firm to make use of the "just in time" strategy delivery at exactly the right time, so that stocks are no longer necessary.

Benetton's success is not based on "internal expansion", but on an extension of a network of companies under its control. It has a "*flexible system*", which - according to Belussi - combines a network with a propulsive core and an adaptable periphery. Such firms can make rapid changes in their organizational borders by "recentralizing" or "decentralizing" the production process.[7] New technology , of course, is decisive.

In his study of "network firms", Antonelli (1988) found that the influence of microelectronics on the production function is basically centrifugal in nature, because it decreases the importance of economies of scale by reducing the minimum effective size of productive units. Conversely, the influence of telematics on the management function is primarily centripetal in nature, increasing the importance of economies of scale and the size of effective administrative structures. The overall result of the conflicting effects of centrifugal and centripetal forces when telematics are introduced is shown in the increasing importance of the network firm. It has a management structure over an extensive area, with small individual production functions and business units managed by hierarchical coordination and quasi-integration (*ibidem*).

This example represents the manifestations of globalization and individuation in space: response to the world market and closer attention to the local conditions in the different areas where the production units operate. What still remains an open question is whether the greater dispersion of the workforce is a sign of greater flexibility and individuation, or of subjugation, following the principle of "divide and rule".

3.5. The destructuring of the multi-level territorial hierarchy

The study of the integration processes in Europe (Mlinar, 1990) shows that similar tendencies are now appearing within larger states, as the units at the lower levels of territorial and social organization endeavour to circumvent the "intermediate levels" to gain the closest possible links with the centres of supranational structures. Examples are: Ljubljana dealing directly with Brussels, not via Belgrade; Cardiff and Edinburgh avoiding London; Bratislava bypassing Prague. These are symptomatic of a general pattern of long-term trends towards individuation and globalization. By contrast, recent practice in Yugoslavia has focused on "direct democracy", in the sense of locally exclusive autonomy - influence on trivial matters within a narrow, local framework. Closed state borders promoted the hierarchical structures of territorial organization. The sequence of superordination and subordination of individual levels was assumed. The political centre of the state was the highest and the final arbiter.

By opening out towards a wider area, as is happening in Europe today, the state loses its supremacy: New supranational institutions are emerging. Within the state borders the trend towards the autonomy of sub-national units is becoming more pronounced. There are increasingly frequent cases of *"indiscipline" and deviation* from the traditional order and from the characteristic lines of communication between the given levels. Such deviations may take the form of conscious revolt against the traditional hierarchical organization. This happens first where the interests of a smaller territorial unit are least adequately represented at the higher levels of the territorial hierarchy. This is, in turn, still more likely in more heterogeneous socio-spatial structures of the state and in more subordinate positions of given territorial units. "Desertion", in the sense of linking up across state borders - whether in the form of *direct links* with supranational structures or direct mutual linkages between individual regions - certainly relativizes but also undermines the hierarchical structure of the territorial organization within the nation-state.

3.6. Changes in the relations between the world core and the periphery

How far does today's socio-spatial restructuring follow the characteristic patterns of relations between the centre (the core) and the periphery? If there are deviations, the question then is - under what circumstances and conditions?

Multinational companies began to move industrial production from locations with relatively highly-paid labour in the richer countries to those with low wages in poorer ones. This had far-reaching consequences for the conditions of life and work of people in all parts of the world (Frobel et al., 1978). It began to undermine the traditional division of the world into a few industrial countries on the one hand and, on the other, a large majority of developing countries, whose contribution to the world economy was exclusively that of a producer of raw materials. Frobel and his associates described the changes which took place as the "*new international division of labour*". This, effectively, is only another way of saying that we are witnessing changes in the relations between the (global) core and the periphery.

A comparative study of the expansion of the electronics industry in Scotland and in some "newly industrialized countries" in Asia, came to the conclusion (Henderson, 1989), that it is impossible to explain what is happening today with old ideas about a global core and peripheries. It is becoming obvious that at the global level we no longer have one dominant core, but rather the beginnings of "*polycentrism*", which is again a deviation from the model. At the same time, the increase in the number of centres is relativizing the domination and subordination relationships in each concrete situation and thus contributing to a resurgence of territorial identities.

It is necessary to move from general explanations of the relationship between the core and the peripheries to a detailed *multi-level analysis*. This shows that the predominance of the centre at one level - a town in relation to surrounding villages - is diminishing, while at the global level it may be increasing.

Another change in relations between the core and the periphery is the role of the dominant culture, in a particular language. While on the one hand there is a kind of "cultural imperialism" in the form of "Americanization" and of the increasing dominance of the English language, we must not ignore the influences in the opposite direction. American culture and the English language are also *absorbing more and more* elements of other cultures and languages and are thus themselves also subject to transformations, which will likewise diminish the distances between the core and the peripheries. This again indicates the limited explanatory power of a "zero sum game" model.[8]

3.7. From domination by the majority to cooperation among minorities

Restructuring the relationships between autonomy (individuation) and integration (globalization) across the borders of state territories, can be seen in the changing relationships between the majority and minorities. One hypothetical explanation is that the *predominant position of the majority* and the *subjugation of the minority*, inflexible in a closed territorial system, are *relativized* with the opening of borders and the linkage to larger environments. In the case of the inflexible structures of a closed system, the minority is somehow condemned to its role as a "permanent minority"; its subjugation in a more porous system is no longer as absolute. In a bigger system the former majority becomes a minority. In a discussion of "education in a multi-cultural society", Nigel Grant (in: Corner, 1984) came to the conclusion that today we are actually all in the position of minorities, including even the English, the French, the Germans, etc. Even the "big ones" are going to have to get used to different relations, not on the basis of domination, but on the basis of cooperation.

The former *de facto* minority position of the Slovenians - within the Yugoslav state or as a small nation in relation to the Austrians, Italians or Serbs - has greatly changed in the wider European context, where these nations are also, in a sense, in the position of minorities. A sign of this is the use of English as a language of communication within the area, making it less likely that one of the "bigger" countries will try to enforce homogenization (assimilation) on the basis of unilateral domination. If there is homogenization, it is the result of the participation of all those involved, rather than domination.

3.8. Territorial and generational differences

Differences among generations within territorial communities are becoming greater than differences between nations. As different international channels of communication and influence from expanding areas increase, the laten restraining force of the local cultural heritage becomes weaker. Discontinuities between generations weaken their specific territorial culture and territorial identities. This opens the spread of new cultural patterns derived from elsewhere and accepted by younger generations without regard to their *territorial* or *national origins*.

Folk music for example is linked to an area and is relatively exclusive. This is not true of the dissemination of jazz or rock. The tastes, music and art of young people can thus in decreasingly lesser measure be explained by reference to their territorial affiliation. Research has shown (Findahl, 1989) that younger generations are more exposed to global communications, experiencing a culture which they adopt "from outside", as their own. As the older generations die out, many cultural characteristics which developed in the past in a narrow, local context, are irrevocably lost. A convincing example is the disappearance of local dialects.

4. Concluding remarks

The main intention of this chapter was not to test some hypotheses, but rather to outline the possible application of a sociological conceptualization which could provide a possible guideline in identifying the trends and regularities of the transformation of territorial social organization. This was done at two levels: firstly, at the most general level by presenting the paradigm of socio-spatial development, i.e. the dimensions of the concepts of individuation and globalization and by interpretation of the interdependence of the two processes; and secondly, in terms of the limited application of this paradigm to the selected processes of restructuring and destructuring of the inherited (pre-)industrial types of territorial organization of society now at the threshold of the "information era" and postmodernity.

Both may represent a step forward, giving a way out of the idiosyncratic descriptions and fragmentary observations that clash with the rapid processes of globalization of a world society. We are trying to avoid simply continuing the prevailing practice of treating our subject in the form of exemplification or by aggregation of the various observations (as in the discussions of the concepts of postmodernity and of post-fordism). Thus, the general conceptualization provides the basis for sensitizing ourselves to the relevant changes at all the levels of territorial social organization and particularly in terms of their changing interrelationships. Such a theoretical framework enables us to identify long-term processes, even if their empirical manifestations are still very limited or appear as irregularities or as deviant cases.

The territorial organization of society is presently undergoing a radical transformation. We have disclosed that this transformation is much more complex than had earlier been expected. Many questions were raised. Neither common sense nor research have yet provided a clear response, regardless of the importance of these questions.

Notes

1 A similar conclusion can be taken from Hirschman's, (1970) "exit, voice and loyalty" model. Those who have greater opportunities for exit are more effectively able to make their voices heard.

2 One reason, for the disintegration of the Communist movement is that socialization without individuation was promoted; "privatization" was seen as a general withdrawal from society as a whole.

3 The individual may sink into mediocrity, uniformity, as collectively there is "ethnocide", the submergence of a specific ethnic group, or loss of identity with a type of regional architecture.

4 The relationship between diversity and integration as a core dynamic of developmental change, see: Teune, Mlinar, (1978).

5 How many foreign things a person finds in his "homeland" and how many similar things "abroad" depends on the size and stage of development of the territorial community. An American will find "Newsweek" or "Time" in Europe, Japan, Australia or in Latin America. A Slovenian will have a considerably more difficult time.

6 In spite of the acts of formal "establishment" of various "communities", a true community in the sociological sense cannot be established but can only arise in the course of time.

7 This involves a sharp division between "internal" labour, which numbers about 1,600, and external labour, which numbers 15,000 to 20,000 workers employed in almost 400 smaller enterprises (Belussi, 1989).

8 Robinson and collaborators (1991), on the basis of extensive international research into popular music have confirmed the continuing dominant influence "of the West over the Rest"; on the other hand, this has not reduced the great diversity of music production in different parts of the world. Our own data on rock groups in Europe show that they do not simply imitate but also rely on elements of their own heritage.

References

Albrow, M. and King, E. (1990) Globalization, Knowledge and Society, London, Sage Publications.
Alger, C. (1984) Effective Participation in World Society: Some Implications of the Columbus Study, in: Banks, M. (ed.) Conflict in World Society, Brighton, Wheatsheaf Books-Harvester.
Alger, C.F. (1988) Perceiving, Analysing and Coping with the Local-Global Nexus, International Social Science Journal, August.
Almond, G. and Bingham, P. (1966) Comparative Politics: a Developmental Approach, Boston, Little Brown.
Antonelli, C. (1988) The Emergence of the Network Firm, in Antonelli, C.(ed.), New Information Technology and Industrial Change: The Italian Case, Dordrecht, Kluwer.
Banks, M. (ed.) Conflict in World Society, A new perspective on international relations, Brighton, Harvester Press.
Belussi, F. (1989) Benetton Italy: Beyond Fordism and Flexible Specialisation. The Evolution of the Network Firm Model, Paper Presented at the UMIST Conference, Manchester, 29-31 March.
Berman, M. (1982) All that is Solid Melts into Air, New York, Simon and Schuster.
Blau, P. (1977) Inequality and Heterogeneity, New York, Free Press.
Boulding, K. (1985) The World as a Total System, London, Sage Publications.
Brotchie, J.F. et al. (1987) The Spatial Impact of Technological Change, London, Croom Helm.
Burton, J. W. (1972) World Society, Cambridge, Cambridge University Press.
Cameron, D.M. (ed.), (1981) Regionalism and Supranationalism, Montreal, The Institute for Research on Public Policy.
Castells, M. (1985) High Technology, Space and Society, London, Sage Publications.
Cecchini, P. (1988) The European Challenge - 1992, Hants, Wildwood House.
Corner, T. (1984) Education in Multicultural Societies, London, Croom and Helm.
Dahl, R. and Tufte, E. (1973) Size and Democracy Stanford, Stanford University Press.
De Stefano, J.S. (1989) The Growth of English as the Language of Global Satellite Telecommunications, Space Communication and Broadcasting 6.
Dicken, P. (1986) Global Shift, London, Harper and Row.
Dore, R. (1984) Unity and Diversity in World Culture, in Hedley, B. and Watson, A. The Expansion of International Society, Oxford, Clarendon Press.
Featherstone, M. (1990) Global Culture: Nationalism, Globalization and Modernity, London, Sage Publications.
Findahl, O. (1989) Language in the Age of Satellite Television, European Journal of Communication, vol. 4, no. 2.
Frobel, F., Heinrichs, J. and Kreye, O. (1978) The New International Division of Labour, Social Science Information, London, Sage Publications, Vol. 17, No.1.
Giddens, A. (1990) The Consequences of Modernity, Cambridge, Polity Press.
Haegerstand, T. (1975) Survival and Arena: On the Life History of Individuals in Relation to their Geographical Environment, in Carlstein, T., Parkes, D. and Thrift, M. (eds.), Human Activity and Time Geography, Vol. 2, London.
Henderson, J, (1989) The Globalisation of High Technology Production, London, Routledge.
Hirschman, A. (1970) Exit, Voice and Loyalty, Cambridge, Harvard University Press.
Jusawalla, M. at. al. (eds.), (1989) Information Technology and Global Interdependence, New York, Greenwood Press.
Knight, R. and Gappert, G. (eds.), (1989) Cities in a Global Society, London, Sage Publications.
Knorr-Cetina, K. and Cicourel, A.V. (1981) Toward an integration of micro and macro-sociologies, London, Routledge.
Kuklinski, A. (ed.), (1990) Globality Versus Locality, Warsaw, University of Warsaw.
Lichtenberg, J. (1981) National Boundaries and Moral Boundaries: A Cosmopolitan View, in Brown, P.G. and Shue, H. (eds.), Boundaries, Totowa, N.J., Rowman and Littlefield.
Luard, E. (1979) Socialism Without the State, London, The Macmillan Press.
McKinlay, R.D. and Little, R. (1986) Global problems and world order, London, Pinter.
Mlinar, Z. (1989) Sociološki odzivi na probleme okolja (Sociological Response to the Problems of Environment) Ljubljana, Teorija in praksa, Vol. 26, No. 11-12.
Mlinar, Z. (1986) Protislovja družbenega razvoja (Contradictions of Social Development), Ljubljana, Delavska enotnost.

Mlinar, Z. (1990) Autonomija in integracija v evropskem prostoru (Autonomy and Integration in Europe) Ljubljana, Teorija in praksa, Vol. 27, No. 12.
Mowlana, H. (1986) Global Information and World Communication, New York, Longman.
Robinson, D. at. al. (ed.), (1991) Music at the Margins, London, Sage Publications.
Rosow, J. M. (ed.), (1988) The Global Marketplace, Oxford, Facts on File.
Roszak, T. (1981) Person/Planet, London, Granada.
Scott, A. and Storper, M. (eds.), (1986) Production, Work, Territory, Boston, Allen and Unwin.
Simmel, G. (1955) Conflict; The Web of Group-Affiliations, The Free Press of Glencoe.
Sklair, L. (1991) Sociology of the Global System, London, Harvester Wheatsheaf.
Smith, B.C. (1985) Decentralization, London, Allen and Unwin.
Smith, M.P. and Feagin, J.R. (1987) The Capitalist City: Global Restructuring and Community Politics, Oxford, Basil Blackwell.
Teune, H. and Mlinar, Z. (1978) Developmental Logic of Social Systems, London, Sage Publications.
Wallerstein, I. (1974, 1980) The Modern World System I, II, New York, Academic Press.
Watts, R.L. (1981) Federalism, Regionalism and Political Integration, in Cameron, D.M. (ed.).

3 Globalism and localism: Theoretical reflections and some evidence

Raimondo Strassoldo

1. Introduction

This paper is divided into two main parts. In the first, some theoretical arguments are developed on globalism and localism (world unity and local diversity) and their dialectical nexus, in the framework of what is called post-modern society. In the second part, two packages of evidence from Northern Italy are presented. The first is an account of the sudden emergence - in the middle eighties and in the most developed part of Italy - of a strong regional political movement ("Lega Lombarda"), challenging the foundations of the centralized Nation-State. The second is a review of the results of a "localism-globalism scale", administered in a series of sociological surveys, from 1970 to 1988, in the Friuli region. In the conclusion, an attempt is made to link the empirical findings with some of the theoretical arguments, and a nod is made towards federalism, as the political doctrine aimed at a harmonious composition of the local-global antithesis.

The main substantive points of the paper are: 1) the trend toward globalization is very old; in social-ecological theory, it has long been known as "ecological expansion"; what is new is the sheer amount of power of communication (information and transport) technologies propelling it in our days; 2) however, there are two new elements in contemporary globalization processes: one is the ecological world-view, according to which humankind should unite in the effort to save the biosphere; the second is the "post-modern" aspiration to a pluralist, non-hierarchical, de-centered world-society; 3) the growth of globalism does not correlate with a corresponding decline of localism; on the contrary, many new forms of localism are cropping up. "New localism" seems an emergent feature of "postmodern society"; space and place, though transformed, are not going to disappear in the "constitution of society"; 4) the main transformation is from necessity and determinism to free-choice; space and place are going to be less relevant as constraining factors and more as objects of social processes. This is due mainly to the liberating effects of the communication technologies ("from a space of places to a space of flows"); 5) in the studied area, small-scale local community (life-world) is the most important "level of territorial attachment" (loyalty, identification, etc.); nation-state comes a distant second, while the regional and especially the European levels are much weaker; globalism (cosmopolitanism) tends to increase with higher education, SES, urbanization, and younger age; thus suggesting an historical trend in this direction; 6) localism is based not only on traditional "Gemeinschaft" features, but also (marginally) on factors typical of modernity.

PART I: THEORETICAL REFLECTIONS

2. Globality

The awareness that the World is something "unitary" ("One World") is not new; on the contrary, it seems to be a cultural universal and a psychological necessity (see the concept of "Weltanschauung"). Primitive societies, insofar as they were isolated from other human groups and had no knowledge of them, tended to identify themselves with Mankind and their local habitat with the World. Ancient empires too pretended to be universal, and so did and do major religions. However there was and is a gap between belief and aspiration on the one hand, and reality on the other. In fact, tribal isolates, empires and religions covered mere portions of the ecumene. It was only with the European expansion in the continents and the assembling of the capitalist "world economy", from the XV century, that a real world system began to take shape, and reality began to match universalistic ideas and values.

Thus, one-world conscience and globalization are pretty old stuff. On the other hand, we are living in an era in which these processes are in many ways different. One of these differences, in the role of technology, is essentially quantitative, but so large as to become perhaps qualitative; the other two - the binding force of the ecological perspective and the aspiration to a pluralist and polycentric world system - seem quite new.

2.1. The role of technology

The world-wide transfer of information, mass-energy and persons has increased beyond the wildest expectations. The World-Economy developed for three centuries (1500-1800), on the age-old means of the legs (of man and animals) the sail, and printed paper. Since then, a number of completely new means have been invented, slashing by several orders of magnitude the cost and the time of communication, and at the same time releasing huge new amounts of energy for communication purposes. The question is whether in our days the "new technologies" - by which is usually meant the synthesis of information processing and information-transmitting technologies, which does not do justice to the wealth of new technologies of quite different type (Teune, 1986) - have brought forth a quantum leap, a qualitative change, in terms of socio-cultural consequences; or whether it is merely "more of the same". We tend to maintain that two real modern communication "revolutions" occurred around 1450, with the invention of the printing press and more efficient navigation devices, and between 1840 and 1950, when a rapid sequence of inventions freed mankind from the limitations of his organic endowment and of a few other "natural" sources of energy (wind, water): train, telegraph, telephone, motorcar, radio, television and computers. What we have been witnessing since 1950 is only a phenomenal growth along established paths. But the difference between evolution and revolution, growth and development, continuity and change is largely a matter of subjective definition; there are no established criteria to test the dialectical law of "transition from quantitative to qualitative change".

2.2. The ecological world view

What is completely new, as a force towards the unification of the globe, is World-Ecology. Up to 1960, the world was being pulled together mainly by World-Economy, i. e. the extraction transfer, combination and consumption of natural resources. Nature was conceived often as an enemy to be conquered. Very few had foreseen that, in so doing, mankind would disrupt life-supporting equilibria and jeopardize its very existential bases. Awareness of ecological problems is something distinctly new and environmentalism is entitled, in our opinion, to be called a revolution.By its emphasis on the planetary nature of ecological interdependencies ("biosphere" the world ecosystem, "spaceship Earth", "the Gaia hypothesis"), it has contributed mightily to the spread of "one-world awareness". There is now a deep and widespread feeling of responsibility, involvement, and care towards our little blue planet, the only home of man, which gives a quite new flavor to contemporary strivings toward world unity.

2.3. Cultural pluralism and structural polycentrism

The third new aspect of the contemporary phase in the globalization process is harder to define. It pertains to the social, cultural and political realm, and may be defined negatively as the "Loss of the Center" or, positively, as the possibility of co-existence of an authentic, real diversity and plurality of civilizations.

The Modern World System has been structured around a core area, Europe, and its core values. Civilization and Modernization (and other such concepts, like Growth and Development) have been thinly disguised synonyms for Europeization (Westernization). The growth of world-level structures has gone hand in hand with the growth of the European, and then Western, (and/or Northern) centrality, and the peripheralization (marginalization) of other areas and cultures.

In the last decades however this process has elicited growing criticisms and reactions, both from the affected peripheries and also from intellectuals of the Center itself. We cannot analyse here the structural-cultural dynamics propelling this protest; basically, it seems to be the effect of the continuing driving force of the Christian and Enlightenment values of "liberté, egalité, fraternité", plus the more modern recognition of "equal dignity" to non-European, non-Western civilizations and, more generally, the new interest and care in the preservation of pre-modern, pre-industrial cultures. Some of these aspirations have fuelled powerful political movements, when and where they have been able to control important resources (e.g. oil, and Islamic "fundamentalism"). Within the West, those countries formerly considered homogeneous in "race", ethnicity and culture are now being asked to accept enclaves of heterogeneous immigrant groups (not to be "melted in the pot"). They are also being asked to tolerate all sorts of sub-cultures and lifestyles formerly considered deviant with respect to some of the old "core values" (e. g. homosexuality).

The new consensus - well expressed in the manifesto of the XII World Sociological Congress in Madrid - emphasizes the possibility and desirability of basic cultural diversity within world (societal) unity. This entails a tolerance for cultural relativism. The world thus envisioned bears little resemblance to anything mankind has known until now; it is also different enough from the "modern world system" as to be considered the beginning of a new era, "post-modernism ("postmodernity"). The sociological debate on this issue is very lively, and understandably so, given the magnitude of the (alleged) historical transition, the vague, confused and contradictory evidence available, and the scope of the moral problems it posits. Tolerance and relativism are old issues in philosophy, and it is well known that perfect tolerance implies perfect lack of moral principles, and cultural relativism easily ends up in moral nihilism. A genuinely polycultural world would be rather inhospitable, for instance, to the idea of "human rights" as codified in the UN Declaration, because these are premised on a culture-bound (Western-Christian) idea of human nature. The well-documented difficulty of making Western-type liberal-democratic systems work in non-Western cultures also bodes ill for a "post-modern" global society.

One traditional way of framing the issue is to ask whether "one can be civilized in more than one way", whether a plurality of civilizations can be woven into an authentically integrated whole (Konecny, 1962). In more sociological terms, one can ask whether shared core values are a necessary requirement of social (societal) order (integration), or whether the latter can rest on other bases, like mere communication or material interests (economy and ecology). We tend to stick to the traditional sociological thesis, that a world society, like any other society, cannot function without a set of core values. Of course the sharing of a minimum set of central values leaves ample room for the tolerance of diversity of more "peripheral", sub-cultural values, pertaining lifestyles and so on.

A further question, at a more structural level, would be whether a world system can be genuinely polycentric, or whether "centredness", centralization, is an unavoidable feature of societal systems. This has partly to do with the former problem since central values tend to be embodied in certain individuals and groups, who tend to dwell in certain places; thus spatial-territorial organization and the structure of the cultural system do mirror each other to some extent. But it also has to do with the mechanics of the communication systems, and modern communication technology seems to enlarge the possibilities for decentralization. But the issue is rather complex and controversial; it can be argued a) that spatial decentralization at the surface (distribution and utilization of "compunication" networks) is accompanied by a growing functional centralization at the core (control of know-how for production of hardware and software of the same networks); b) that the "real" centers of societal (political-economic) power are by definition better equipped to take full advantage of the compunication technologies, and thus, in one way or the other, the latter will end up reinforcing the former.

In sum, contemporary (post-modern) "globalism" rejects older visions of world unity based on the spread of a single set of core values (European, Western, modern) and the dominance of a single core area (the North). It emphasizes instead the equal dignity of a wide plurality of cultures and civilizations, and enshrines cultural diversity and spatial equality (symmetry, equilibrium) as basic features of the proposed world system. But there is no guarantee that this is a possible or viable world societal system, and not merely a collection of loose, competitive, hostile subsystems, as it was in pre-modern history. In order to make such a polycentric, morally diverse system function peacefully, an extraordinary amount of human virtue and institutional ingenuity seems required.

3. Localism

One of the main "laws" of social theory, expressed in many ways by an impressive roster of authorities, is that "modernization" entails the broadening of spatial horizons, the transition from "localism to cosmopolitanism" as an aspect of the more general change from particularism to universalism; and that "progress" is accompanied by the "communication and mobiletic (Russett, 1967) revolution" and the withering away of the spatial determinants of social behavior. To structural-functional sociology, space and place are increasingly marginal variables.

Positions have changed in the last twenty years, for a number of reasons. One is the role of "structural" studies on development, which brought to the fore the importance of urban poles, the continuing dichotomy between town and country ("dual economies"), the growing opposition between "center and periphery", the persistence of old and the emergence of new regional differentiations, etc. Another source seems to be the growth of modern environmentalism, with its stress on the material, and hence also spatial, bases of social life; and the ensuing revival of the "human-ecological" approach in sociology. A further source is the involvement of sociology in the processes of spatial (architectural, urban, regional) planning and design. Finally, a new sensitivity towards the spatial dimension is also the result of developments in micro-sociological theory (symbolic interactionism, phenomenology etc.), with their emphasis on face-to-face relations, "silent" body language, concrete situations and behavior settings, etc. In the eighties, a number of theorists, such as A. Giddens, and R. Collins, drew on both the macro/structural, and micro/phenomenological approaches to build synthetic theories in which space is given back the central place it once held (Giddens, 1985; Collins, 1981).

These theoretical developments have an elective affinity with a number of phenomena occurring in contemporary societies and which often share the label of "new localism". We shall try below to sketch some of them; given the nature of the material, and the highly synthetic account, we shall not attempt to refer systematically to the wide-ranging literature behind it.

3.1 Localism in economic development

Homo Oeconomicus does not exist in the void, nor only in the abstract space of the market. Development depends not only on natural physical conditions, like land, raw materials and climate, but also on transport and communications infrastructures, settlement patterns, political institutions, cultural values and social relations prevailing in the specific locales. Thus even modern economies show a variety of spatial patterning. One instance are the so-called "economic islands", based on a multiplicity of small firms, growing by mithosis, flexibly linked by a variety of "externalities", deeply rooted in the local conditions, but technologically advanced and fully oriented to the world markets. This type of economic development, according to many analysts, can only be explained by the specificity of local conditions; in turn it may enhance community pride, regional identity, etc. Another, related, instance is the stress on the "certified regional origin" of products, especially of agriculture (wine, liquors, fruit, cheese, etc.), but extending also to others (shoes, garments). The national origin has been long used as a guarantee of quality, especially of industrial products: "Made in Germany" for machinery and chemicals, "Made in Japan" for electronics, "made in Italy" for fashion, etc. Now some regional chambers of commerce, at least in Italy, have established their own systems for guaranteeing, marketing and publicising worldwide the produce of their area. Finally, it can be recalled that in the competition for attracting residents and investments, the localities and regions often engage themselves in PR and advertising campaigns ("urban and regional marketing"), stressing their locational advantages-services, amenities, infrastructures, social climate ("business environment") etc. This inevitably contributes to the liveliness of at least "official", institutional, and mercantile regional identity, pride, etc. Intellectuals and believers in "authentic" identity may sneer at such "fabricated" images, but it is neither new nor *per se* objectionable that cultural values ride on material interests.

A quite different version of "new economic localism" concerns less developed regions. New doctrines of "self reliance", "self-centered development", "community development", gained popularity in the seventies as a reaction to established and largely bankrupted (literally) approaches to development in the "Third World". They stress the "de-coupling" of the "dependency" links between the poor and the advanced economies and technologies, and the full use of local potentials both in terms of natural and of human resources, for meeting basic local needs; a return to some degree of self-sufficiency and autarchy. They favor the use of "appropriate", "small-scale", "intermediate" technologies, often derived from local traditions ("ethno-technologies"). These theories are an outgrowth (and an important component) of the ecological, populist and "nativist" doctrines of that decade, and it is not at all clear how far they have proved their use and viability in the following years. They have found some favor also in the conservative, isolationist circles of the North (the temptation of "benign neglect" of less developed countries), but, some rhetoric notwithstanding, they seem to have nowhere persuaded the elites of the poor countries, unable and unwilling to "opt out" of their links with the developed world.

3.2. Localism in politics

There are several arguments on the enduring importance of place in politics. At a more general level, it is hard to counter the famous dictum of Tip 0'Neill, that "all politics is local politics"; at the international as well as the domestic levels it is mainly a struggle for the geographical distribution of resources. The control of territory ("der Nomos Der Erde", as Carl Schmitt (1950) put it) is still one of the central objects, as well as determinants, of political life.

At another level, electoral studies show a high degree of spatial variation, as well as of stability in time, in voting behavior; there are local traditions in voting, which endure for generations, and in some cases even centuries, however much socio-economic conditions may change; they point to underlying longue-durée, space-rooted structures. The "nationalization" thesis of voting behavior, according to which local variations would converge toward national averages, has been falsified again and again (Agnew, 1987). A third, enduring source of localism in politics is the persistence, at least in liberal-democratic regimes, of the principle of self-government of local communities, administrative decentralization, etc. Although the forces of centralization are ever more powerful, they meet continuing resistance - though often only rhetorical and ineffective; but the underlying values continue to be professed. A fourth factor is the growing scope of the physical, environmental planning functions of public administrations, which forces them to dedicate a fair part of their attention and activities to spatial, local problems. Finally, it has also been pointed out that common regional roots still play a role also at the higher levels of politics. It is well known that national leaders often surround themselves with "inner circles" of personal counselors drawn from their home region, as though this type of bond (in which space has a mediating role, of facilitating intimate, enduring personal bonds, developed through common early experiences in residence, school, business, profession, and often reinforced by family relations, sharing of speechforms and folkways, etc.) would provide maximum trust and loyalty.

3.3. The revival of smaller settlements

In most advanced countries, the secular cycle of large-city growth has subsided, and smaller towns (within metropolitan regions) are experiencing a healthy growth trend. This is connected to the increasing dis-amenities of big-city life (pollution, crime, overcrowding, etc.), the reduction of distances caused by communications technologies,and the changing patterns of work. A growing number of people can enjoy the advantages of small-town and rural life, without giving up the advantages of metropolitan jobs and services. These "exurbanites" often become strongly protective of their newly-found locale, fight to preserve its local flavor, and promote a revival in community-feelings.

3.4. Ethnic-regional movements

One of the biggest surprises of the sixties and seventies has been the revival of ethnic-regional- (micro)national consciousness within some of the oldest, and most advanced, national societies. The Quebeçois separatist movement in Canada, Scottish and Welsh nationalism in the United Kingdom, Celtic revival in Brittany, Catalonian nationalism in Spain, Occitan movements in Southern France, Friesian identity in the Low Countries and northern Germany, Sardinian and Friulian regional movements in Italy, etc. are just a few examples. In Eastern Europe, ethnic-regional and national differences, far from melting in the class-internationalism and the socialist melting pot, seem to have been exacerbated and now appear as the most explosive problem in the area. Here as elsewhere, however, it is difficult to distinguish the "level" of the claim. Much of the struggle in this field concerns precisely the self- and hetero- definition of a collectivity as a "people" "race" "minority" "nationality" "nation" "language group" "ethnic group" "regional group", etc., because legal and political claims are variously attached to each of them.

In the US, ethnic groups have not (yet?) managed to "spatialize" their claims, to identify themselves with particular regions; due partly to the exceptionally high mobility of the US population. But some districts and areas are getting more and more ethnically "colored", and bilingualism (still unofficial) is spreading in some areas; so that ethnic regionalism is a distinct possibility in the US too.

The persistence or resurgence of ethnic-regional differentiation is a highly diversified and complex phenomenon, and in the past three decades several sociological interpretations have been advanced. Some of the most popular relate it with socio-economic dynamics (the "internal colonialism" thesis); others see it as a displacement of the revolutionary spirit; and so on. In most advanced countries, regional-ethnic differences - at least at "folkloric" levels - are cultivated and emphasized also for political reasons (enhancement of loyalty and participation) and economic ones (as we have seen above).

Ethnic-regional movements, at least in Western Europe, do not necessarily have a closed, inward- and backward-looking, parochial outlook. One of their aims is to translate traditional cultural forms into modern media of expression. They do not reject modern society, but try to select and adapt what is valuable in the old culture; therefore they are often actively engaged in the invention of cultural innovations. Among their leaders, one often finds younger intellectuals, well acquainted with the latest fashions in the arts, as well as in the technologies. This is what makes "modern" ethnic-regional movements distinct from the "old", merely conservative, ones.

They are not isolated either. They link up across boundaries, hold international meetings, build coordinating bodies and federations, so that at least in Europe one may speak of a "trans-national ethnic-regional movement". They actively lobby the European institutions (Council of Europe, European Community) who have promptly seized the issue, because of its clear implications for the "softening" of the rigid structures of centralistic nation-states. A federalist "Europe of the Regions" is a basic official goal of many Western European ethnic-regional movements.

Whatever the factual weight of these phenomena (and there are grounds to believe they are rather light: their heydays were in the sixties and seventies; the eighties seem to have witnessed a decline in their momentum, at least in most western-European countries) they are certainly among the clearest evidence in favor of the individuation-globalization (in this case, regionalization-europeization)nexus.

3.5. Environmental movements

We have already seen that ecological consciousness is a force toward globalism. But here it must be stressed that it is also, at the same time, a force toward localism. Usually, concern and mobilization in this field start from very local, "backyard" problems. Throughout industrial societies, in thousands and thousands of cases, people unite at the grassroot level to defend their drinking water, their air, their landscape, the quality of their neighborhoods and regions. Almost automatically, however, local environmental movements become vehicles for the spread of global ecological conscience. It is obvious even to children that air, water and life-forms found in one particular place are but cross-sections of world-wide flows; that what we breathe depends on the workings of the tropical rain forests, that our woods die because of far-away industrial fumes, etc. The double bind of the ecological movements is perfectly expressed by their widespread slogan, "think globally, act locally".

It is common for environmental movements to coalesce with ethnic-regional ones, since in many countries the environment comprises both natural and man-made features; the defense of the natural environment cannot easily be set apart from the defense of the cultural landscape.

The attribution of a collective name, "new localism", to these apparently disparate (but, as we have seen, in many ways linked) phenomena implies that they can be subsumed under a common theory. Perhaps the simpler way to express it is that they manifest the transformations in the "social nature of space". In modern conditions, structured mainly by communication technologies, space has indeed lost many of its old functions in the organization of society, but has acquired new ones. The roles of space have deeply changed ("from the space of places to the space of flows") but have not dissolved. Some spatial constraints have disappeared, and man is now more free to structure space according to his own whims and needs; but this makes space even more an object of conscious choice and discussion, private as well as public. More than ever, space has become a social problem.

4. Globalism, localism, and post-modern society

It is maintained that localism and globalism (individuation and globalization) grow simultaneously because they are really not opposites, but dialectically linked. An alternative explanation may be that they both grow at the expense of a third party. This is - according to such a view - the old model of Society, identified with the Nation-State. This identification, long taken for granted in modern sociology, as well as in most common discourse, is now subject to growing criticism, both for conceptual theoretical and for empirical-historical reasons. There is a growing consensus that the Nation State is in "crisis", and that its decline as the main level of social organization is a component (cause and effect) of a larger crisis, that of Modernity (modern society), which, in turn, is correlated with the contemporary technological and economic triumphs. According to some theorists, we are living in an epochal transition from Modernity to Post-Modernity. The theory of post-modernism has been developed - so far, mainly at the "micro" level (individual consciousness and everyday life) - but it is not difficult to see its "structural", "macro", correlates, and some of them are actually being developed by scholars of political science and international relations.

Modern society, as we have known it for a few centuries, was based on 1) emphasis on instrumental rationality; 2) economicism (emphasis on "material" values of production and consumption); 3) "nationalization", i.e. concentration of social power in the hands of the Nation State, marked by centralization, hierarchization, drive for internal cultural homogeneity, maximum differentiation from other Nation States, strict control of boundaries, "totipotency" (or autarchy), ability to defend its independence by military force ("sovereignty"), etc. Now, so the theory runs, the very success of that system has generated its own contradictions, and unleashed its antithetic forces. Of course, the theory takes into account mainly phenomena occurring in the most advanced parts of the world.

Instrumental rationality has created a scientific-technological industrial system able to produce unlimited amounts of goods and to satisfy all basic material needs, so that it is now no longer necessary to focus all activities on "getting a living"; now it is possible to liberate other human faculties, e.g. capacity for enjoyment, emotions, altruism, phantasies, solidarity with nature. That the very success of rationalization would open the gates for a new wave of sensualism, emotionalism and irrationality, and that the bouurgeois-capitalist system would be contradicted and betrayed by its scions, is a rather old sociological observation: it runs from Weber to Mannheim throught Sorokin and Schumpeter to Marcuse to Bell, (just to drop a few names).

Also, the success of the Nation-States has created the conditions for their own decline ("nothing fails like success"). States became so overwhelming on peoples' minds as to induce them to die by the tens of millions in the name of the Nation; eventually, this caused a moral revulsion against "ethical" nationalism. But the nation state is also losing its capability to provide basic services, to perform its traditional functions. With the development of the air force and the nuclear-missile complex, the state ceased to guarantee the physical survival of people within its boundaries. The nation-states have also lost some of their powers in the economic spheres, with the internationalization of economies, the growth of multi-national corporations, etc. In cases where they are unable to provide the expected amount of goods and services (economic failure) nationstates can easily suffer loss of loyalty (Teune, 1990). With the dramatic growth of electronic communications, states have almost completely lost their control of the flows of information reaching their citizens. The importance of this loss can hardly be exaggerated; we would argue that the most powerful single factor behind the dramatic collapse of Communist regimes in Eastern Europe was television, through which some very attractive features of the West had become quite familiar to the "socialist" masses. The improvement of the educational level of the citizenry, in order to provide the skills required by a modern industrial society, has also made it more difficult for central governments to exert hierarchical controls and to maintain legitimacy (Rosenau, 1990).

Thus, while established Nation-States formally still occupy the center stage in the political arena - both domestic and international - they have generally lost their hold on their citizens' hearts as well as in some of the basic social processes. Portions of power are leaving the national centers and moving "upward" and "sideways"; the weakening of national centers also encourages claims for devolution "downwards", toward sectoral, regional and local levels. Crises of authority, of legitimacy, are common features of nation-states in late-modern, or perhaps already post-modern, society.

From the micro (subjective, psychological) point of view, the basic fact is the huge increase of information available to the individual. The "communication revolution" gives him access to persons, things, places or events regardless (almost) of physical distance. Individuals are free to build relations and communities across space, throwing into disarray the old hierarchical order of local communities. They can belong to a growing, almost unlimited number of "social circles", which is a basic condition for individuation. They are free (with all the necessary qualifications) to choose from among a wide range of information sources, and can structure their own information environment; which allows for a (potential) further increase in individual differentiation, to the limits where the individual is so thinly extended as to break up into pieces. Communication and information can be so abundant as to lose their original instrumental functions; post-modern man is characterized by his playful, random, aimless use of the information and communication resources. In the extreme case, they become ends in themselves, and the prospect of the "disappearance of the subject" and the "end of man", wholly melted in the flow of information through him, is a favourite theme of post-modern theorists. This also reminds us that excessive focus on the individual subject can vaporize it.

But there are also less exotic, negative sides of the situation. To begin with, the information supplied by the communication industry is inevitably partial, selected, and follows its own rules; fears of conditioning and feelings of manipulation are widespread. The fact that the media still command a surprisingly high level of popular trust, according to most studies, only compounds the anxiety of some social critics. Its very quantity easily results in confusion, overload, stress, and rejection. People are bombarded by an excess of disordered messages, and the overall image of the world often is one of threatening chaos. Secondly, freedom is not an unqualified boon. It requires decisions taken in uncertainty; it can be psychologically tiring and demanding; it can lead to random, chaotic behavior, to loss of identity, and to flight reactions (Fromm). People also need the security and comforts (Burke's "resting places") of an external constraining moral order, familiar customs, trustworthy authority.

Finally, the world of electronics and print may well be highly diversified, and pointing to growing "customization" and individuation; they can well be bended to enhance the vitality of local, regional and minority cultures. The overall impression remains one of an essential difference between that "virtual" world and the one that results from face-to-face interactions and conversations, from the bodily, sensory experience of people, things and places. The electronic media operate, basically, at a level different from everyday life; they bear the mark (on their hardware, as well as in their contents) of the national and transnational society, and thus belong to "large scale society", with its inevitable connotates of massification, homogeneization etc. (this applies much less, of course, to some newer technologies, like the telefax, the videocam, etc.)

Post-modern society, like all antitheses, in part brings to the extremes some of the trends of the preceding one, and in part represents a reaction to it. Cultural pluralism, polycentrism and localism seem to belong to the latter category. Post-modernism is marked, among other things, by the rejection of the value of uniformity (equality, homogeneity) which characterizes the old thinking and which descends from the requirements of the rule of law, of bureaucracy and of mass production. Instead, it extols the values of diversity and multiplicity, which are characteristic of ecological thinking.

Post-modernism is characterised, further, by the loss or rejection of the one, necessary, and transcendent Center - be it God, the Nation-State, or any other value; perhaps, even Man, substituted by a supermarket surfeit of arbitrary, contingent, fluid, multiple centers.

Post-modernism is also marked by a revival of localism. Localism represents one of the possible ways out of anomy, alienation and identity loss, typical of modernity. The New Localism is the search for a refuge from the unsettling confusion of the larger world. Modern man/woman has created a global system, which has many advantages and values but which is certainly too complex to survey and manage, even though only intellectually. Post-modern man/woman, just because he/she is so deeply embedded in global information flows, may feel the need to revive small enclaves of familiarity, intimacy, security, intelligibility, organic-sensuous interaction, in which to mirror him/herself, contrary to the process occurring in front of the subjectivity-effacing TV screen. The possibility of being exposed, through modern communication technology, to the whole infinity of places, persons, things, ideas, makes it all the more necessary to have, as a compensation, a center in which to cultivate one's self . The easy access of the whole world, with just a little time and money, gives new meaning to the need of a subjective center - a home, a community, a locale - from which to move and to which to return and rest.

Traditionally, localism and rootedness have been considered backward, if not reactionary, attitudes, since history seemed to unfold towards cosmopolitanism , universalism, and mobility.

Territorial *Gemeinschaft* seemed bound to be destroyed by functional *Gesellschaft*. This has happened to some extent, but the trend could not run full course. It has found inner limits in some basic human needs, and it has generated dialectically its own limiting contradictions and countervailing forces.

Of course, as the qualifiers make clear, neo-localism is different from old localism. The essential differences are two. The first is that while old localism was"primordial", unthinking, the new one is the outcome of free will, conscious choice; the former is "necessary and natural", the second voluntary and intentional (rational). The second difference is that the old localism tended to minimize contacts with the exterior, to maintain a strong closed boundary, while the new localism is quite aware of the rest of the world, and is quite open to interactions with it.

PART II: SOME EMPIRICAL MATERIALS

5. Regionalism in Italy: the Lega Lombarda

According to most usual socio-economic indicators, Italy is a modern society; it vies with the United Kingdom in industrial output and living standards. Like most countries, it shows strong regional variations, especially along the North-South axis. The traditional dichotomy between the Mezzogiorno and the North seems to be widening, at least at the structural-economic level. More recently, a three-fold partition has been suggested, with the growth of a "third Italy" comprising the North-East and some central areas, marked by a diffuse network of small and medium industries.

It is not easy to assess the extent to which "objective" regional variations in geographical conditions, in historical experience, in culture (values, language, style of life), in productive structures, translate into feelings of regional identities in Italy. After national unity (1860), the State was set up along strictly centralistic lines, and regional differentiations were officially negated; every effort was made to build a common national identity. After the fall of Fascism, regionalist political doctrines re-emerged, and 19 regions were granted some degree of administrative autonomy (1948 Constitution). Five of them were peripheral regions, marked by special problems (insularity or presence of national minorities) and these were given special, broader autonomy: Sicily, Sardinia, Valle d' Aosta, Trentino-South Tyrol, and Friuli-Venezia Giulia. The former four were set up even before the 1948 Republican Constitution; the last only in 1963. The other, "normal" regions, were instituted in 1971. This staggering fact indicates how hard it was to turn the old centralistic state into a regional one; and the difficulties are still by no means over. In the eighties, many political observers saw a tendency of the Central State to undermine regional autonomies and reclaim its powers.

For a long time, regional variations had no political meaning and little cultural legitimacy. They were relegated to the low-brow level of dialects, jokes and prejudices. With the strong immigration waves from the South to the North-West, in the fifties and sixties, some manifestations of ethnic prejudice and "racism" emerged; but the issue was not taken seriously. Very few sociological studies on ethnic-regional relations have ever been done in Italy. Regional variations were considered a matter for ethnologists and anthropologists, i. e. scholars of premodern societies. It was assumed that they would wither away with modernization and "progress".

Such phenomena were considered more important in the frontier areas, where historical ties with the entities beyond the border, cultural affinity, presence of minorities and claims for autonomy were more significant. And it is in such areas that some scholarly interest in these issues emerged, and a small tradition of regional-ethnic studies was built in the seventies and eighties.

In Italy, regional identity feelings translated into political movements and organizations only in a few cases. In Sicily during the Allied occupation (liberation) and immediately thereafter, a separatist movement arose; it had murky ideological bases, and was short-lived. Since the setting up of the regional autonomous government, there have been no talks of a "Sicilian autonomist movement". By contrast however, separatism in Sardinia - which always housed a "Sardinian Action Party" - has been at times fairly strong; and even more so in the Valle d'Aosta, whose Union Valdotaine has always been the ruling party. The Region Trentino-South Tyrol has been practically split in two. In South Tyrol, the local regional party (Sudtiroler Volkspartei) dominates political-administrative life, and the Province enjoys a large degree of autonomy. The Trentino question is less linear. Its autonomist movement was rather strong at the end of the war, but was subsequently mostly swallowed up by the Christian Democratic party. It lingered on for thirty years, and more recently seems to have partly contributed to the success of the Green party.

Likewise, in Friuli-Venezia Giulia one has to distinguish the two parts of the region. Venezia Giulia is the Trieste metropolitan area, characterized by a sizeable Slovene minority, which is of the "national", and not merely "ethnic-regional" type.

Friuli has long nurtured a cultural-historical identity, but only after 1945 was this translated into political terms. The inclusion of Friuli among the "Special Autonomy Regions" was bitterly fought, also by the local power elite, fearful of any "separatist" tendency. This also helps to explain the 15-year lag between formal institution and factual implementation. The autonomist feeling was very weak, and limited to a handful of lay and priestly intellectuals. With the setting up of the regional institutions, the ethnic-regional awareness suddenly exploded; a Movimento Friuli was founded in 1964, which at the 1968 elections won 12 % of the vote. It became a significant political force, but after a few years it began to decline; in the eighties it was reduced to about 3 %, and in the nineties dissolved.

The example of Friuli was probably not without significance for the neighboring, much larger Veneto. In the seventies, the Liga Veneta (Venetian League) was founded. While the issues on which the Movimento Friuli built its success were mostly of the economic type (the familiar "internal colonialism" argument: Hechter, 1975), it seems that the main motivation of the Liga Veneta is the threat to local culture and way of life posed by recent immigration from the South, especially in the public service sector. One of the more characteristic rally cries of the Liga has been "Fuori i terroni" - "Southerners go home".

6. The "Lega Lombarda"

Finally, in the eighties the mighty Lombards got the ethnic-regional message. In the most prosperous, well-organized, orderly, and modern province of the whole country - bordering on Switzerland, engaged in internationally-oriented industrial and service production - a mass ethnic-regional movement suddenly exploded, the Lega Lombarda. In the 1990 municipal elections, it ravaged all "national" parties, reaching an average of 18-20 % in many provinces, and even the relative majority in many townships. In the 1992 elections, having changed its name to Lega Nord (Northern League), it skyrocketed to 25-30 % in Lombardy and caused landslides also in neighboring Piemonte and Veneto, where it became, in many areas, the second largest party. At the national level, with 9 % of the vote, it ranks only in fourth place (after the Christian Democratic party, the Socialists and the ex-Communists, newly renamed Party of the Democratic Left), because the Center and the South stuck to traditional voting patterns.

The Lega Lombarda has also shattered most socio-political theories on the "stability" of the Italian electorate, and has caught social scientists quite unprepared. A spate of instant-researches on the phenomenon has been contracted out, and some longer-term and more systematic studies on motivations, ideology, expectations, social position, political origin, etc. of the Lega supporters are under way (Mannheimer, 1991). The most frequently cited factors are the following (not necessarily in order of importance):

a) the hostility towards Southerners, especially because of (fears of) the encroachment of organised crime (Mafia, Camorra, N'drangheta). In particular the "kidnapping industry", based in Calabria and Sardinia, has struck hard in the North, causing a veritable wave of resentment against Southerners. In more recent times, however, the Liga has officially muffled these feelings, and vigourously rejects charges of xenophobia or "racism"; to some extent, these feelings have been re-targeted against Third World immigrants;
b) the hostility towards the Central State, seen as fiscally oppressive, arrogant, corrupt and inefficient. Some observers emphasize this anti-statist motive, and see the Lega essentially as a fiscal revolt, an expression of the dissatisfaction of autonomous workers and small businessmen with the stifling bureaucracy and bad

public services; others stress the coincidence of anti-South and anti-State animosity, since the Italian State is manned disproportionately by Southerners (up to 80 %, by some accounts);

c) the aspiration to more effective self-government, especially with regard to financial matters (fiscal and investment policies); there is a widespread feeling in Lombardy and the North generally of being bled in order to support the Roman parasitic bureaucracy and the Mezzogiorno waste;

d) the impatience (certainly not peculiar to Lombardy) with the somewhat Byzantine practices of a seemingly unreformable system of parties, centered in the national capital and thus often sneered at as "Roman Parties";

e) the dissolution of the moral grip of the two main national church-parties, the Christian Democrats and the Communists. Their ideological "raison d'être" slowly eroded by the secularization of society, on one side, and the withering away of revolutionary, millenaristic expectations on the other. The PCI (now PDS) has long ceased to appear as a threat; correspondingly, the Christian Democratic party has also lost its credibility as the "dam" and "shield" against Communism. Thus, other grounds for political action and conflict were free to emerge.

It is unclear whether the Lega Lombarda can be called a localistic and/or an ethnic-regional movement. One reason for the difficulty is the speed of change both in the real composition of the movement and of its official ideology. Undoubtedly it began, in the late seventies, as an ethnic-regional movement, after the pattern of the Liga Veneta. But its promotion of a Lombard identity and conscience has met with several difficulties, among which is the lack of a common linguistic code (Lombardy is a hodge-podge of widely different dialects). The concept of a "Lombard nation" failed to be taken seriously. Thus, in a second stage (ca. 1985) the Liga dropped such "vernacular-folkloric" objectives; thereby ceasing, we would say, to qualify as an ethnic-regional movement. It began to talk in more politico-economic terms, stressing the commonality of concrete interests of the whole of Northern Italy. Its leadership was acknowledged by other ethnic-regional movements in that area, coalitions were formed, and the Lega Lombarda effectively became the Lega Nord. At this stage, the startling proposal was made (ca. 1990) of splitting up latitudinally the Italian unitary state into three federate republics, North, Center and South. It met with some cries of horror and even charges of high treason, but also with extensive scepticism. Presently (1992) the Lega seems bent on becomeing, first of all, a nation-wide force intent on capturing the national power center in order to reform from there the whole of the Italian system. The energy and efficiency with which this goal is being pursued is one of the reasons for the huge success of the Lega; but it may weaken its original, local-ethnic roots and transform it into another nation-wide party. It is not difficult to imagine that, as the Lega representatives in Rome become increasingly involved in political bargaining with the System, and work to reform the Italian State, their followers should become impatient and fall back on local, short term, emotional, maybe even ethnic-regional issues. Because, as some pieces of research show, the objective defining feature of the Lega electorate is indeed localism (Mannheimer 1991).

But there is also a second feature, which is perhaps more ideological, but which is stressed almost obsessively in Lega rhetoric: the appeal to Europe. According to the Lega, Northern Italy is already a fully European (Central European) area, in economic, social, and cultural terms; but it is weighted down towards the Mediterranean and the Third World. Northern Italy is ready to meet the requirements of the European Unity act, and the deadline of Dec. 31, 1992; it will not tolerate the thought of missing the "European train" because of the inefficiency and backwardness of the Center-South. This is the main argument for the "secession" hypothesis. Thus, integration into a larger whole becomes a possible cause of the disintegration of lesser systems.

The Lega Lombarda/Nord may be only a passing historical contingency, or it may take root and stabilize as one of the many small and ineffective ethnic-regional parties which dot the voking maps of the Italian nation, as well as those of other nations. Or it may be able to develop into a fully-fledged national party of significant dimensions, thus gaining the ability to deeply transform the Italian system. Nobody knows yet.

As a social phenomenon, at any rate, it seems to bear out nicely some of the theories on the relations between localism and globalism, (regionalism and Europeanism), in the framework of advanced (post modern?) societies, as sketched above.

7. The localism-cosmopolitanism scale: applications in Friuli

Empirical sociologists have sometimes tried to measure the position of individuals on a localism-cosmopolitanism scale. This is not exactly the same as the localism-globalism dimension - since cosmopolitanism, like universalism, has more a moral, cultural-substantive meaning than a spatial one - but it seems close enough. One such scale asks respondents to state their "attachment" or "feeling of belonging" (membership, loyalty, etc.) to several levels of "socio-spatial organization", ranging from the neighborhood (village) to commune, province (district, county), (sub-national) region (state, in federal polities), nation-state (federal state), continent (international region) civilization ("block"), and the world (mankind). As is the case with most sociological scales, this too presents many problems. The main charge it elicits is that responses cannot avoid being highly context-dependent. People feel more attached to one or the other level according to the situation in which they find themselves when the issue arises. It is common knowledge that when a person is abroad, he identifies himself more readily as a national (citizen of his nation-state), while when "at home", he may feel more strongly his regional or local loyalty. Another difficulty is the different meaning (content) of terms like "attachment" "belonging", "identity" and others, commonly used to describe the relationship between the individual and "place". Such psychological relationships are indeed complex and volatile, and the semantics of the scale may massively influence the answers. But this is inevitable in all attempts to measure attitudes. Much truth must be attributed to the statement that what counts is behavior, and not attitude, and that the correlation between the two may be rather low. However, this is the predicament of most sociological surveys.

In a series of studies spanning almost twenty years (1972-1988), a localism-globalism scale (with very slight changes in wording and in responding techniques) was administered to samples in North-Eastern Italy (Friuli). The overall results are shown in fig. l. For more information on the studies, see the Appendix.

The main comments, taking into account also the variables and associations wich are not shown in the figure and cannot be presented here because of space limitations, are as follows:

7.1 People "feel attached" ("report to belong", "identify with", "are loyal to", etc.) mainly to the smaller-scale locales: the neighborhood (in cities), the hamlet or village (in rural areas), the township or commune (on the average, amounting to a few thousand people). The term however poses a difficulty, because it is more an organizational-administrative than a spatial entity. The second main locus of attachment, much weaker than the first, is the nation-state. The intermediate levels ("district", province, region, sub-national area) and the supra-national levels (Europe, the World) attract weaker feelings. It seems that people feel attached above all to the primordial "life-world" of everyday life, the place where they have their homes, property, jobs, primary relations, service structures and infrastructures. But they are also much influenced by the most powerful element of the system in which they are embedded - the Nation State - loyalty to which is the goal of much institutional effort, beginning with the school.

7.2 In all cases, Europe kindles weaker feelings than the State and the World. It appears that there is no smooth progress in the broadening of horizons. People jump directly from national attachments to cosmopolitanism-universalism, which appears to be, as indicated above, a moral rather than a spatial category; it appears to be the negation of any territorial attachment whatsoever, a declaration of "world-citizenship", of lack of roots, of readiness to move, of refusal to accept the partition of mankind, etc. In spite of all the historical links of Friuli to Europe (migration, business, etc.), the efforts of European Institutions, and the rhetoric of Europeanism (very strong in Italy), Europe has a very weak place on the mental horizon of the respondents.

7.3 The levels between the local (neighborhod, village, township) and the national have variable positions in the different pieces of research. The Region comes out badly in the older research, but fares far better in some of the more recent. This may be evidence of the strengthening of the administrative region (only nine years old when the first survey was done) in the consciousness of people, and/or of the (relative) weakness of the merely cultural-historical regional entity.

7.4 In all cases "Northern Italy" gets a very low score. At the time of the surveys, there was not much popular support for a "Republic of Northern Italy", as proposed by the Lega Lombarda.

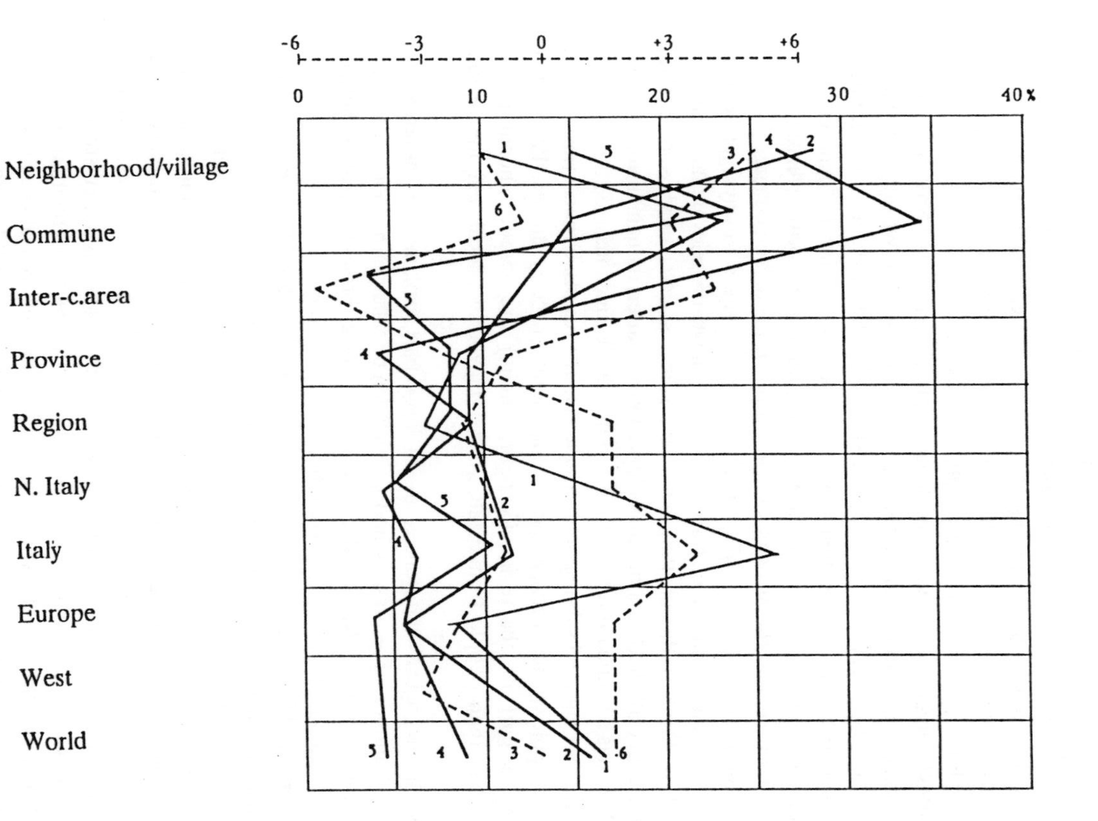

Figure 1 Attachment to levels of territorial organization in six studies in the Friuli-V.G.region, 1971-1988 (see notes)

7.5 While most studies yield rather similar patterns, two of them diverge widely. In both cases, the difference may be easily explained by contextual, ad-hoc factors. In the 1972 survey, the Nation State (Italy) scored very high. That survey concerned the problems of "living at the border", and many of the questions concerned the past difficulties between Italy and neighboring Yugoslavia, the problem of the Slovene minority, the role of armed forces and border militia, and so on. Thus the focus was very much on state-level problems, and it is reasonable to think that the respondents' minds were also focused on the positive role of the Nation State in embodying basic cultural values, warranting security, etc.

The 1988 survey also shows a prevalence of attachment to the Nation State, but also - at exactly the same level - to the region, Europe and the World. Here too the focus of the whole survey - a pre-election study of political perceptions, attitudes, values, opinions, party alignments etc. - was on regional, national and international problems. No mention was made of strictly local, everyday issues. Little wonder then that the higher spatial levels of social life loomed large.

7.6 Medium-low levels, like the "area" and the "province", always get very low marks. This is understandable, since the former have no relevant administrative structure in Friuli (although they may have some socio-cultural and historical existence, especially in the mountain valleys) and the latter, though historically well-established, has few and rather marginal administrative functions.

7.7 There are marked sub-regional variations in the results. Urban areas are much more cosmopolitan than rural, and especially mountain, communities. People from the Eastern part of the region (Venezia Giulia) are more nationalistic and cosmopolitan than people from Friuli, who tend favour the local and the regional levels.

7.8 Such "ecological" differences are in large part explained by differences in education (number of years in school), which can be taken as a good indicator of socio-economic status. More educated people have broader mental horizons (systems of spatial reference) than the others.

7.9 Gender differences are not very prominent. Females, who generally have lower education, have a rather narrower breadth of horizon.

7.10 Age makes a strong difference. Younger people have markedly broader horizons than their elders. Age is highly correlated with longer schooling, so that it may be assumed that this is, again, the relevant factor; but statistical tests show that it has an influence of its own may; so other age-related factors have to be invoked. An obvious one is the shorter span of time passed in the place: as many studies have shown, length of residence is strongly correlated with local attachment. If this is the case, generational patterns of territorial identification could be stable across time: as each younger generation grows older, it becomes more "rooted". This runs counter to the theory according to which cosmopolitism-globalism is a characteristic of the present historical context, and the generations on which it is imprinted would bear on these cultural orientations in their future course. The evidence discussed here does not allow the testing of these theses, although other sources of data would tempt one to favor the latter. One clue is that localism is very much stronger in small mountain settlements than in urban areas; and urbanization can be taken as a good indicator of the complex set of variables that can be also called modernization.

7.11 Experiences of migration for work in other countries does not appreciably improve one's position on the cosmopolitanism scale.

7.12 Evidence from one of the surveys (1985) indicates that localism is associated with: 1) (low) degree of knowledge of other Italian regions; 2) length of stay; 3) spatial extension of the primary relations network; 4) overall characteristic of the community: localism is stronger in the mountains and the rural plains, much weaker in the coastal areas and in the city; 5) degree of residential satisfaction; 6) type of attachment: the "existential-biological" one produces smaller areas of attachment, while other types of attachment fail to show this association.

7.13 The 1985 study suggests that there are different "types" of "territorial attachment" (which is something very close to localism, even though not wholly coincident), in terms of "motivation". The more common is, of course, the "primordial" or "existential" type, based on birth and upbringing in the place, having there one's family network, etc. The second is "attachment because of social integration" (feeling to be a person in a community, having friends and colleagues, feeling useful to the community, etc.). A third type of attachment, much less common, refers primarily to the qualities of the physical environment (beauty of landscape and townscape, good climate, etc.). Finally there are some who explain their local attachment in terms of pride in the "image of progress and modernity" beaconed by their community.

7.14 Evidence from another of the surveys (1988) indicates that cosmopolitism/globalism is also associated with higher income, reading of national instead of regional dailies, higher interest in politics, leftist leanings, and even more with support for the Communist party (as it was then known) and for the Greens. But also the conservatives ("neo-Fascists"), with their strong emphasis on the Nation-State, raise their position on the scale. On the contrary, localism is associated with votes for the ethnic-regional party ("Movimento Friuli") and the Christian Democratic party.

8. Summary and discussion

As usual in sociology, our empirical research raises more questions than it settles. The somewhat different techniques by which the localism measures were presented, the differences in sample designs and, more crucially, in our opinion, the different "universes of discourse" (context of research issues and "problem-areas") in which they were presented, prevents the "longitudinal" use of the evidence. In other words, it is impossible to extract from our evidence an answer to the crucial question: is localism declining, as conventional wisdom maintains?

Other answers are more clear-cut. First, also in a modern (or at least a recently modernized) society, as the one we have studied, the absolute level of localism - in factual-behavioural terms - of common people is very high: almost 70 % have been born in the same commune as their fathers; almost 60 % live in the same commune in which they born; the mean length of residence in the same place is 30 years (the average age of the sample, in the 1985 an 1988 studies, is 42 years); the mean radius of the area where family members were born or live in is between 3 and 9 kilometers; and the mean radius of mobility for work, shopping, services, etc. does not exceed 50 kilometers. Secondly, also the attitudinal (verbally reported) levels of localism ("how much do you feel attached to your locale") is also very high. Thirdly, it is also clear that localism is more a moral-social than a spatial phenomenon: people are attached to place because it is the locus of their existential, primordial, family relations. The locale is basically the life-world, the primary community. However, it is interesting to note that a minority stresses the physical aspects (landscape, environment) as the relevant motives for their attachment; this points to the "ecological" roots of localism, old or new.

Spatial mobility, per se, does not appreciably increase the levels of localism, especially if it is related to work reasons. People who had fairly long experience abroad as migrant workers are no less localistic than the others.

Fourthly, it is also interesting to note that there is a type of local attachment which is based on pride in the "progressive and modern" character of one's locale. This means that localism need not be limited to traditional societies and communities, and based on features as history, speechways, folkways, etc. This suggests that it can also survive - to some extent, and certainly with somewhat different contents - in modern societies.

The studies reviewed above do not, for instance, address the issue of the possibility of a positive correlation between localism and cosmopolitism. It is clear that some places base at least part of their fascination on their cosmopolitan character - their being world capitals, or tourist landmarks drawing visitors from all over the world, their cultural pluralism, their ethnic heterogeneity etc. The case of the Big Apple comes readily to mind. And it seems also clear that such characters foster pride and attachment in their inhabitants, and thus some sort of localism.

The same can be said, perhaps, of towns and regions that find themselves at the crossroads between different cultural and political areas. There are many such locales, along the frontiers of continental European states, that emphasize their functions as "bridges" and meeting places. A veritable "ideology of frontier regions" has been developed. It is reasonable to think - although here we can present no hard evidence - that this can be a source of community pride and attachment, and therefore of a new sort of localism. In other words, people can develop particular affection to their locale precisely because it is spatially or functionally close to (or harbors) a multiplicity of other cultures, and is wide open to them. As already suggested, localism is not necessarily correlated with closure, nor with the other features of Toennesian community.

Finally, it should be clear that the "levels of attachment" scale is a crude attempt to measure and test the Federalist doctrine. Roughly, two basic models of political organization can be confronted: the Jacobin-centralist-nationalist, and the federalist. In the first, there are only three subjects: the citizen, the State and Humanity, and the

State sits at the center of this political universe. In the federalist view, between the individual and mankind there is a very complex web of social forms, grown out of historical experience: family, local communities of various levels (from neighborhood to state to supra-national entities), associations and organizations of all kinds. Each of them is the product of spontaneous social interaction, and each has its function and worth. "We belong to all levels of Communities, and owe our loyalty to each of them" (Doxiadis, 1969). The system is subject to continuous change, mainly in the direction of enlargement, differentiation, integration and complexification. The Nation-State has been a very important phase in this development, but cannot claim any special ethnical status. It grew out of special social conditions, and should go with them. Various societal tendencies push for the devolution of its powers both upwards, to supra-national agencies, and downwards, to regional and local entities. The Federalist doctrine envisions a complex, organic, hierarchical, nested system of political entities; geared on the one hand to the global unity and the integration of humankind, and on the other hand to the protection of the diversity, identity and rights of all individual and collective subjects. Regionalism is another name for federalism. The trend toward global unity should be balanced by the upgrading of local communities, for, as Mumford (1967) put it, "To assemble peace-making power into a world authority, without a revitalization of autonomous smaller units capable of exercising local and regional initiatives, would be to rivet together the ultimate megamachine". And interest in the infinite plurality and differentiation of individual regions is what makes people love to travel freely around the world. Local and regional diversity is what makes it worthwhile to strive for global unity.

The federalist model certainly lacks the clarity and power of the stato-centric one, and in fact runs into all sort of difficulties. But it seems the only one capable of bridging, in an acceptable way, the two eternal polarities: the individual and the world, the subject and the system, local identities and global identification; and capable of weaning man out of his primordial fixation with his "national tribe" and making him tolerant of the inescapable complexities of the world system.

Some notes on the six studies

All studies were based on "structured" questionnaires administered by trained interviewers in the respondent's premises. All have used standard statistical multivariate procedures for analysis. The first three were carried out within the framework of the Institute of International Sociology of Gorizia, at the instigation of its founder and first director, Prof. Franco Demarchi; the fourth is part of an inter-university research program on "territorial attachment", funded by the Italian Ministry of Education and directed by Prof. R. Gubert, one of Demarchi's disciples. Study no. 5 was the responsibility of Dr. J. Pohl of the Institute of Geography of the Technical University of Munich, an institute whose director, Prof. Robert Geipel, led a number of surveys in the Friuli region, following the 1976 earthquake. The study was done in cooperation with the Sociological Section at the University of Udine. This latter team also carried out study no. 6.

Study 1 was done in 1970 in the provinces of Trieste and Gorizia (total population about 380.000). The random sample was 1215. The general theme was "living at the border": perceptions, attitudes, opinions and behavior regarding the border, its functions and meanings; the neighboring state; ethnic and national minorities; the boundary-maintaining institutions (the guards, armed forces, the State) etc. It was published in full as R. Gubert, La situazione confinaria, Lint, Trieste, 1972.

Study 2 focused on reciprocal perceptions and attitudes of 11 different groups, defined ethnically and spatially, living along the whole Italian-Yugoslav boundary (provinces of Udine, Trieste and Gorizia; population considered, ca. 430.000). The sample is not representative of the overall population, but only of the defined groups; in each, 100 individuals were selected, regardless of the group's widely different size. The questionnaires were administered in 1973; the results were published in A.M. Boileau, E. Sussi, Dominanza e minoranza. Immagini e raporti interetnici al confine Nord-orientale, Grillo, Udine. 1981.

Study no. 3 is based on a doctoral thesis done by Mr. A. Spetich, who in 1980 administered a short questionnaire to a random sample of 400, representative of the population of the province of Gorizia (with the exclusion of the capital town). The main topics were the attitudes toward a proposed reorganization of administrative districts, the attraction of the three main centers of the area (Udine, Trieste, Gorizia), and ethnic-regional identification. The results were published in two articles by R. Strassoldo, Legami territoriali nella provincia di Gorizia. Un sondaggio demoscopico, in "Studi Goriziani", 62, 1985; and Sociologia spaziale e apppartenenze terrritoriali, in "Sociologia urbana e rurale", 16, 1985.

The institutional framework of study no. 4 has been indicated above. The questionnaire, though rather large (over 200 variables), was strictly focused on the spatial dimensions of the "lifeworld", and the "feelings of territorial belonging", attachment, etc. The research involves 4 different regions in North-eastern Italy (Emilia Romagna, Veneto, Trentino, and Friuli). The field research was done in 1985. In Friuli, the research group based at the University of Udine includes B. Cattarinussi, N. Tessarin, B. Tellia, and the present writer. Four areas were selected for their sharp difference in "ecological" structure and morphology (a town of 100.000, Udine; two villages in rural plains; two coastal settlements; and a cluster of villages in a mountain valley). In each, 1.00 individuals were interviewed. The results of the first analyses have been published: R. Strassoldo, N. Tessarin, Le radici del localismo. Indagine sociologica sull'appartenenza territoriale in Friuli. Reverdito, Trento 1992. For a brief account in English, see N. Tessarin, Socio-spatial patterns of territorial identity, in "Proceedings of the 11· IAPS conference", Metu, Ankara, 1990.

Study 5 focused on the topic of "feelings and symbols of regional identity in Friuli". It is based on questionnaire interviews (n = 521) carried out in 1986 by a team of German scholars in five small communities in Friuli. It is still in the early stages of analysis. A preliminary publication is: J. Pohl, La coscienza regionale dei friulani all'interno e all'esterno dell'area terremotata, in G. Valussi (cur.) L'identità regionale, Quaderni dell' Istituto di geografia, Università di Trieste, 1990.

Study 6 , carried out in 1988, is a pre-electoral opinion poll commissioned by local politicians, on a sample of 1200 , representative of the whole of Friuli (provinces of Pordenone, Udine and Gorizia, with a total of ca. 1.000.000 people). The questionnaire dealt with a wide variety of political issues (international, national and regional problems; opinions on parties, institutions, etc; dynamics of electoral choice; socio-cultural attitudes, etc.). The research team included F.Buratto, G. Delli Zotti, B. Tellia and the present writer. Only a small part of the data has as yet been published, and none in scientific journals.

Selected references

Agnew, J. (1987) Place and Politics, Boston, Allen and Unwin.

Alger, C. (1990) Local response to global intrusions, Paper presented at the session on Globalization, Technology, and Territorial Identities, Madrid: XII World Congress of Sociology.

Buehl, W. (1978) Transnationale Politik, Internationale Beziehung zwischen Hegemonie und Interdependenz, Stuttgart, Klett-Cotta.

De Rosnay, J. (1974) Le macroscope, Paris, Seuil.

De Rougemont, D. (1977) L'avenir est notre affaire, Paris, Stock.

Doxiadis, C.A. (1968) Ekistics, an entroduction to the science of human settlements, London, Hutchinson.
Collins, R. (1981) On the microfoundations of macrosociology, American Yournal of Sociology, Vol. 85, No. 5.
Featherstone, M. (ed.), (1988) Post Modern Society, Theory, Culture and Society, Vol. 5. No. 2-3.
Giddens, A. (1985) The constitution of society, Oxford, Univ. Press.
Gottmann, J. (ed.) (1980) Centre and Periphery, Spatial Variations in Politics, Beverely Hills-London, Sage Publications.
Konecny, F. (1962) On the plurality of civilizations, London, Polonica.
Lemert, C. (1979) Sociology and the twilight of man, Carbondale and London, Southern Illinois Univ. Press.
Luhmann, N. (1975) Die Weltgesellschaft, in Luhmann, N. Soziologische Aufklarung, Opladen, Westdeutscher.
Magnaghi, A. (1990) Politiche ambientali e sviluppo locale, in Trevisiol, E. (ed.) Territorio e società nella transizione ambientale, Bologna, Esculapio.
Mannheimer, R. (1991) La lega lombarda, Milano, Feltrinelli.
Milbrath, L.W. (1984) Environmentalists. Vanguard for a new society, Albany, State Univ. of New York Press.
Mlinar, Z. and Splichal, S. (1988) Globalization and Individuation in Social Development and Comparative Research, Paper presented at the ISA conference, Cross-cultural and International Research, Ljubljana (mimeo), published Slovene version, Primerjalno raziskovanje in razvojni procesi, Družboslovne razprave, Ljubljana, No. 6.
Moore, W. (1966) Global sociology: the world as a singular system, The American Journal of Sociology, Vol. 71.
Mumford, L. (1964) The Pentagon of Power, London, Secker and Warburg.
Piore, M. and Sabel, C.F. (1984) The second industrial divide, New York, Basic Books.
Poche, B. (1979) Movements regionaux et fondements territoriaux de l'identité, in Cahiers Internationaux de sociologie, No. 66.
Rosenau, J.N. (1990) Turbulence in World Politics: a Theory of Change and Continuity, Princeton, Princeton Univ. Press.
Russett, B. (1967) International regions and the international system, Chicago, Rand McNally.
Sedlmayr, H. (1948) Das Verlust der Mitte, Wien.
Sernini, M. (1990) Ancora: materiali critici sul localismo, in Trevisiol, E. (ed.) Territorio e società nella transizione ambientale, Bologna, Esculapio.
Shils, E. (1975) Center and periphery, Chicago, Chicago Univ. Press.
Simonsen, K. (1990) Planning in post-modern conditions, in Acta Sociologica", No. 33.
Strassoldo, R. (1979) Temi di sociologia delle relazioni internazionali, Gorizia, ISIG.
Strassoldo, R. (1981) Center and Periphery. Socio-ecological Perspectives, in Kuklinski, A. (ed.) Polarized Development and Regional Policies, The Hague-Paris, Mouton.
Strassoldo, R. and Delli Zotti, G. (eds.), (1982) Cooperation and Conflict in Border Areas, Milano, Angeli.
Strassoldo, R. (1985) Ethnicity and regionalism. The case of Friuli, International Political Science Review", Vol. 6, No. 2.
Strassoldo, R. (1986) Thinking Globally and Acting Locally. A Study of Environmental Opposition to Growth Projects in Friuli (Italy), paper presented at the session on Ecological Crisis, Growth and Development, XI World Congress of Sociology, New Delhi (mimeo).
Strassoldo, R. (1987) The Sociology of Space. A Typological approach, Discussion Paper n. 90, Syracuse, Dept. of Geography, Univ. of Syracuse (mimeo).
Strassoldo, R. and Tessarin, N. (1992) Le radici del localismo. Indagine sociologica sull'apparteneza territoriale in Friuli Trento: Reverdito.
Teune, H.(1990) Multiple Group Loyalties and the Security of Political Communities, Paper presented at the session on Globalization, Technology and Territorial Identities, Madrid, XII World Congress of Sociology (mimeo).
Thompson, W.R. (ed.), (1983) Contending Aproaches to World System Analysis, Beverly Hills-London-New Delhi, Sage Publications.
Williams, C. (ed.), (1982) National Separatism, Vancouver and London, Univ. of British Columbia Press.

4 Turbulence and sovereignty in world politics: Explaining the relocation of legitimacy in the 1990s and beyond

R. B. A. DiMuccio and James N. Rosenau

1. Introduction

Although the tension between interdependence and sovereignty in world politics has not been ignored by thoughtful observers,[1] neither has it been a central focus of international relations (IR) theorists. Such tensions appear especially acute in the post-Cold War era, but many theoreticians continue to treat as unproblematic state sovereignty and the related issue of public loyalties, as constants that are in no need of in-depth study. Increasingly, however, presumptions of constancy loom as unacceptable. They fly in the face of new patterns in world politics which point to the erosion of the hold states have had on the loyalties of their publics and the legitimate control they have had within their borders. As one analyst puts it, "We are witnessing the decline of the great collective forms of identification and the emergence of fragmented and multiple collective actors" (Melucci, 1990). It can readily be concluded, in other words, that world politics is marked by a global authority crisis which is sustained by shifting sovereignties and loyalties at all levels.

For theorists, this problem is complicated by the fact that the redirection of legitimacy sentiments is multi-directional. That is, while in some instances they are being redirected "outward" toward supranational or transnational entities, in other cases the loyalties of populations are shifting away from state structures "inward" toward subnational bodies, groups and institutions.[2] In any event, whatever the direction, the implication is that publics are looking toward an increasingly wide range of sources for the satisfaction of their needs. For theorists as well as citizens, therefore, the fact that the underlying dynamics of change in world politics are related to integrational *as well as* disintegrational tendencies creates a conundrum which begs to be resolved.

In this essay, we briefly describe the limitations of two theoretical approaches - identification theory and neofunctionalist theory - that have been used to address the problem of loyalty shifts, and outline a perspective that offers a comprehensive means for explaining multi-directional shifts in identity and loyalty under conditions of extensive transformation. We call it "turbulence theory." According to this approach, the same dynamics that foster global interdependence are conceived to operate also as the root causes of various types of loyalty shifts, even those that develop in diverse and opposite directions. The same factors which induce publics to press their national governments to cede some of their autonomy to supranational institutions, also prompt segments of some populations to reduce, even to renounce, their allegiance to state authority structures and to redirect their legitimacy sentiments toward transnational groups or to make demands for their own political sovereignty. In sum, centralization and decentralization - integration and fragmentation - in world politics are outgrowths of the same processes. What follows seeks to show that turbulence theory can help to resolve the problem of multi-directional loyalty shifts.

2. Loyalty shifts as multidirectional phenomena: the global authority crisis

Among the most compelling recent trends in world politics is the wide-spread authority crisis which has been at the core of the problematization of previously unproblematic issues in world politics. Indeed, authority is being challenged on a global scale and in a scope and magnitude never before witnessed. Of course, the revolutionary period in Europe (during which many of the old monarchies were overthrown in favor of democratic forms of government) demonstrates that challenges to state authority are not new phenomena. However, the specifically global nature in which authority is being challenged today denotes that the present era can be seen as a break-point in the development of world politics (Rosenau, 1990:5).

More important for present purposes are the effects of this authority crisis on the locus of public loyalties. Ever since the notion of sovereignty was enshrined in the treaties of Westphalia and Utrecht, the legal competence of state governmental elites within their borders and the loyalties of mass citizenries have existed, by and large, in a stable symbiosis. That is, elites have generally been able to assume that their authority would go uncontested, and citizens have tended to link the satisfaction of their welfare and security needs to the directives of state authorities, a linkage that over the years has come to find expression through largely automatic habits of compliance.

Within this context, the import of the evolving global authority crisis becomes abundantly clear. As authority is increasingly challenged, it becomes increasingly difficult for state elites to claim or exercise legal competence and autonomous rule within their own borders. Accordingly, if effective governance depends - at least in part - on the loyalties of citizens, the dissipation of citizens' compliance habits and the redirection of their legitimacy sentiments correspond to a trend toward the erosion of sovereignty and the relocation of authority in world politics.

3. "Inward" vs. "outward" loyalty shifts

How then, to classify and categorize the types of challenges to authority and corresponding loyalty shifts that are taking place? We argue that there are at least two types of shifts in legitimacy sentiments: those in which loyalties move toward subnational groups or institutions; and those in which loyalties are redirected toward supranational or transnational entities. As noted, we refer to these respectively as "inward" and "outward" loyalty shifts.

A few examples illustrate the distinction between the inward and outward redirection of legitimacy sentiments. Consider, first, the recent challenges to authority in, say, Poland and the former Soviet Union. In each case, mass publics or subgroups within mass publics have directly challenged the authority of state elites in an effort to achieve a more effective satisfaction of their needs. In Poland, essentially the entire citizenry's allegiance was redirected away from the central institutions of the state and toward "Solidarity," a subnational group. In addition, subgroups within the former Soviet Union successfully challenged central authorities and gained their own political autonomy; allegiance among the citizens of the Republics toward the central authorities of the former Soviet state were redirected towards the Republics themselves.

While there are significant differences among these cases, they both constitute examples of an "inward" redirection of legitimacy sentiments since loyalties toward system governments are giving way to loyalties toward subsystem entities or entities which reside within the old whole system. That is, each case reveals the fragmentation of wholes into parts or the splitting away of one or more components of a collectivity (Rosenau, 1990:403).

However, not all shifts in legitimacy sentiments become manifested in inward movement. In some instances, publics are shifting their loyalties toward entities lying wholly or partly outside the realm of the whole system or of the sub-systems within it. In Gaza and the West Bank, subgroups have challenged Israeli authority and have thrown their loyalties toward a transnational group, the PLO. The movement here is outward in that a transnational body is the recipient of loyalties which the state, Israel in this case, previously had enjoyed. In Europe, to state another example, the integrative experiment of the European Communities (EC) has grown and developed - not without periods of stagnation or retrogression - for over 30 years. Gradually, the EC states have ceded autonomy in a growing range of issue areas to common decision-making procedures and increasingly they have submitted to binding agreements and laws laid down by central institutions. Integration in Europe is therefore related to the gradual relocation of authority, outward from the governmental bodies of the member states, to the supranational bodies of the EC.

4. Explaining the relocation of loyalties

There is, of course, a rich literature in which problems related to the shifting of legitimacy sentiments have been addressed. One approach which might be useful is identification theory, which is founded on "a universal psychological dynamic" whereby "through identification and internalization" the individual gets linked to mass publics (Bloom, 1990: 129). Holders of this theory argue that it has the "ability to explain both political integration and national mobilization. It provides a coherent explanation for a spectrum of mass social behavior, running from a low-key and agreeable sense of national solidarity through to actions of mass terrorism from a mixture of aggregated states of individual members of a system to a global characteristic of the system" (Bloom, 1990: 129-30).

There is a major difficulty with identification theory, however. It is not suited to the present period of rapid global change, in which the conventional lines of authority are continually fluctuating and simultaneously moving in the direction of both more and less encompassing political entities. Identification theory posits a stable process which culminates in identification with the national state and, as such, it lacks the postulates needed to account for the evolution of loyalties toward either subnational or supranational collectivities.

Another framework which accounts for some of the difficulties found in identification theory derives from regional integration theory. Scholars within this tradition are foremost among those who have sought to grasp the dynamics which underlie loyalty shifts in an interdependent world. A significant group of academics saw the emergent forms of post-World War II cooperation among the states of Europe and later the founding of the European Communities (EC) as the initiation of a "great experiment" in international integration and supranationalism (Haas, 1970). This opened many scholars' eyes to the possibility for major, peaceful transformations and relocations of sovereignty at the regional level, even as enmity and power struggles surrounded such regions. Thus, "a major bloc" in the American discipline of IR turned its attention to these phenomena, and regional political integration emerged in the late 1950s as an important area of concern in the discipline of international relations (Little, 1980:22).

The primary expression of the effort to explain the conditions under which the member states of the EC tend to cede sovereignty to central institutions, emerged in the form the neofunctionalist theory of integration.[3] As integration theorists increasingly began to question the validity of the older functionalism in the 1950s and 1960s, a considerably revised version of functionalist theory appeared in the form of neofunctionalism. Whereas the older functionalism, for example, envisions a homogeneous community ("Gemeinshchaft"), neofunctionalists see a society ("Gesellschaft"), which is defined by a complex network of competing interests. For neofunctionalists, integration means the harnessing of pressures produced by competing interest groups (especially economic interest groups, but also transnational political parties) and a consciously political stimulation of the desire on their part for further integration.

In other words, integration is not accomplished so that the community or "Gemeinschaft" can harmoniously realize general gain, but rather so that interest groups can realize egoistic gains through the greater capacity of international institutions (Taylor, 1983:6). The main motor of integration for neofunctionalists comprises a change in the behavior and loyalties of elites, not of mass publics, as the older functionalists argued. Integration is seen as requiring the existence of a framework of existing institutional structures in which economic elites are persuaded to shift their legitimacy sentiments and thus to orient their activities towards this larger supranational setting.

Neofunctionalists focus, therefore, on the attempt by interest groups to pursue their goals by demanding task expansion on the part of central institutions. Through this mechanism, supranational governance in areas of "low politics" spills over into areas of "high politics." The consequence of this dynamic is that as governments are essentially forced to yield to central institutions to satisfy diverse lobbies, new problems are created which can only logically and practically be solved by granting further supranational powers to those institutions (Heathcote, 1975:40). The redirection of legitimacy sentiments, the erosion of state sovereignty, and the "forward march"[4] of regional integration all become self-perpetuating processes.

The ways in which neofunctionalists conceptualize public loyalties and their relation to sovereignty in world politics are readily manifest in the recent history of the EC. Neofunctionalists have concentrated on economic elites and the relationship between member state governments and the European Commission, the EC's primary supranational body. The contention is essentially that as the Commission's range of formal powers is legislatively increased, its capacity to act in a variety of areas affecting state elites increases correspondingly. Increased function leads to increased capacity, which in turn leads to increased interest group loyalty. The combined effect of these means a transfer of legal competence or sovereignty. Put differently, neofunctionalism involves the expectation that the pressures of the post-industrial world and the pressures of spontaneous and imposed interdependence will lead to a quality of supranationalism in the central regional institutions, to the redirection of loyalties, and finally to an erosion of some aspects of the sovereignty of the member states (Taylor, p. 26). The ineffectiveness of states feeds into the shifting of loyalties, which becomes related to a relocation of sovereignty.

Despite its initial success in explaining European integration, regional integration theory was rejected - *en masse* - by scholars of international relations in the middle 1970s as integration in Europe came to a halt and as the global economic and energy crises compelled them to think in the more general terms of interdependence, hegemonic stability, international regimes, and the like. The fall from grace of regional integration theory also highlights several reasons why it is not particularly helpful in explaining the multi-directional character of loyalty shifts in world politics today. Three interrelated difficulties can be noted: its normative content, its teleology, and its geographical specificity.

The normative content of regional integration theory poses a problem because of two especially influential elements: 1) the underlying premise that regional integration is a value which should be sought after and prescribed; 2) the assumption that regions can and must be thought of as analytically and factually self-contained units (Haas, 1976). That is, for regional integration theorists the outward relocation of loyalty has been a goal as well as a perceived empirical tendency. Accordingly, once the regional dynamic of integration is set in motion, developments which occur at the extra-regional level are not seen as affecting integration in any way. Theories of regional integration are deliberately absent of attention to the global developments which may impact "negatively" upon the regional processes of political integration. Since integration is rooted in the rationality of various groups, functionalists and neofunctionalists see integration as an insulated process which enjoys the quality of automaticity.

In other words, the value orientations of regional integration theorists have tended to blind them to the prospect that periods of integration may be followed by periods of disintegration, or that the "end-state" which they prescribe might not in fact obtain. Therefore, both the automaticity and regional self-containment of integration theory stand at logical odds with the global simultaneity which accompanies the multidirectional loyalty shifts occurring in the world today. Primarily because of their value orientations, regional integration theorists have not generally recognized variations in the destination of loyalty relocations. Though they tend to agree that the ineffectiveness of states compels citizens or groups to look elsewhere for the satisfaction of their needs, it is assumed that they will inevitably look to supranational institutions. For integrationists, the loyalty shift is a form of teleology and therefore a distinctly uni-directional phenomenon.

A final problem comprises the specific geographical focal point of regional integration theory. The functionalist and neofunctionalist logic of integration presupposes the existence of liberal, democratic, capitalist member states whose populations have direct and indirect access to the information made available by interdependent relations with similar, neighboring states. By focusing so parochially on the European case, integration theorists have rendered their frameworks incapable of explaining loyalty shifts among populations of non-democratic, non-capitalist, non-Western states.

It follows from this brief review of neofunctionalism[5] that its explanatory range is, in fact, somewhat narrow. Integration theory cannot explain the simultaneity with which structurally similar events tend to occur in diverse parts of the globe and within the context of diverse societies and political cultures; nor can it capture varieties in the redirection of legitimacy sentiments in world politics. While neofunctionalism may be helpful in explaining outward loyalty shifts, it is of little use as a vehicle for addressing the problem of inward shifts. In sum, though neofunctionalism retains a certain degree of heuristic value, the problems outlined above severely limit its value in explaining the central puzzles of this paper.

5. Turbulence theory and the redirection of legitimacy sentiments

The primary object of this paper is to articulate a parsimonious framework which can explain, based upon a few simple assumptions, multidirectional shifts in loyalty wherever they may occur in the world. The approach which we argue overcomes the inadequacies of previous attempts to explain loyalty shifts is turbulence theory.[6]

Turbulence theory seeks to offer a broad explanation for why previously given aspects of world politics - among them, the orientations of citizens toward public authorities - have now become problematic. It posits world politics as in a state of flux, with its implicit structures and parameters underlying dramatic alterations. Profound changes are occurring on a global scale as authority structures come under challenge and as uncertainty increases. More specifically, the well-established patterns that sustained the three basic parameters of world politics in the past have given way (Rosenau, 1990:101). All three have entered a state of high "complexity" and "dynamism," a condition which is defined as that of "turbulence." Any international system is "turbulent" when its parameters undergo substantial increases in the number of actors, in the extent of dissimilarity among the actors, and in the scope and depth of the interdependence among such actors (complexity), while at the same time there is a high degree of variability across time in terms of the goals and activities of such actors (dynamism) (Rosenau, 1990:62-3).

The basic premises of turbulence theory are simple. The transition from the industrial to the "post-industrial" world - as evidenced by the onset of a microelectronic revolution - has fostered the emergence of world political issues of an inherently transnational nature, e.g., environmental issues, terrorism, the drug trade, currency crises, etc. Such issues are direct products of increased interdependence resulting from the development of new technologies. The growing preponderance of these fundamentally transnational issues has, in turn, served to reduce the capacities of states and their governments to provide satisfactory solutions to the new problems they face.

As a result, whole systems (states, for example) have been weakened and their subsystems have been correspondingly strengthened, a trend Rosenau (1990) calls "subgroupism." Even more important, however, is the feedback of the consequences of such dynamics for the skills of the world's adults. The combination of increasing interdependence, the microelectronic revolution, and the emergence of inherently transnational issues, has been associated with a corresponding increase in the abilities of individuals to think in multi-variate terms and to locate themselves within the context of the emerging opportunities and barriers created by global interdependence and turbulence. Since individuals (because of their increased skills) are no longer as susceptible as they once were to the coercive capabilities of the state, and since legitimacy is decreasingly based on traditional habits of compliance and increasingly on performance criteria, the enlargement of the skills of individuals fuels the turbulence which brought on the skill enhancements in the first place.

Turbulence theory has a multi-level quality in that it demonstrates the interrelationships between "micro-" and "macro-level" factors and posits a synergism between them. But although there is a feedback among and between each of the above factors, micro skills "have comparatively the most important influence" (Rosenau, 1990:14). Macro changes (the microelectronic revolution, interdependence, etc.) bring about micro changes (increased intellectual and cathectic capabilities of individuals) which serve both to reflect and accelerate turbulence (dynamism and complexity) in world politics. Therefore, turbulence is both cause and effect. That is, systems and actors become more specialized as a result of the introduction of new knowledge and technologies, as a result of which they must rely on others for support; hence interdependencies increase and new technologies become more effective through specialization. As communication and transport technologies become refined, geographic distances shrink and events cascade rapidly through and across diverse political systems, adding to the complexity, interdependence and dynamism as the turbulence mounts and feeds on itself (Rosenau, 1990:65).

But what are the overall effects of turbulence on world politics? At the broad structural level, it has resulted in the bifurcation of the global system into a state-centric world and a multi-centric world, two subsystems that compete, cooperate, or otherwise interact with each other even as each retains its autonomy. Within both systems authority crises are pervasive as people increasingly question the legitimacy of leaders at all levels of society. The result is a continuing process of the disaggregation of whole systems and the aggregation of diverse sub-systems either within whole systems, around certain issues, or between whole systems (Rosenau, 1990:159-73). In short, authority relationships in a vast array of contexts have become unsettled on a global scale. An important resultant of this development has been the problematization of previously unproblematical issues and structures (Rosenau, 1990:390). Most important for present purposes, it poses for individuals a continuing challenge to their political identity, in determining what organizations should serve as the focus of their highest loyalties.

A simple but powerful question follows from this formulation of turbulence theory: assuming that the capacity of every adult in every country to think in multi-variate terms is improving, and assuming also that the macro changes of the post-industrial order have brought about a sharp decrease in the abilities of national governments to satisfy the security and welfare needs of their citizens, what effects can be expected to emerge in terms of authority relationships? As previously implied, the answer involves the replacement of traditional criteria of legitimacy with performance criteria. Now people have both the motives and the skills to judge the conduct of their leaders, and their reliance on these motives and skills goes a long way toward explaining the course of world politics in the present era. A redirection of legitimacy sentiments can thus be seen as a shift in micro orientations caused by the failure of macro structures and institutions to meet the needs and goals of adults. That is, the combination of macro changes (interdependence) and micro changes (increased skills) is directly related to the increased employment of performance criteria on the part of citizens and to the withering away of their traditional habits of compliance. The global trend toward the shifting of loyalties is the clear result of the confluence of interdependence and the increased skills of adults.

6. Turbulence and outward loyalty shifts

It follows that turbulence theory explains simultaneous occurrences of outward and inward loyalty shifts as distinct but structurally connected events. The combined impact of interdependence and increased skills can be demonstrated by looking, first, at the outward relocation of loyalties in the case of regional political and economic integration in Western Europe.

For centuries, political philosophers have sought to prescribe methods through which the European states could end their warring ways and join together into some or another form of federal or confederal contract involving the exchange of some aspects of sovereignty for the peace and security unavailable under conditions of anarchy. Variations on this theme were proposed by Dubois in the 13th century, Podebrad in the 15th century, de Sully and Cruce in the 16th century, William Penn and Immanuel Kant in the 17th century, and the Abbé de Saint-Pierre in the 18th century.[7] Among those carrying on the tradition of proposing the creation of supranational organizations to establish peace in Europe was Woodrow Wilson, whose post-World War I notion of collective security was derived in part from a reading of these and other supranationalist texts.

Far from being a new idea then, integration in Europe - broadly defined - has been a goal of political thinkers for quite some time. Yet, it is only in the period following WWII that substantial, concrete movement in a supranational direction has occurred. The movement has been sporadic and some even question whether any has occurred.[8] But on balance, it seems clear that Europe is more integrated today than it was in, say, 1945. Notwithstanding the opinion of many European Unionists and European maximalists that the central institutions of the EC have not obtained an adequate level of supranational powers, there has been significant movement in this area, especially since the inception of the "plan for 1992" and the amendments to the Rome Treaty embodied in the Single European Act (SEA) of 1987. The member states of the EC, many quite recalcitrant in terms of movement toward political integration,[9] have relinquished aspects of their sovereignty and have participated in the creation of structures and procedures which have tied their own well-being into that of their European neighbors.

Why is it that the plan for supranationality embodied in the Treaty of Rome and its later amendment by the SEA has realized significant success when previous efforts along similar lines have failed? In addressing this puzzle within the bounds of turbulence theory, the intersection of global interdependence with the enhancement of the skills of the world's adults is an extremely consequential factor. It helps explain the outward shift of loyalties in Europe in several ways. Most notably perhaps, a challenge to state authority of the type we have seen in Europe in the second half of the 20th century presupposes an openness on the part of the member states' citizens to the idea that their own governments may not be able to solve the problems which impact on their welfare and security. This, in turn, presumes the availability of alternative sources of satisfaction and the knowledge on the part of individuals of how to access these alternative sources.

Therefore, according to turbulence theory, supranationality is an exclusive product of the post-industrial era. While in previous eras, there has been a wide range of plans to create supranationality in Europe, and while a certain degree of interdependence - broadly defined - has always existed among the European states, only as such factors have coincided with markedly intellectually enhanced populations has there been the real and logical possibility of the public support necessary for a transfer of national powers to supranational institutions. Because of the tendency on the part of national governments to protect their sovereignty and autonomy whenever possible, the norms of traditional authority patterns - of unthinking patriotism - are incompatible with challenges to authority of the type which result in supranationality. In the absence of the flexibility and openness enabled by skill-enhancement, a crucial basis for an outward loyalty shift is not present.

In what senses, then, have we seen a redirection of legitimacy sentiments in the example of the European Community? While average citizens have not renounced their loyalty to national governments,[10] many groups have been at the forefront of efforts to pressure governments to enact the so-called "White Paper" program,[11] which most in the business community consider critical to their viability in the increasingly competitive European and world markets.[12] In their struggle to forward the internal market, though, business elites have had to confront the recalcitrance of national governments. While few in the business community doubted the urgency for reform in the early 1980s, fewer still knew how to mobilize the support of such governments whose conservatism had been demonstrated in their dilution of the Genscher-Colombo initiative for a draft European act (Lodge, 1986). Thus, the SEA must be seen against the backdrop of the inherent reluctance of many member governments to go beyond rather limited notions of European integration. Whereas the European Parliament had sought to supplant existing treaties with its draft European Union Treaty, governments engineered the retention of the old policy-making system with as few amendments as possible (Lodge, 1986).

Whenever national governments perceive that their positions might be weakened in relationship to supranational organizations, they often take steps to reinforce their ultimate preeminence with a view towards maintaining the status quo (Lodge, 1986). Indeed, there is some evidence that national governmental actors may even work to "sabotage" the integrative process when national goals seem to come into conflict with Community efforts (Feld & Wildgen, 1975). For this reason, the relocation of the activities and legitimacy sentiments of economic actors has played a central role in the movement towards higher supranationality in the EC, even in the face of recalcitrance on the part of national governments.

To illustrate this dynamic, it is instructive to take an in-depth look at a specific case. One of the most recalcitrant and "minimalist" member governments of the EC has been Great Britain. The general perception among the British business community during the early and mid-1980s was that Britain stood to gain considerably from the changes represented by the SEA. British industry was shocked to discover, when Britain entered the Community in 1973, not a free market, but one with a range of subtle barriers to trade. Freeing the market would help Britain's exporters, the

Confederation of British Industry (CBI) reported, without at the same time opening up a floodgate for foreign imports. The CBI estimated that frontier delays cost European industry 7 billion pounds a year or 5 to 7 percent of the unit costs. British exporters had long complained of the delay and cost involved in getting a product tested and certified for sale in another EC member state. Furthermore, the CBI argued that the freeing of trade in services, particularly financial services, would greatly favor British companies. The adoption of mutual recognition on standards would remove the excuse for national bias in public procurement and, in the view of the CBI, open up new markets for British exporters. The public procurement policies of the EC in the mid-1980s, cost the Community 25 billion pounds a year the CBI estimated. In the absence of action to correct procurement costs, British firms would be at a disadvantage compared to heavily subsidized competitors.[13]

Important lobbies made it abundantly clear, therefore, that they favored EC reform and the transfer of aspects of British sovereignty in those areas important for establishing the single integrated market. Against this backdrop, it is not surprising that the general opinion of British businessmen has been fairly clear on this issue of reform. Two surveys, one by the European Commission and another by Business International magazine, found that European (and British) businessmen placed frontier delays high on their list of difficulties in trading across Europe. Most mentioned progress against obstructive standards when asked to identify the opportunities and barriers connected to business in Europe.[14] According to the surveys, there was a clear perception that the effort to create the single integrated market presented businessmen with a gradually expanding opportunity in the European market. There followed a general consensus on the part of most British businessmen that the economic environment in the EC would have to change and that Britain would have to accept amendment of the Treaty of Rome and the invigorated supranationality that came with it, in order to achieve its objectives in the EC.[15]

Despite the fact that the British government fought and fervently resisted the program for EC reform in the mid-1980s, the fact that Britain eventually agreed to the transfers of autonomy provided for by the SEA serves as a strong indication that pressure from the business elites played a major role in this development. Great Britain is a case study in the employment of performance criteria of legitimacy on the part of an important subgroup to circumvent its national government in order to secure a more effective satisfaction of its needs.

In many ways, the turbulence theory explanation of European supranationalism is conspicuously similar to a neofunctionalist explanation. Both approaches argue that the inability of states to satisfy needs fosters a relocation of legitimacy sentiments among population groups. Both approaches emphasize the friction between the supranationalist tendencies of self-interested population groups and the inherent conservatism of national governments. In short, both turbulence theory and neofunctionalism recognize the essential tension between interdependence and sovereignty in world politics.

But the above analysis also demonstrates that turbulence theory subsumes neofunctionalism, since it accounts for what neofunctionalism cannot explain. The most important factors which elude neofunctionalism as characterized in this essay are two. First, there is nothing in neofunctionalist theory which can readily explain the success of European integration in the late 20th century, as against the failures of previous attempts to create supranational bodies in Europe. If, according to neofunctionalism, economic actors will always throw their loyalties toward whichever body best serves their interests, why was it only after World War II that such actors successfully compelled their governments to cede sovereignty to supranational institutions? Turbulence theory accounts for the timing of successful integration in Europe by placing skill enhancement at the micro level and the evolution of performance criteria at the center of causality. The norms of unthinking national patriotism, prevalent in Europe for many hundred of years, are incompatible with challenges to authority of the type which foster supranationality.

Thus the success of supranationalism in Europe and the growth of the nascent norm of performance criteria induced by the macro-changes of the post-industrial world are developments which share much more than mere simultaneity. According to turbulence theory, they are causally linked through the increasing skills of individuals. To repeat, where legitimacy once derived from habitual and traditional norms perpetuated by macro structures and processes, today the enlarged analytic skills and cathectic capacities of citizens, increasingly enable them to ascribe legitimacy on the basis of performance activities that they perceive as appropriate (Rosenau, 1990:381).

The second deficiency of neofunctionalism is that it is not equipped to account for the other side of the loyalty-shift coin, subgroupism. It is the argument of turbulence theory that instances of supranationalism and subgroupism are outgrowths of the same global dynamics that have led to the bifurcation of the system and the onset of pervasive authority crises. Since it is the goal of this paper to account for the multidirectional nature of legitimacy shifts, and since most of these shifts in world politics are of the inward type, neofunctionalism's lack of attention to subgroupism can be considered a fatal flaw for the purposes of the present analysis.

7. Turbulence and inward loyalty shifts

While we have outlined turbulence theory's ability to explain supranationalism, it is perhaps even more central to an explanation of inward loyalty shifts. As people become more skilled at locating themselves in an ever more complex world, at seeing through authorities who claim to have the answers, and at identifying subgroups that seem to offer greater hope, they are less likely to accept as legitimate the directives issued by the leaders of national governments. When turbulence sets in, then habits related to compliance to authority begin to crumble, and new networks of loyalty begin to emerge (Rosenau, 1990:389).

These new networks tend to manifest themselves in the fragmentation of wholes into parts. This is the case either because decentralization is believed to allow the system to achieve its goals more effectively or because its subsystems become increasingly sensitive to the differences that set them apart. Subgroupism, then, is the splitting away of one or more components of any collectivity as a result of the interaction among turbulent micro and macro pressures (Rosenau, 1990:403).

The devolution of authority and the processes of subgroupism that accompany it can take several forms. It can occur wholly within the context of public structures and, in turn, this form can follow two different paths. First, it can be authorized and implemented within a legal and constitutional framework. France and the United States are examples here, as both countries pursued policies of decentralization or deregulation in the early 1980s that shifted considerable authority from the national to state or local levels. Second, the devolution of authority within public structures can occur informally, without authorization and in opposition to prevailing policies. The authority crisis of China, for instance, is exactly one in which provincial governors and Communist party secretaries attract foreign investments on liberal terms that they are not authorized to grant or, on other issues, simply ignore the directives coming out of the central government in Beijing (Kristof, 1990a, 1990b). In some cases the rebellion of local officials against the central authorities is even expressed through physical actions:

> One sign of the cavalier attitude that localities take toward national policy is the increase in illegal roadblocks set up by local governments. Peasant Daily, an official newspaper, recently carried a letter from three truck drivers who ran into nearly 100 such illegal roadblocks on what should have been a three-day journey along the coast. Local officials seized all the drivers' money and much of their cargo, and when the drivers ran out of money even detained them in nine places for periods of up to several days at a time (Kristof, 1990b).

Perhaps even more conspicuous than the relocation of authority in the public arena is the subgroupism that originates in the nongovernmental realms of societies and either seeks to establish new loci of authority or forces the adoption of new arrangements within the public arena. A striking example can be discerned in the Black Panther Militia, an organization formed in Milwaukee in 1990 which said it would take the law into its own hands in five years unless $100 million was invested in Milwaukee's black community (Maraniss, 1990). No less noteworthy are the diverse developments in the Soviet Union that are transforming that society into a plethora of subgroup entities, from breakaway proclamations by urban neighborhood councils to the establishment of parliaments by regional groups that have "no borders, no money, and no legal authority" (Bohlen, 1990), from republics that use their highway policemen as customs guards charged with stopping shipments to neighboring republics to the insistence of the Ukrainian Orthodox Church's insistence on self-government within the newly revived Russian Orthodox Church (Clines, 1990).

Indeed, subgroupism has been so rampant in parts of the former Soviet Union that it is reasonable to speak of what might be called "sub-subgroupism": not only, for example, did the Republic of Moldavia press for greater autonomy from the old Soviet state, but within Moldavia two regions. Trans-Dniester and Gagauz, declared themselves to be autonomous republics. As one observer notes, "Power, once tightly held by Moscow, has not just been decentralized; it is being pulverized, as different groups and regions assert their sovereignty, autonomy or simply their desire to do things their way" (Bohlem, 1990).

That these dynamics confront citizens with enormous problems as to the directions in which they should channel their loyalties can readily be demonstrated. Consider, for example, bankers in the Russian Republic when its Parliament voted to reduce its contribution to the USSR's budget by more than ninety percent. A large part of the 261-billion-rouble Soviet budget comes from taxes and other revenues collected by the republics and deposited in their banks, an arrangement which now places the Russian bankers in the agonizing situation of having to decide whether to abide by the decision of the Russian Parliament or to maintain the established procedure of turning the funds over to the central government.

8. Conclusion

For most students of international relations, the relocation of legitimacy in world politics is not a consequential factor. According to turbulence theory, however, the redirection of legitimacy sentiments is a central fact of the late 20th century, one which is readily explained in terms of the intersection of interdependence and the increasing skills of individuals. From the viewpoint of turbulence theory, the disaggregation of old whole systems and the reaggregation of old sub-systems will become increasingly important theoretical givens as the global authority crisis continues to undermine previously held micro-macro assumptions in the study of international relations.

Turbulence theory, then, embraces the realization that the political map of the world is undergoing rapid change. If different colors are used to depict its political jurisdictions, a veritable rainbow of endless shadings will be needed to keep the map up to date. At the surface, this rainbow may seem confusing and unpredictable. Most frameworks are capable of perceiving only some of the hues, leading to inaccurate or only partially correct predictions regarding the levels of saturation and brightness which may emerge. However, the problem is not that reality lacks an underlying order. Rather, the lenses used to capture the rainbows as they are formed and transformed are merely insufficient.

Turbulence theory enables a unified characterization of the many directions of the relocation of legitimacy in world politics. By focusing our attention on the intersection of macro-level and micro-level factors, turbulence theory reveals both inward and outward loyalty shifts as distinct but structurally related phenomena. As interdependence and the microelectronic revolution collide with the enhancement of the skills of individuals across the globe, it follows that the range of possible sources for the satisfaction of needs will subjectively and objectively expand. Thus, turbulence theory sees the simultaneity of integration and disintegration, fragmentation and aggregation, centralization and decentralization, not as a paradox but an expectation.

In sum, even though some of the shadings may be collapsed into one color as the dynamics of turbulence give rise to supranational entities, the accompanying proliferation of subnational and transnational entities seems bound to promote dazzling maps, assuming the world's cartographers can find sufficiently differentiated colors to portray the vast new structures of authority.

Notes

1 Long ago Jean Jacques Rousseau grasped that the autonomy and legitimacy of a civil society tend to be disrupted in proportion to the extent of its interconnections with other societies. See Jean Jacques Rousseau's unfinished manuscript on "The State of War," and his "Summary and Critique of the Abbe de Saint Pierre's "Project for Perpetual Peace" for an articulation of Rousseau's views on this subject.

2 So as to minimize terminological repetition, throughout we treat "loyalties" and "legitimacy sentiments" interchangeably even though the term "loyalty" may suggest a more enduring set of orientations than does "legitimacy sentiments." We understand both concepts to refer to the predispositions and priorities whereby people resolve conflicts between the demands of the diverse collectivities and organizations to which they belong. Both loyalties and legitimacy sentiments are seen as firmly held but as nevertheless subject to change if fundamental economic, social, and political conditions undergo alteration. That is, loyalties and legitimacy sentiments are not so deeply ingrained as are the unchanging cultural affinities that last a lifetime for most people. For an elaboration of the nature of legitimacy sentiments, see Eckstein (1973).

3 Other frameworks generally included under the rubric of regional integration theory are pluralism and federalism, and the older functionalism. The historiography of regional integration reveals that by the middle 1960s, that approach to integration which seemed to be the most useful and accurate in terms of explaining European integration was neofunctionalism. See Pentland (1973) for a cogent review of all four approaches to integration theory. For an explanation of why functionalism, pluralism, and federalism were not considered "viable" approaches, see Haas (1970, 1976). For an in-depth historiographical account of the development of regional integration theory in international relations, see DiMuccio (1990).

4 An allusion to Hansen (1973).

5 Of course, the framework initiated by Haas (1958) went through numerous reformulations by several scholars in a general attempt to account for the perceived failure of the original neofunctionalist theory to account for developments in European integration in the late 1960s and early 1970s. In particular, the works of Lindberg (1963), Lindberg & Scheingold (1970), Nye (1971), and Caporaso (1972) attempted to correct the apparent flaws in Haas' initial construct. Nevertheless, for simplicity, the conception of neofunctionalism utilized in this paper has been confined to earlier formulations.

6 For a full explanation of turbulence theory, see Rosenau (1990). The following summary of the theory is derived from this volume.

7 For in-depth discussions of these "peace plans," see for example Hinsley (1967), and Jacobson (1984).

8 See Juliet Lodge (1986) for a cogent argument for why recent developments in EC policymaking are not, in her view, indicative of any movement towards meaningful supranationalism. See also Calingaert (1988) for an even appraisal of the implications and significance of the Single European Act of 1987.

9 Great Britain, Denmark, and Greece are generally considered the most "recalcitrant" states in terms of reluctance to relinquish their autonomy to the central institutions of the EC.

10 It is for this reason that functionalist theory has proven to have less and less relevance for explaining integration in Europe. Since the loyalties of mass publics have not tended to shift toward the EC central institutions, functionalism's focus on "Gemeinschaft" has been more or less

falsified. For a neofunctionalist critique of the older functionalism, see Haas (1970). For a discussion of the apathy of European citizens toward the EC's central institutions, see "Europe's Internal Market: What Are They Building?" in The Economist, July 8, 1990.

11 A long list of proposals (initially around 300) drafted by the European Commission in 1985 meant to foster the development of the single integrated market.

12 For example, the President of Phillips once lamented that the EC's inability to complete the internal market - as mandated in the Rome Treaty - was the cause of Europe's deteriorating competitive position in the 1970s and early 1980s, and that Europessimism should give way to a Eurorealism which would be rooted in the effort to complete the single integrated market. He was among the first to coin such phrases as "Europe 1990." This anecdote is related by Calingaert (1988). Another example comes from the head of Siemen's microchips division who in 1981 was quoted as saying, "If only the EEC would stop trying to spend a few pfennigs here and there on industry and give us a real break by creating really free competition for European telecommunications contracts, then, with a huge home market, we might be able to take on the Japanese and Americans and beat them." See "Saving the EEC," in The Economist, November 28, 1981.

13 This account of developments in Great Britain is drawn from "Trade Barriers: Britain Hopes to Free the Market from its Fetters," The London Times, June 28, 1985.

14 See "Europe's Internal Market: What are they building," in The Economist, July 8, 1989.

15 See "Britain May Have to Change Tune to Realize European Objectives," in The London Times, July 7, 1985.

References

Bloom, W. (1990) Personal Identity, National Identity and International Relations, Cambridge, Cambridge University Press.

Bohlen, C. (1990) Ethnic Enmity Governs A New Soviet Republic, New York Times, October 15.

Calingaert, M. (1988) The 1992 Challenge from Europe: Development of the European Community's Internal Market, Washington, National Planning Association.

Caporaso, J. (1972) Functionalism and Regional Integration: A Logical and Empirical Assessment, Beverly Hills, Sage Publications.

Cecchini, P. (1988) The European Challenge: 1992, The Benefits of a Single Market, London, Wildwood House Ltd.

Clines, F.X. (1990) Soviet Union is Reeling with Dizzying Disunion, New York, Times, October 26.

Commission of the European Communities (1987) The Single Act: A New Frontier for Europe, Bulletin of the EC, Supplement, January.

Corbett, R. (1989) Testing the New Procedures: The European Parliament's First Experiences with its New Single-Act Powers, Journal of Common Market Studies, Vol. 27, No.4.

DiMuccio, R.B.A. (1990) Neorealism, 1992 and Integration Theory: Historiography of a Once (and Future?) Field, Paper presented at the annual convention of the International Studies Association, Washington D.C., April.

Eckstein, H. (1973) Authority Patterns: A Structural Basis for Political Inquiry, American Political Science Review, vol. 67, December.

Feld, W. and Wildgen, J. (1975) National Administration Elites and European Integration: Saboteurs at Work?, Journal of Common Market Studies, Vol. 13, No. 3.

Haas, E. (1959) The Uniting of Europe, Stanford, Stanford University Press.

Haas, E. (1964) Beyond the Nation State, Stanford, Stanford University Press.

Haas, E. (1970) The Study of Regional Integration: Reflections on the Joy and Anguish of Pretheorizing, International Organization, Vol. 24, No. 4.

Haas, E. (1976) Turbulent Fields and the Theory of Regional Integration, International Organization, Vol. 30, No.2.

Hansen, R. (1973) European Integration: Forward March, Parade Rest, or Dismissed?, International Organization, Vol. 27, No. 2.

Harrison, R.J. (1978), Neofunctionalism, in Taylor, P. and Groom, A.J.R. (ed.), International Organization: A Conceptual Approach, London, Frances Pinter.

Heathcote, N. (1975) Neofunctionalist Theories of Regional Integration, in Groom, A.J.R. and Taylor, P. (eds.), Functionalism: Theory and Practice in International Relations, London, Univ. of London Press.

Hinsley, F.H. (1963) Power and the Pursuit of Peace: Theory and Practice in the History of Relations between States, Cambridge, Cambridge Univ. Press.

Jacobson, H.K. (1984) Networks of Interdependence: International Organizations and the Global Political System, New York, Alfred A. Knopf.

Kristof, N.D. (1990a) In China, Too, Centrifugal Forces Are Growing Stronger, New York Times, Section 4, August 26.

Kristof, N.D. (1990b) Fear Abates Among Chinese But Few Find Cause for Hope, New York Times, November 24.

Lindberg, L. (1963) The Political Dynamics of European Integration, Stanford, Stanford Univ. Press.

Lindberg, L. and Scheingold, S. (1970) Europe's Would-Be Polity: Patterns of Change in the European Communities, Englewood Cliffs, Prentice-Hall.

Little, R. (1980) The Evolution of International Relations as a Social Science, in Kent, R.C. and Nielsson, G.P. (eds.), The Study and Teaching of International Relations: A Perspective on Mid-Career Education, New York, Nichols Publishing Co.

Lodge, J. (1986) Single European Act: Towards a New Euro-Dynamism?, Journal of Common Market Studies, Vol. 24, No. 3.

McAleese, D. and Matthews, A. (1987) The Single European Act and Ireland, Implications for a Small Member State, Journal of Common Market Studies, Vol. 26, No. 1.

Maraniss, D. (1990) Trouble Brewing in Milwaukee, Washington Post National Weekly Edition, July 30/August 5.

Melucci, A. (1990) Frontierland: Collective Action Between Actors and Systems, Paper presented at XII World Congress of the International Sociological Association, Madrid.

Mitrany, D. (1945) A Working Peace System, Chicago, Quadrangle Books.

Nye, J. (1971) Peace in Parts: Integration and Conflict in Regional Organization, Boston, Little, Brown.

Pentland, C. (1973) International Theory and European Integration, New York, The Free Press.

Rosenau, J.N. (1990) Turbulence in World Politics: A Theory of Change and Continuity, Princeton, Princeton Univ. Press.

Taylor, P. (1983) The Limits of European Integration, New York, Columbia Univ. Press.

5 Local response to global intrusions

Chadwick F. Alger

Introduction

We live in an age in which technological change, as exemplified by satellite communications and jet engines, has magnified the global reach of worldwide military, political, communications, production, marketing distribution, advertising, banking, research, educational and religious organizations (Alger, 1974). There is a growing literature on the impact of these global organizations on local places by scholars who identify with anthropology, urban political economy, world systems and women's studies (Alger, 1988). David Barkin writes of the impact of "the new global system on daily life," as reflected in consumption patterns, organization of production, and in the creation of a new proletariat (Barkin, 1985, 38-41). Steven Sanderson illuminates the way in which "The 'New' Agriculture" has threatened peasant survival, diminished the production of basic foods, diminished peasant nutrition, and forced mass migration to cities (Sanderson, 1985, 65). June Nash explicates the effect of global integration of production on the work force, as in the shift from craft to routinized jobs, the shift from assembly to automated or computerized work processes and the impact of shifts (or threats to shift) of production to areas in which labor is cheaper (Nash, 1985, 253).

There is no doubt that new technology is in some cases fundamentally transforming the worldwide linkages of local places, but insightful understanding of these phenomena requires recognition that worldwide intrusions on local places is not something new (Alger, 1984-85). Criticizing those who have portrayed local communities as though they were isolated from the world, anthropologist Eric Wolf declares that the central assertion of his analysis of the world since 1400 is "that the world of humankind constitutes a manifold, a totality of interconnected processes, and inquiries that disassemble this totality into bits and fail to reassemble it falsify reality. Concepts like 'nation,' 'society,' and 'culture' name bits and threaten to turn names into things" (Wolf, 1982, 3). Historian Fernand Braudel puts the encounters between human settlements and the world into long historical perspective, particularly as he describes the "centerings and decenterings" of the European world economy, observing that this economy centered on Venice in the 1380s, with the center shifting to Antwerp about 1500, to Genoa between 1550 and 1560, and to Amsterdam where it remained for two centuries. Behind Amsterdam, he notes, the "United Provinces were but a shadow government" (Braudel, 1977, 95). Portes and Walton also underscore the significance of historic roots in their study of urbanization in Latin America: "The study of determinants of the current forms of urban poverty in Latin America must start with the colonial beginnings of present cities. ...by 1580 the creation of a continent-wide urban scheme was completed" (Portes and Walter, 1976, 7, 10).

The mainstream of social science has been very slow to recognize the linkages between local places and world systems and organizations. Traditional paradigms which have guided inquiry have tended to make such linkages "unthinkable." The units under investigation have been "societies;" for the most part, these societies have been treated as the equivalent of states. Thus, world relations have been conceptualized as relations between societies/states. The linkages between local places have been assumed to occur *within* societies/states. Only recently have social scientists begun to illuminate the worldwide linkages of local places. But this scholarship has tended to focus on the ways in which world systems and organizations impact on local places, thus creating the impression that influence is only one-way. There is, of course, good reason for this emphasis, in that these global intrusions appear to be far more powerful than any apparent possibility for local response or resistance. On the other hand, one-way influence should not be assumed without empirical investigation.

Despite the widespread neglect of inquiry on local response to global intrusions, people in many parts of the world are struggling to cope. In the Third World local response is creating "new culture" and "alternative political space." Largely in the industrialized countries, local movements are attempting to "Think Globally: Act Locally." There are efforts by local movements to establish transnational networks with movements in other countries. It is the purpose of this paper to begin to gather together scattered information on local response to global intrusions, toward the end of illuminating evidence of the "unthinkable" which can then serve as a base for further inquiry. This evidence is to be found in scattered research off the mainstream of several social science disciplines and also in the reports of local organizations attempting to mobilize response to global intrusions.

It is important for the reader to understand that in our search of the literature we have not been looking for insight on information on local efforts to cope with all kinds of external intrusions. Rather, we have limited our search to literature which explicitly deals with linkages between local people and systems and organizations whose activities transcend societies/states. The report which follows is organized under the following topics: (1) Creating Culture, (2) Households, (3) Political Movements, (4) Local Action on Foreign Policy Issues of States, (5) Creating Worldwide Movements.

1. Creating culture

Some anthropologists emphasize local creation of culture as a means for overcoming and diminishing the impact of external intrusions. Barri Anne Brown places her concern for the "culture of resistance" in the context of Kathleen Gough's 1968 characterization of anthropology as a "child of Western imperialism" (Gough, 1968, 403; cited by Brown, 1985, 131). She identifies with those who "attempt the development of an anthropology which could propose alternatives to the cultural obliteration that accompanied the spread of Western society" (Brown, 1985, 131). Noting that "dominated people have resisted the cultural erosion that accompanies development," she writes:

> While I would argue "culture of resistance" is often defensive - the resistance to dominant culture for purposes of survival is not the same thing as militant political activity, and at times may be a reactionary response - in a revolutionary context, this maintenance of indigenous culture could be pivotal in restructuring oppressive power hierarchies. Preservation of traditional meanings, initially a response to destructive forces, may be translated into a changed consciousness by the people being dominated; those people could then be provoked to deconstruct dominant cultural categories and regain control over the production of meaning (133).

In her study of "dependency and exploitation in Bolivian tin mines, June Nash argues that "Eurocentric categories" produce studies which fail to recognize the capacity of people in "less developed countries" to understand and respond to the challenges of industrialization. In studying the cultural roots of working-class identity among Bolivian tin miners, she views culture not only as "something that is transmitted from the past to present and future generations" but also as a "generative base" for adapting to changing conditions and for transforming these conditions. In this way myths and rituals from pre-hispanic times, help to prevent alienation among the miners. Says Nash: "When we conceive of culture in this historical structural framework, it becomes a tool for analyzing processes of change rather than an ideology for confirming the status quo" (Nash, 1979, 311). Remarkable is the way in which these miners combine their pre-hispanic cultural identity with keen awareness of their ties to global markets:

> ...their class consciousness is intrinsically tied to an awareness of the world division of labor, in which they feel themselves to be exploited not only as a working class in opposition to a managerial elite, but also as nationals of a dependent economy subject to domination by developed centers. As a class, they are more aware of international relations than are their counterparts in the United States. As a cultural enclave they are less alienated than the majority of the working class of industrial nations... (Nash, 1979, 311).

Based on a study of plantation workers in Colombia and Bolivian tin mines, Michael T. Taussig has reached somewhat similar conclusions. In a study of the social significance of the devil in the folklore of plantation workers and miners, he observes that the "religion of the oppressed can assuage that oppression and adapt people to it, but it can also provide resistance to that oppression." He observes that magical rights "stimulate the vision and sustain the morale upon which (class struggle) depends." At the same time he notes that pre-colonial beliefs are "as dynamic and everchanging as the network of social relations that encompasses the believers, and their meaning mediates those changes" (Taussig, 1980, 231).

John Bennett draws somewhat similar conclusions in his research on agrarian society in North America. He sees that "the most important missing theory segment in anthropology concerns the macro/micro nexus of relationships" (Bennett, 1985, 48). This perspective, he believes, "focuses our attention on what is really going on in the world - the incorporation of communities into larger and larger systems." (50) When he focuses on the "micro" in agrarian North America, he discerns "the ability of 'traditional' social systems to withstand pressures and modify outcomes of the general processes of industrialization and urbanization." Thus the local "community is seen not as a tribal isolate, but as a population nucleus that owes much of its continuing existence to its dealings with the outside." He sees that "the local spatial system retains many of its 'traditional' institutions and utilizes these to manipulate and control the external forces" (Bennett, 1967, 441-442).

In his research on Miskito Indians in the Atlantic region of Nicaragua, Richard Adams also roots his analysis in the local creation of culture. But his "preliminary model for emergent phenomena in complex societies" is much more explicit in spelling out the characteristics of this culture, and very provocative in suggesting how its organizational products extend into larger social systems. Adams' thesis is that "the great leveling of culture that capitalism engendered and the leveling of society that socialism has sought are two processes that work against a basic and primal adaptive tendency in human beings. This tendency is to seek survival through the elaboration of culture" (Adams, 1981, 18). One aspect of this elaboration is technological innovation, and another is the elaboration of social organization. It is "this constant tendency to sprout new survival vehicles" which is the concern of Adams, who sees this as creating "new cultures with their complex symbols and form-meaning attachments that have allowed the human species to find ways of dealing with totally new problems" (Adams, 1981, 18). Adams recognizes that older cultures have been destroyed by the spread of mass culture but declares that "it cannot ever be expected to inhibit the emergence of new cultures" (Adams, 1981, 18).

At the core of Adams' view of human social relations are "primal survival vehicles" which individuals create and sustain in order to survive. Included are domestic units, associations of domestic units (communities) and associations of communities. (Figure 1) An assembly of primal survival vehicles comprises a "primary coaxal structure," which provides "the basis of an individual's primary identity" (Adams, 1981, 5). Eventually population pressures and resource scarcities produce problems that require new "higher level political survival vehicles." In turn, simple political vehicles

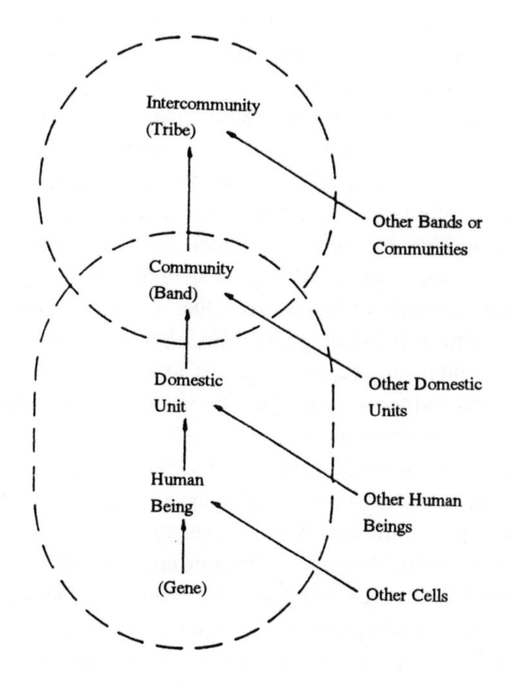

Figure 1 Primal survival vehicles
Source: Adams, 1981, p. 6

(chiefdoms, kingships and states) confront problems which require "agencies" which endeavor to regulate the activities of primal survival vehicles in terms of their view of what is required for survival. Important in Adams' scheme is a broad definition of "political," inclusive not only of government, and political organizations and movements, but also of capitalist enterprises, and institutionalized religious organizations. "These organizations are designated political vehicles to draw attention to the fact that, irrespective of the problems with which they deal, they are alike in seeking individual conformity to practices that perpetuate themselves " (Adams, 1981, 8).

When political survival vehicles and their agencies fail to satisfy a substantial number of people, those who are frustrated create "new survival vehicles and new secondary coaxes." These may be created in order to cope with problems left unattended by political vehicles or they may attempt to reform or replace existing political vehicles. (Figure 2) Examples of the creation of secondary vehicles are responses to the Industrial Revolution which are now essential parts of modern societies: labor unions, mutual aid societies, and pressure groups. Because the emergence of new survival vehicles is inevitable, Adams believes that "it is inevitable that we should witness constant generation of new culture" (Adams, 1981, 11). Adams cites as current examples, evangelical, Catholic and other religious cults, pro-abortion and right-to-life groups, Black power movements, Ku Klux Klan, environmentalists, and nuclear hawks.

In applying his scheme to the survival vehicles of Miskito Indians in Nicaragua, Adams'analysis ranges from primary survival vehicles to the Nicaraguan state, to other states and even to international agencies. Illuminating for our purposes is his diagram of relations on the Nicaraguan Atlantic coast in 1979. (Figure 3) The ties of Spaniards lead through the local Sandinista Committee of Defense, to the Junta, and then to the non-aligned international movement of states. But the local survival vehicles fashioned by the Indians lead through different organizational paths. Those of the Miskito and Sumu link to the National Assembly of the Miskito and Sumu peoples (ALPROMISU), but those of the Creole, Rama and Carib lead to the Southern Indigenous Creole Community. Eventually all local Indian survival vehicles are represented as having some kind of access to regional and world councils of indigenous peoples and the World Council of Churches. This diagram, with its dual linkages to world systems, is a challenging departure from traditional portrayals of inter-societal relationships.

2. Households

In introducing a volume of readings on Households and the World Economy, Smith, Wallerstein and Evers observe that households of today are not "responses" to a capitalist world, but part and parcel of that world. Households are seen neither as isolates nor as small units of social organization related to national economies, but instead as basic units of an emerging world system (Smith, Wallerstein and Evers, 1984, 7-8). Consistent with this perspective is Friedman's view of households as an integral part of a transnational process, thereby challenging "studies on the sociology

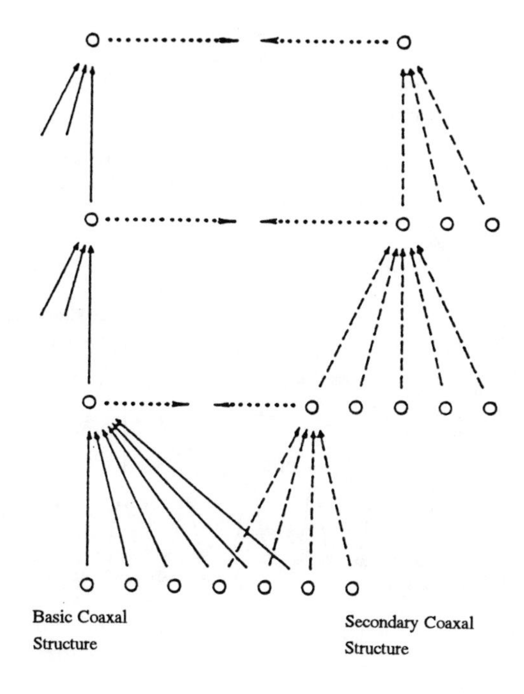

Figure 2 Formation of secondary coaxal structures
Source: Adams, 1981, p. 10

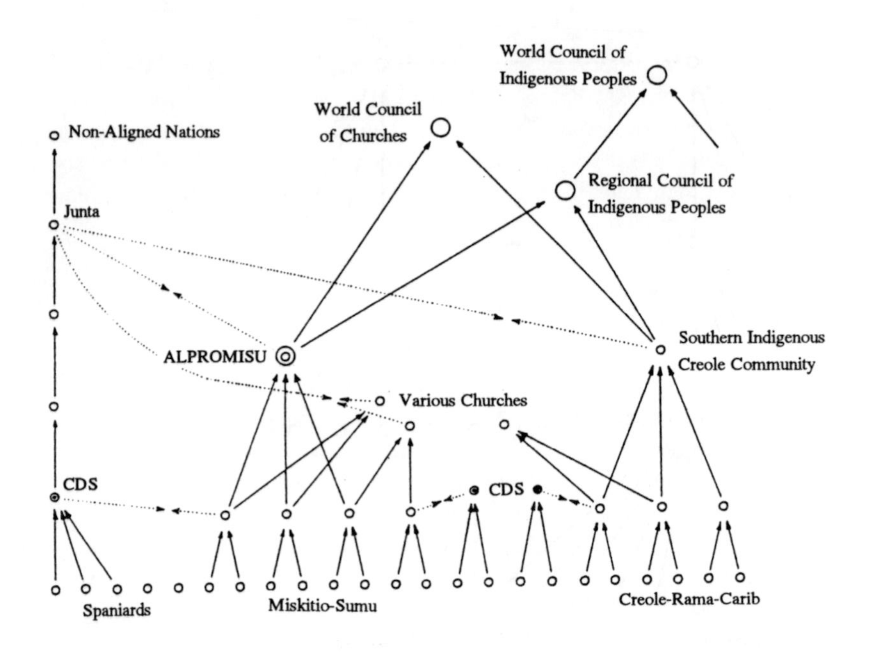

Figure 3 Some Nicaragua Atlantic Coast relations, September-October 1979
Source: Adams, 1981, p. 14

of families, which view their "structure and function" as the consequence of a single straight line of development from the terminus of "industrialization"." The "relationship between households and labour-force patterns in the capitalist world economy would then be viewed as shaped by these long-term undulating economic transformations within which they are situated and to which they are in large measure a response" (Friedman, 1984, 43).

Much of the literature dealing with the growth in worldwide linkages of households focuses on the external impacts on the household. But Wallerstein notes that "the household as an income-pooling unit can be seen as a fortress both of accommodation to and resistance to the patterns of labor-force allocation favored by accumulators" (Wallerstein, 1984, 21). His conclusion is supported by illuminating studies of households in Oaxaca, Mexico and Davao City, Philippines, that offer insight on the capacity of households to resist efforts by the state to 'help' marginal and poor workers to cope with the intrusion of worldwide economic processes into their daily lives. In this study, Hackenberg, Murphy and Selby criticize dependency theorists and, implicitly, most world systems theorists, by noting that their kind of theory is "less interested in the reactions and striving of the exploited than it is in delineating the historical, sociological, cultural and economic forces that coadjust to exploit them." Because dependency theory portrays the urban household as 'fairly helpless,' the authors "take leave of dependency theory" and depict the household as a vital institution that endeavors to protect its interests by resisting state programmes that would undermine the integrity of the household by "opportunities generated by development" which would exploit "the desires of some household members to better themselves economically at the expense of other members" (Hackenberg, Murphy and Selby, 1984, 189-190).

After delineating household strategies employed for resisting external intrusion, the authors divide the population of Oaxaca into marginal, poor and middle economic categories and then apply a regression model that tests the effect of specific household strategies. The results tend to support the efficacy of household strategies that resist state programmes such as population reduction and education: (1) The key to raising household income in each economic category is increasing the number of household workers. (2) The key to survival for the marginal households is the insertion of workers into the informal economy. (3) While the poor and middle groups may do well to invest in education for the head of household, such investments are wasted on secondary workers in these groups, as they are for all those in the marginal category. (4) The key to effective deployment of a larger number of workers is household organization, specifically budget management that takes advantage of economies of scale in consumption. (5) Household organization involves the organization and even manipulation of kinfolk as well, especially sons and daughters-in-law. Thus the authors conclude that efforts by the Mexican government to reduce fertility in the belief that "the small family lives better," is not valid in the light of contemporary distribution of income and wealth in Mexico:

> ...the marginal and poor groups have but one recourse: to withdraw into themselves and organize themselves into large, closely related collectivities that work together in order to survive. Children and their begetting are important facets of this strategy...the large household lives better, for good and sufficient reason (Hackenberg, Murphy and Selby, 1984, 212).

At the same time the government encourages households to make sacrifices in order to educate their children. But this study reveals that "to the degree that households in the marginal and poor groups embrace the 'informal economy' strategy, education is largely wasted." And this strategy seems prudent because the informal economy is expanding more rapidly than formal sector employment. Of course there are individuals who escape from poverty through education. "But when educated members of households depart, they leave behind the ruins of the only strategy that could possibly have assisted their families out of the poverty they are themselves escaping (with luck and perseverance)." In conclusion, under present conditions, the authors see a "continuing hostile dialogue between the households of the majority and the apparatus of the state" (Hackenberg, Murphy, and Selby, 1984, 212-213).

3. Political movements

Critics of both urban political economy and world systems research look to political movements as the source of city resistance to the intrusions of global capital. Richard Child Hill, in an overview of the "emergence, consolidation and development of urban political economy, "makes this parting declaration:

> If, as some scholars imply, the city has become the "weak link" in the world capitalist system, then the most pressing urban research issues today center upon investigation of the conditions under which global-local contradictions... give rise to political movements and public policies directed toward changing the structure and dynamics of the translocal system (Hill, 1984, 135).

Craig Murphy makes a similar criticism of world systems research in the title of a 1982 paper: "Understanding the world-economy in order to change it: A plea for including studies of social mobilization in the world system research program" There is extensive evidence that powerful actors in transnational production systems (Timberlake and Kentor, 1983), and in global cities (Ross and Trachte, 1983), do understand the world economy and they are changing it. But Murphy has a different kind of concern, noting that "the trouble comes when world systemists are asked to define what dynamic role, if any, Third world cultures have in the transformation of capitalism." But before this can be done Murphy sees the need for "a theory of the role of political consciousness and social mobilization in the dynamics of world capitalism" (Murphy, 1982, 1).

Some insight into the "stuff of actual social mobilization" is to be found in studies of grassroots movements in the Third World. Snow and Marshall offer particularly acute observations on the way in which Islamic movements have been provoked by "cultural degradation and desecration" caused by the "market-expanding efforts of Western multinational corporations" (1984, 146). Not very encouraging is Gilbert and Ward's study of community action among the poor in Bogota, Mexico City and Valencia (Venezuela). They found that regimes in each city were successful in deflecting opposition, by making concessions, by providing services and by coopting leaders. But they report that "service provision in each city is shaped more by governmental constraints and needs than by local or settlement conditions."

> this conclusion is discouraging if not unexpected...The truth seems to be that in Bogota, Mexico City and Balencia the state has developed highly effective methods of channeling and controlling participation. there is certainly little sign of participation in the sense of growing control by poor people over the resources and institutions that determine their quality of life. The state in each city has been successful in containing discontent (Gilbert and Ward, 1984, 921).

The results of Gilbert and Ward's study would tend to confirm the conclusion of Manuel Castells, based on his cross-cultural study of grassroots urban social movements: "...the state has become an overwhelming, centralized, and insulated bureaucracy...local communities are, in reality, powerless in the context of world empires and computerized bureaucracies" (Castells, 1983, 329).

Basing his analysis on Indian experience, Rajni Kothari is somewhat more encouraging. His starting point is a view similar to that of the world systems analysts, in that he perceives tendencies:

> that seek, on the one hand, to integrate the organized economy into the world market and, on the other hand, remove millions of people from the economy by throwing them in the dustbin of history - impoverished, destitute, drained of their own resources and deprived of minimum requirements of health and nutrition, denied 'entitlement' to food and water and shelter - in short, an unwanted and dispensable lot whose fate seems to be 'doomed' (Kothari, 1983, 598).

In response he sees "grass-roots movements and non-party formations" springing "from a deep stirring of consciousness and an intuitive awareness of a crisis that could conceivably be turned into a catalyst of new opportunities" (Kothari, 1983, 604-605). These new movements are attempting to "open alternative political spaces" outside the traditional arenas of party and government.

Kothari observes that the very content of politics has been redefined. Issues that "were not so far seen as amenable to political action...now fall within the purview of political struggle" (Kothari, 1983, 606). These include people's health, rights over forests and other community resources, and women's rights. Not limited to economic and political demands, the struggle extends to ecological, cultural and educational issues. Examples include people's movements to prevent the felling of trees in the foothills of the Himalayas, the miners' struggle in Chhattisgarh (a predominantly tribal belt in Madhya Pradesh), an organization of landless activists in Andhra Pradesh, and a peasant's organization in Kanakpura in Karnataka against the mining and export of granite.

While basing his analysis on Indian experience, Kothari sees these movements as part of a "phenomenon (that) has more general relevance." They are, in his view, responsive to

> a new...phase in the structure of world dominance, a change of the role of the state in national and sub-national settings, and a drastically altered relationship between the people and what we (half in jest and half in deception) call 'development' (Kothari, 1983, 613).

Kothari sees the emergence of these new grassroots movements as very "important in shaping the world we live in, including the prospects of survival." Therein, he says, "lies hope." Nevertheless, he cautions that "No one with any sense of realism and any sensitivity to the colossal power of the establishment can afford to be an optimist, either for these movements or for any other transformative process at work" (Kothari, 1983, 610).

4. Local action on foreign policy issues of states

As the global context of cities and towns has been transformed, changes have been taking place in the ways in which local people attempt to cope with the foreign policy issues of states. Although these changes are not necessarily confined to specific parts of the world, the most obvious changes seem to be centered in Europe, North America and Japan. Those involved tend to be a small minority of people, who are middle class, have had some international education and sometimes have had some kind of international experience that sustains their concern for international issues. The traditional activities of these local "internationals" in the United States has been of three main types: relief and aid, exchange programs and international education.

Overall these traditional international programs for local citizens have been in the spirit of creating positive background conditions for a peaceful and humane world. They have operated comfortably within the context of the state system and its ideology, permitting a tacit division of labor in which the state makes foreign policy and voluntary organizations create favorable background conditions which will help the state system to run smoothly. Most local international programs have tended to avoid taking positions on foreign policy issues. Certainly individual local leaders of international programs have often disagreed with national foreign policy. But in the past they have tended not to form local movements to push their views. And, they also have had a tendency to defer to the expertise of national foreign policy leaders.

But dramatic changes are now taking place in the willingness of local people to become actively involved in "foreign policy" issues. The fact that some employ the slogan "Think Globally and Act Locally" is one indicator that people are becoming aware that the intrinsic character of a global issue is that it affects all human settlements. This being the case, they insist that it ought to be possible to act on local manifestations of that issue, whether it be distrust of the "enemy," local military bases, local lack of concern for "distant" poverty or deprivation of human rights. In the following section the reader will encounter a diversity of strategies which citizens have created for coping with global intrusions. They have developed their own citizens exchange and diplomatic corps. They struggle to create their own "island of peace," free of weapons of mass destruction and military production. They practice deterrence by "pledging resistance" to certain foreign ventures of their state government. They struggle to implement global human rights standards in their own community and in distant places. They endeavor to understand the ways in which world economic processes link them to distant poverty and struggle to make these ties more equitable. They offer local sanctuary to the victims of the policies of their own state, as well as the policies of other states. An overview of these local movements can best be approached in the context of three issues: (a) war prevention and disarmament, (b) poverty and (c) human rights.

4.1. War prevention and disarmament As we have already stated, traditional citizen exchange activity has had the purpose of creating a general background of intersocietal relationships that would facilitate peacemaking among states. Some exchange programs have now evolved into activity more pointed at foreign policy issues. An example would be the Citizen Exchange Council which was founded in 1962 as a response to US- Soviet tensions that resulted in the Cuban Missile Crisis. Each year the CEC sent hundreds of US people to the Soviet Union and Eastern Europe. The CEC believed that "the experience sharpens participants' abilities to analyze daily news reports and discern rhetoric from fact. It was believed that better understanding of Soviet society would be passed on to participant's neighbors, friends, students, or classmates, helping more Americans make informed judgments about international events." Other examples of more issue-focused exchanges were Peace Pilgrimage to the USSR, Peace Study Tour to Russia, the Volga Peace Cruise and the Iowa Peace Mission to the USSR. A Scandinavian counterpart was the peace marches of Scandinavian women. In 1981 they walked to Paris, in 1982 to Moscow and in 1983 to Washington. In 1985 they walked to all UN countries in Europe where they put basic peace questions to European governments (Warner and Shuman, 1987).

Somewhat similar were numerous programs in which US citizens visited Central America, particularly Nicaragua. Many of these visits were arranged by church-related organizations. As a result, leaders in churches and voluntary organizations in many communities throughout the country observed conditions in Central America for themselves and offered information and policy advice to local people that supplemented the normal sources of information and opinions on foreign policy issues - the national government and the media. It is reasonable to conclude that this first-hand citizen experience contributed to widespread citizen resistance to US government efforts to escalate US military involvement in Nicaragua.

Thus the evolution of adult exchange programs into issue-focused investigations is adding a new element to local dialogue on foreign policy issues - local people who have had significant issue-related experiences abroad. In a sense, these people can be viewed as a "people's foreign service" that does not accept the traditional state system assumption that people should defer to the experts in Washington on issues such as Soviet and Nicaraguan relations.

One form of "citizen diplomacy" is the city twinning movement, now including efforts directed toward the development of sustained relationships through which people from the two cities attempt to cope with issues which have created animosity between their national governments. John Lofland's (1987) study of these city twinning efforts places them in the context of social movements, classifying them as consensus movements, as distinguished from conflict movements. A key feature of consensus movements is that their programs of action imply conflict with certain aspects of social policy, but they "phrase their aims and programs ... in ways that achieve a facade of consensus" (Lofland, 1987, 3). Thus they are able to obtain mainstream community support, from politicians, media, business, and churches. From Lofland's perspective, "the prime aim of consensus movements (is) the *alteration of awareness* rather than of social conditions" (Lofland, 1987: 32). He concludes that consensus movements "*mystify social causation and social change* by portraying social problems as merely isolated matters of incorrect awareness, ignorance, and lack of direct or personal relationships" (Lofland, 1987: 39). Although Lofland's critique raises penetrating questions, we are inclined to believe that he does not give adequate attention to those city twinning programs which serve as an alternative "foreign service," ones that links cities (not states) and ones that links a great diversity of occupations (not just the professional foreign service). Unlike conflict movements within societies, whose primary goal is to change government policies, the city twinning movement is establishing its own transnational institutions. One example is the eighty-five US-Nicaragua sister city programs (Trubo, 1988) in which citizens from US cities deliver humanitarian aid and at the same time acquire first-hand knowledge of conditions in Nicaraguan cities. Another example is the over thirty US-Soviet sister city programs which are developing sustained ties between US and Soviet cities (Bulletin of Municipal Foreign Policy, 1987, 1989). Of course, a long-term goal of these programs is also to change the policies of national governments.

As local citizens have become more knowledgeable about military strategy, arms races and arms production, they have also become increasingly informed about their personal support of military production and deployment, the conflict between military expenditures and the ability of a society to satisfy human needs and the explicit ways in which their own local community is a part of military production and deployment (Arkin and Fieldhouse, 1985). They are learning how much people in their local community contribute to military budgets through taxes, about specific local military contracts, about local production of military equipment and about the kinds of activities at local military bases (Center for Economic Conversion, 1984). Increasingly local groups are developing strategies for making these local manifestations of military policy widely known. When feasible they are attempting to develop strategies for bringing these local military activities into line with their personal values and policy preferences.

Local plans for conversion from military to civilian production appeal to the self-interests of workers by citing studies such as one by the US government indicating that investment of one million dollars in "defense" production creates 76,000 jobs whereas the same investment in civilian production would produce over 100,000 jobs (US Department of Labor, 1972, cited by Lindroos, 1980). The US trade unions most active in studying conversion have been the International Association of Machinists and Aerospace Workers and the United Automobile Workers' Union. Groups in numerous cities have developed conversion plans (Gordon and McFadden, 1984; Christdoulou, 1970). Perhaps the best known conversion effort was the Corporate plan published by the Lucas Aerospace Workers in England, in 1976. In some 1000 pages the plan identified 150 new products along with suggestions for reorganization of production. The goals of the plan were the safeguarding of jobs and the production of goods that are useful to society. Said the plan, "our intentions are . . . to make a start to question existing economic assumptions and make a small contribution to demonstrating that workers are prepared to press for the right to work on products which actually help to solve human problems rather than create them" (Wainright and Elliott, 1982: 243).

Another local approach has been prevention of weapons deployment. Perhaps the most reported effort to prevent deployment of weapons has been the efforts of the Greenham Common Women in the United Kingdom to blockade US bases. They also brought a suit in the US courts charging that cruise missiles are unconstitutional. They argued that the missiles, capable of being quickly and secretly launched, deprive Congress of its right to declare war, threaten to deprive life and liberty without due process, in violation of the Fifth Amendment, and violate several canons of international law because of their indiscriminate and long-lasting potential effects. Hundreds of US and British churches, disarmament groups and labor organizations joined the suit as "friends of the court." A US court dismissed the suit. (*Defense and Disarmament News*, March-April 1985). In Nebraska a coalition of Western environmental and peace groups filed a legal suit to block the deployment of MX missiles, in Western Solidarity v. Ronald Reagan. Ground Zero in Bangor, Washington has blockaded a local naval base in a campaign against the Trident submarine which they perceive to be a first strike weapon. In April 1985 community organizers in eight US cities pledged their resistance to deployment of sea-launched cruise missiles (SLCMs). Most of the representatives came from cities which the Navy had considered as possible homeport sites for battleship surface action groups. These ships have the potential for carrying the Tomahawk SLCM (*Disarmament Campaigns*, May 1985).

A final local approach to military policy is the application of deterrence by citizens. In the Pledge of Resistance campaign people agreed to engage in either legal vigils or nonviolent civil disobedience in case the US invaded, bombed, sent combat troops, or significantly elevated its intervention in Central America (Butigan, Messman-Rucker, Pastrick, 1986). By January 1985 some 42,000 had signed the pledge. Local groups created local plans of action for civil disobedience and trained people for nonviolent action (*COPRED Peace Chronicle*, February/April 1985: 5).

A significant departure in new forms of local activism on "foreign policy" issues has been the tremendous growth in efforts to put international issues on the agendas of city government and to put foreign policy questions before the electorate in local referenda (Shuman, 1986-87). The nuclear weapons freeze campaign put much of its efforts into nuclear freeze votes by city, town and county councils and local referenda. The freeze called for a bilateral (US-Soviet) freeze on the production of nuclear weapons. Based on figures from the Nuclear Weapons Freeze Campaign National Clearinghouse in St. Louis, Newcombe (1983) reported that 240 city councils, 466 New England town meetings and 63 county councils passed freeze resolutions, a total of 769. In addition, referenda were passed in over 50 cities and counties. This effort was followed by a comprehensive test ban campaign which had received support from 154 cities by 1987.

Cities have also declared themselves to be nuclear weapons free zones (Takayanagi and Shioya, 1983; Takahara, 1987). The nuclear weapons free zone approach was originated in the context of continents, such as Antarctica and Latin America and regions, such as the Indian Ocean, Pacific, Middle East, Central Europe and Scandinavia. Perhaps frustrated by lack of progress in obtaining support of states for nuclear free zones over these large areas, the movement was moved to the grassroots. A nuclear-weapons free municipality is generally one that does not permit the stationing of nuclear weapons and also does not permit transit of such weapons, including through surrounding water and air space. It may also mean nonstationing or non-transit of weapons systems associated with nuclear weapons and refraining from the production of these related weapons systems. A few cities have extended the nuclear weapons free zone to a "nuclear free zone" which prohibits civilian nuclear power stations as well as nuclear weapons.

The CND (Campaign for Nuclear Disarmament) started the municipal nuclear free zone movement in Britain where 192 local councils have approved the proposal, over 60% of the population. Nuclear Free America, Baltimore, Maryland (*The New Abolitionist*, October 1988) reports that there are 4222 nuclear free zone communities in 23 countries: Argentina (1), Australia (111), Belgium (281), Canada (176), Denmark (20), Finland (3), France (1) Great Britain (192), Greece (70), Ireland (117), Italy (700), Japan (1315), Netherlands (100), New Zealand (105), Norway (140), Philippines (21), Portugal (105), Spain (400), Sweden (7), Tahati (1), USA (155), Vanatu (1), and West Germany (200).

For those who view these local involvements in international issues from the standpoint of state system ideology, city meddling in issues such as the war in Vietnam, Apartheid, nuclear freeze and nuclear free zones appear to be intrusions in issues that should be handled in Washington, thus producing messy and confusing foreign policy-making that is risky for the "national interest." On the other hand, some view these issues as intrinsically local issues in that the first victims of nuclear war would be cities. How then can it be said that citizen initiatives whose goal is to prevent nuclear war are not appropriately the concern of local government? Bitter experience motivates the extensive anti-nuclear activities of the mayors of Hiroshima and Nagasaki, as exemplified by their personal lobbying efforts in the United Nations. Among many local officials sharing their view is Larry Agran, now on the city council of Irvine, California and former mayor of the city. Viewing the nuclear threat as a local issue, he took the initiative in organizing mayors and council members in California through Local Elected Officials of America (LEO-USA). This organization supports the nuclear weapons freeze, reversing the arms race, a reduction of US military spending and conversion of the funds to more productive civilian purposes. Other interesting indicators of the dynamic interest in municipal foreign policies that is centered in California are the emergence of a *Bulletin of Municipal Foreign Policy* (Center for Innovative Diplomacy, Irvine) and appearance of *Building Municipal Foreign Policies: An Action Handbook for Citizens and Local Elected Officials* (Shuman, 1987).

In conclusion, perhaps the greatest significance of these local approaches to military policy is not in their success or failure but in the way in which people are reconceptualizing both the targets of action and strategies for achieving goals. Instead of only demonstrating against distant officials they have acted against manifestations of their policies in local neighborhoods. Instead of only appealing to these same officials for changes in relationships with other countries, they have established their own relationships with people in cities abroad. In so doing they are significantly challenging traditional norms for the participation of local people in world affairs, both by making the local community an arena of "foreign policy" action and by direct involvement abroad. These changes are also reflected in local activity with respect to poverty and human rights.

4.2. Poverty Over the past couple of decades voluntary programs to relieve suffering abroad have gradually evolved into programs for overcoming poverty through longterm economic and social development. Participation in Third World development has in turn involved leaders of voluntary programs in a complicated political process as they simultaneously attempt to raise funds from affluent people in the industrialized countries and use these funds to serve needs of the poor in the Third World. Lissner's *The Politics of Altruism* (1977) graphically portrays the tension between the expectations of many who donate to aid programs and those administering the programs overseas. As Lissner sees it, donors tend to think of aid in terms of "resource aid" that improves the standard of living by means of various social services (e.g. education, health, agriculture) within the given economic and political structure. On the other hand, people involved in administering programs in the Third World tend to see the need for "structural aid," i.e., transforming the local socio-economic environment by "conscientization through literacy training, establishment of rural credit institutions and rural cooperatives, support of trade unions and liberation movements" (Lissner, 1977: 22). Even more difficult to communicate to affluent supporters is the discovery "that many (but not all) of the problems of the low-income countries originate in and are sustained by factors and policies in the high-income nations; and that many (but not all) of the governmental and voluntary aid efforts "out there" are of little use, unless those root causes located within the high-income countries are tackled simultaneously" (Lissner, 10).

Increasingly voluntary agencies involved in development programs in the Third World have created development education programs in their home countries as a response to these difficulties. US based organizations such as CARE and CROP (Church World Service) now devote a specified portion of their budget to development education (Hampson and Whalen, 1989). Programs for development education are most highly developed in Europe and also in Canada, and US programs are patterned after them (Pradervand, 1982; Traitler, 1984). Canadian efforts include development education centers in cities such as Toronto, London and Kitchener-Waterloo. Although the development education movement is only in its infancy in the United States, it has great potential for transforming the species identity reflected in willingness to respond to famine and poverty into much deeper understanding of the longterm causes of these conditions. In essence, development education is largely education in global political economy that provides a framework for understanding how people in local communities in both Third World and First World countries are linked to the global economy. This can open the way for specifying local policies in First World countries that are responsive to the needs of local communities in the Third World.

It is not surprising that some perceive a relationship between arms expenditures in the Third World and poverty. This, of course, raises concern about sales of arms to the Third World by First World manufacturers and governments. Since 1974 the British Campaign Against Arms Trade (CAAT) has been publishing a newsletter under the same name. In December 1984 they reported on a November 1984 International Conference on the Arms Trade held in The Netherlands. In May 1985 a CAAT sponsored "Bread not Bombs" nationwide Week of Action, publicizing the damaging effects of the arms trade to Third World countries, focused on Britain as the world's fourth largest supplier of arms to the Third World. Emphasis was placed on local action. OXFAM, long active in Third World development programs, has issued a "Cultivating Hunger" report whose suggestions for action include: "Encouraging a transfer of spending from the Arms Race to Development. In particular: cutting out Government encouragement for arms dealing with the Third World, carefully restricting the export of repressive equipment and arms likely to be used for quelling internal disturbance caused by the anger of the hungry" (*Campaign Against Arms Trade*, Newsletter 69, December 1984).

The Towns and Development movement, largely centered in Europe, is an effort to spur Third World development through direct collaboration between European cities and Third World cities. Responding to a suggested outline of the Towns and Development Secretariat in The Hague, a number of European towns/cities have contributed case studies of their relationships with Third World counterparts. (As yet no case studies by Third World participants seem to be available). Because there is no available document that generalizes across the case studies, it is difficult to draw conclusions about the achievements of this program. On the other hand, it is significant that the number of participating towns/cities is growing. Very impressive is the forthright critical approach of the case studies in which both failures and successes are reported. Says Lode De Wilde of Brugge, "Linking with towns in developing countries is fated to be short-lived because of the great differences in mentality between local governments on both sides. The degree of bureaucracy in nearly all Third World countries inevitably confines you to official channels" (Kussendrager, 1988: 17). A report on Oldenburg complains that the relationship with a town in Lesotho had not progressed between 1985 and 1988. More upbeat reports are made on links between Amsterdam and Managua and between Bremen and towns in Namibia, Western Sahara and Nicaragua. Gunther Hilliges, head of the Department of Development of Bremen reports that Bremen is in an ambigious position. "It is part of an economic structure, but it supports the critics of that structure," resulting in much opposition in Bremen to the development cooperation of the Federal Republic of Germany (Kussendrager, 1988: 72). Thus we have some evidence that the Towns and Development program offers a challenging arena for local "hands-on" experience in contending with the complexities of economic relationships between the First and Third Worlds.

In Europe there is a movement for town councils to create policies for development cooperation, as reflected by a conference in Florence in October 1983 organized by the International Union of Local Authorities, the United Town Organization and UNESCO. Emphasis was placed on "Twinning" cities in Europe and cities in the Third World and conscientization of local people to Third World problems. Says the conference report: "Increased interest in these problems and the desire amongst local inhabitants to make their own contribution towards solving them has in many cases led to municipal councils being confronted with these matters. Development cooperation items appear on Town Council agendas more and more" (*IFDA Dossier*, March/April 1984: 27).

The conference report cites examples of municipal Third World policies in Northern Europe. In Belgium there is a campaign to have an Alderman for Development Cooperation appointed in each municipality. In Bruges the Alderman for Development participates on a 15 member Third World committee composed of all organizations in Bruges involved in development cooperation. This committee advises the Bruges Town Council on matters pertaining to development cooperation, conducts awareness building activities for the Bruges population and coordinates initiatives of the various local organizations involved in Third World activity. In Leiden the municipality decided in 1979 to make available an annual amount of 10.000 guilders for informing people about Third World developments. In Tilburg, Netherlands, the Mayor and Aldermen in 1979 produced a draft "opinion" on "foreign affairs" examining the possibilities of municipal authorities contributing to local awareness about the inequality in the relations between industrial countries, such as the Netherlands, and countries of the Third World. This led to the creation of an Advisory Board in June 1980 composed of members of the Town Council and representatives of community organizations. After an inventory of local organizations involved in development cooperation it was decided that development education would be approached from two angles: (1) conditions in the Third World, (2) the domestic situation (textile workers). A fund has been established for local education and for programs directly linked to a Third World situation. The Town Council annually contributes 50,000 guilders to this fund.

In summary, we have seen dramatic changes in local efforts to cope with distant poverty. There has been an evolution from the charitable impulse to send aid to the less fortunate to a concern for long-term development. This has been accompanied by growing concern for the way in which local ties to the Third World have an impact on distant poverty. And the assumption that the role of government in coping with distant poverty is exclusively in the domain of states, is now being challenged by local governments. Whether these changes will have any significant impact on the still growing gap between the rich and poor of the world remains to be seen. On the other hand, there is no doubt that, when compared to the more traditional activities of local "internationals," these new styles of participation have very significantly advanced local understanding of issues in world political economy, and have spurred more self-conscious participation in local efforts to cope with these issues.

4.3. Human rights In conformance with the ideology of the state system, fulfillment of human rights as promulgated in the Declaration of Human Rights is normally perceived to be the task of national governments. But those who follow closely the global struggle for human rights, know that nongovernmental groups have been the prime engines in the struggle. Indeed, the two covenants drafted to fulfill the declaration (one on civil and political rights and one on economic, social and cultural rights) both assert in their preambles:

> Realizing that *the individual, having duties to other individuals and to the community to which he belongs*, is under a responsibility to strive for the promotion and observance of the rights recognized in the present Covenant (emphasis added).

One example of local response to the spirit of this appeal, was the promulgation of the UN International Covenant on the Elimination of All Forms of Racial Discrimination in Burlington, Iowa in an ordinance adopted by the city council (*The Burlington Iowa Hawk Eye*, September 21, 1986). One organization that endeavors to fulfill this responsibility is Amnesty International (AI), particularly through its program in which local AI groups work for the release of prisoners of conscience throughout the world. The primary approach of these AI groups is to bring pressure on foreign governments through publicity, letters, and phone calls (Amnesty International, 1986).

The struggle against Apartheid in South Africa has also been localized through local boycotts of companies and banks doing business in South Africa and efforts to change their policies by participation in shareholders meetings. There are also campaigns on many college campuses attempting to pressure boards of directors of colleges and universities to disinvest in corporations doing business in South Africa. In these cases the investments consist principally of endowment funds. Janice Love's 1985 study of anti-Apartheid campaigns in Michigan and Massachusetts reported that twenty-two local governments in the U.S. had withdrawn investments from corporations doing business in South Africa. By 1986 the American Committee on Africa reported that fifty-four cities had divested (Love, 1985).

Another form of local human rights activity is efforts to provide new homes for refugees from political oppression, war and economic deprivation in other countries. Normally this means settling legal immigrants in local communities, although sometimes it can - either deliberately or unwittingly - involve assistance to illegal immigrants. The Sanctuary Movement in the United States offered sanctuary for refugees from El Salvador and Guatemala whom the movement believed would suffer punishment or death if they returned. But the US immigration service declared them to be illegal aliens which they would return to El Salvador; and in March 1989 the US Court of Appeals in San Francisco upheld the 1986 conviction of eight religious workers who gave sanctuary to aliens from Guatemala and El Salvador. The movement began in 1981 in Arizona and the San Francisco area when church people of many denominations began to assist, feed and shelter refugees fleeing El Salvador and Guatemala. Since then over 300 religious congregations have declared themselves to be Sanctuaries in a movement involving over 50,000 people. The Sanctuary Movement bases its efforts on the Refugee Act of 1980 which provides asylum for those persecuted or having "a well-founded fear of persecution in their own countries," and sees itself as following a US tradition, as exemplified by the Underground Railroad during the Civil War. It is also noted that those helping the slaves were indicted and imprisoned.

Still another local form of human rights action has been the INFACT Campaign against the Nestlé Corporation and its marketing practices for infant formula in the Third World. INFACT action included local boycotts of Nestlé products, disinvestment campaigns and national and international efforts to set standards for the marketing of infant formula in the Third World. This culminated in the approval of recommended standards by the Assembly of the World Health Organization in 1980. There was only one negative vote, cast by the representative of the United States. This led to the acceptance of the WHO standards by the Nestlé Corporation (McComas, Fookes, Taucher and Worsnop, 1985). Although INFACT field monitoring has found significant violations of the WHO standards, they found that marketing of baby food and hospital feeding practices for infants have changed substantially since the code was adopted (INFACT, 1984, cited by Sikkink, 1986, 822). In a study of this case which included field work in Central America, Kathryn Sikkink concluded that "the activities of nongovernmental groups, in particular transnational activist groups, were essential to the final outcome" (Sikkink, 1986).

4.4. Creating worldwide movements A limitation on research and education which might empower people to cope with the impact of worldwide economic, and political, systems on their communities is the absence of theory, and even penetrating descriptions, of how local communities are linked to the world. Nevertheless, we have learned that local people have established transnational ties in attempting to cope with issues such as Apartheid, political prisoners, and marketing of infant formula. In response, some scholars studying grassroots movements in the Third World are attempting to gain insight into what some refer to as the micro-macro dynamic. Perceiving 'macro' and 'micro' as "only differential expressions of the same process," Kothari calls "for a review of ideological positions that continue to locate 'vested interests' in local situations and liberation from them in distant processes--the state, technology, revolutionary vanguards" (Kothari, 1983, 615). Writing out of experience with the Lokayan movement in India, D.L. Sheth concludes that a new politics is required that is "not constricted by the narrow logic of capturing state power." Rather, he concludes:

> It is the dialectic between micro-practice and macro-thinking that will actualize a new politics of the future. ...In brief a macro-vision is the prime need of these groups and movements, and this can be satisfied only by a growing partnership between activists and intellectuals in the process of social transformation (Sheth, 1983, 23).

He perceives a new mode of politics arising across regional, linguistic, cultural and national boundaries. It encompasses peace and anti-nuclear movements, environmental movements, women's movements, movements for self-determination of cultural groups, minorities and tribes, and a movement championing non-Western cultures, techno-sciences and languages.

This bears striking similarity to the vision of two Swedish economists, Friberg and Hettne (1982) who see a worldwide "green" movement emerging that offers an alternative to the "Blue" (market, liberal, capitalist) and the "Red" (state, socialism, planning). From the Green perspective, they see that "the human being or small communities of human beings are the ultimate actors" (Friberg and Hettne, 1982, 23). Rahnema, too, points to the emergence of informal networks that not only link "together the grass-roots movements of the South but also establish new forms of co-action between those and those of the North" (Rahnema, 1986, 43). He concludes:

> To sum up, new ways and means are to be imagined, mainly to allow each different group to be informed, to learn about other human groups and cultures, in terms of their respective life support systems; in other words to be open to differences and learn from them. As such, only a highly de-centralized, nonbureaucratic, *inter-cultural* rather than *inter-national* network of persons and groups could response to such needs (Rahnema, 1986, 44).

Zsuzsa Hegedus has analyzed the transnational wave of protests which responded to the installation of Pershing II cruise missiles in Germany and Western Europe. She observes that the mass demonstrations were only the tip of an immense iceberg consisting of a "veritable explosion of diverse citizens committees, associations, and activist groups" which proliferated after 1981 (Hegedus, 1987, 199). A particularly significant aspect of this "social fabric" is the way it ranges across age, sex, class, occupation, political ideology, and religious affiliation. "Whereas the debate on security was once confined to the cabinets of national governments, today it is as much in the streets and in the media as it is in Western Parliaments (with the exception of France)" (Hegedus, 1987, 204). Significant aspects of developing "capacity for initiative outside the framework of the state," have been both local and regional initiatives, and the transnational spread of this movement across the Western world (except France).

Hegedus observes that the significance of these protests extends beyond their impact on specific policy issues, noting that "the major result of this protest is to extend the democratic process so that the military-statist realm of security is transformed into a transnational public sphere" (Hegedus, 1987, 204). She sees a "new ethic of civilian responsibility" emerging which extends beyond nuclear weapons issues and is inclusive of broader security issues, including famine and liberty. She concludes:

> Will this effort to civilize transnational relations through a transnational movement of civil emancipation which practices an ethic of responsibility and transnational solidarity be able to transform effectively the statist-military world while addressing the problems of peace, freedom, and famine? The answer is far from clear. Yet this movement has at least brought this challenge to light and has made manifest our responsibility to meet it (Hegedus, 1987, 215).

Another perspective on locally based transnational movements is Laurie Cashdan's research on anti-war feminism. For her the significance of the feminist dimension of the antimilitarist movement is its refusal "to separate the quest for new human relations from antimilitarism" (Cashdan, 1989, 81). She believes that the blockade of the Pentagon in 1979 (Women's Pentagon Action) inspired women across the Atlantic, including the Greenham Common Women's Peace Camp. Among specific examples of transnational links are dialogues begun by San Francisco women in 1983 with women from Japan, the Marshall Islands, and Latin America, and marches in New Zealand in support of the women at Greenham Common. At the same time, she notes how young women activists in the United States have been challenged with the way in which "women's resistance to the outside oppressor, in such places as Guatemala, Chile, the Philippines, and South Africa, is combined with the deep desire on their part for new human relations at home" (Cashdan, 1989, 82).

Remarkably similar in perspective is an account of the experiences of native-Hawaiian women in Wai-anae who came together to share their experiences of sexism, racism and economic exploitation. They decided to examine how to deal with and resolve conflict without violence. This led to the conclusion that "the violences that occur on the larger societal and global levels and on the personal level have connections" (Chai and De Cambra, 1989, 61). Eventually they decided to work on disarmament "because we want a future for our children," and to work with local women on women's role in nuclear disarmament. At the same time, they endeavored to employ creative means for dealing with conflicts at home and to develop local peace education curricula. These native Hawaiian women see that "the convergence of Western feminism and Third World women's grassroots politics can be transformed into a global feminism to the purpose of accomplishing world peace to save the whole of humanity" (Chai and De Cambra, 1989, 63).

Conclusion

At least since the age of the Western "explorers," people in towns and cities throughout the world have been linked to distant places, but the tendency to portray the world as consisting of relationships between societies/states has caused the social science mainstream to neglect systematic study of these relationships. More recently, there has been scattered interest in the local impact of global intrusions. Despite scholarly neglect of local response, local people have invented a variety of ways to cope with these intrusions. This chapter has attempted to pull together scattered literature which might offer insight on these efforts and also provide a base for future inquiry.

We have gained insight on how local people have attempted to respond by creating a "culture of resistance" - Bolivian tin miners, North American farmers, and Miskito Indians in Nicaragua. We have learned how households attempt to resist the policies of worldwide economic institutions and their state supporters - in Mexico and the Philippines. We have noted the response to global intrusions by Islamic movements, urban movements in Colombia and Mexico, and grassroots movements in India. We have illuminated the strategies of local movements attempting to "Think Globally and Act Locally," primarily in North America and Europe, as they cope with issues in war prevention and disarmament, poverty and human rights. We have examined efforts to create worldwide human rights, disarmament, and feminist movements.

In many respects, these people are out in front of the social science mainstream in their competence to confront the world around them as it really is. To employ more graphic terms, in transcending the state system view of the world, they have freed themselves from the shackles of a "cast iron grid that exercises a transcendent despotism over reality" (Young, 1976, 6). Nevertheless, there are researchers in anthropology, world systems, urban political economy, political movements and grassroots movements who are attempting to observe and evaluate these efforts. In some cases, the only material which we have are the accounts of participants themselves, particularly in the case of the "Think Locally and Act Globally" activities in the industrialized countries.

No doubt this brief survey of a few arenas is a very incomplete view of human efforts to cope with global intrusions into local space. However, it does reveal that people in all parts of the world are attempting to create new means (cultures of resistance, survival vehicles, household strategies, political, grassroots and worldwide movements, local government foreign policies) for coping with these intrusions. The application of new technology to world relationships, particularly the world economy, has spurred new kinds of local political processes. Like the global economy to which they respond, they do not respect old political boundaries. Most social scientists will be surprised at the ways in which seemingly "ordinary people" are demonstrating competence both in understanding complicated world systems and in creating new means for coping with these complexities. But these people still need our help in fully explicating potential for local response and in evaluating the consequences of alternative strategies. Such inquiries will not only be helpful to specific local movements but will also provide a significant missing link in the knowledge needed if humanity is to cope with a growing array of global problems. To paraphrase Tip O'Neill, former speaker of the United States House of Representatives, "All problems are local problems." None can be solved without the competent participation of local people throughout the world, and without their willingness to recognize the legitimacy of necessary parallel efforts by states and global institutions. (Alger, 1990)

References

Adams, R.N. (1981) The Dynamics of Societal Diversity: Notes from Nicaragua for a Sociology of Survival, American Ethnologist, Vol. 8, No. 1.

Alger, C.F. (1990) Grassroots Perspectives on Global Policies for Development, Journal of Peace Research, Vol. 27, No. 2, May.

Alger, C.F. (1988) Perceiving, Analyzing and Coping with the Local-Global Nexus, in International Social Science Journal, (Paris) 117/August.

Alger, C.F. (1984-85) Bridging the Micro and the Macro in International Relations Research, Alternatives, Vol. X, No. 3, Winter.

Alger, C.F. (1977) 'Foreign' Policies of United State Publics, International Studies Quarterly, Vol. 21, No. 2, June.

Amnesty International (1986) Voices of Freedom, New York, 1986.

Barkin, D. (1985) Global Proletarianization, in Sanderson.

Bennett, J. (1967) Microcosm-Macrocosm Relationships in North American Agrarian Society, American Anthropologist, Vol. 69, No. 1.

Bennett, J. (1985) The Micro-Macro Nexus Typology, Processes and System, in Billie R. DeWalt and Pertti Pelto, Micro and Macro Levels of Analysis in Anthropology: Issues in Theory and Research, Boulder, Co., Westview Press.

Braudel, F. (1977) Afterthoughts on Material Civilization and Capitalism, Baltimore, Johns Hopkins University Press.

Brown, B.A. (1985) Anthropology and the Production of Culture, Dialectical Anthropology Vol. 10, No. 1 and 2, July.

Butigan, K., Messman-Rucker, T. and Pastrick, M. (eds.), (1986) Basta! No Mandate for War. A Pledge of Resistance Handbook The Emergency Response Network, Philadelphia, Pa., New Society Publishers.

Cashdan, L. (1989) Anti-War Feminism: New Directions, New dualities - A Marxist-Humanist Perspective, Women's Studies Int. Forum, Vol.12, No.1.

Castells, M. (1983) The City and the Grass-roots: A Cross-Cultural Theory of Urban Social Movements, Berkeley, University of California Press.

Chai, A.Y. and De Cambra, H. (1989) Evolution of Global Feminism through Hawaiian Feminist Politics, Women's Studies Int. Forum, Vol. 12, No. 1.

Christodoulou, A.P. (1970) The Conversion of Nuclear Facilities from Military to Civilian use: A Case Study in Hanford Washington, New York, Praeger.

Friberg, M. and Hettne, B. (1982) The Greening of the World: Towards a Non-Deterministic Model of Global Processes, University of Gothenburg, Sweden, (xerox).

Friedman, K. (1984) Households as Income-producing Units, in Wallerstein, S. and Evers (eds.), Households and the World Economy, Beverly Hills, Sage Publications.

Gilbert, A. and Ward, P. (1984) Community Participation in Upgrading Irregular Settlements: The Community Response, World Development, Vol. 12, No. 9.

Gordon, S. and McFadden, D. (eds.), (1984) Economic Conversion: Revitalizing the American Economy, Boston, Ballinger books.

Gough, K. (1968) New Proposals for Anthropologists, Current Anthropology, Vol. 9, cited by Brown, 1985.

Hackenberg, R., Murphy, A.D., and Selby, H.A. (1984) The Urban Household in Dependent Development, in Netting, R. McC., Welk, R.R. and Arnould, E.J. (eds.), Households: Comparative and Historical Studies of the Domestic Group, Berkeley, University of California Press.

Hampson, T. and Whelan, L. (1989) Tales of the Heart: Affective Approaches to Global Education, New York, Friendship Press.

Harvey, D. (1985) Consciousness and the Urban Experience: Studies in the History and Theory of Capitalist Urbanization, Baltimore, Johns Hopkins Press.

Hegedus, Z. (1987) The Challenge of the Peace Movement: Civilian Security and Civilian Emancipation, Alternatives XII.

Hill, R.C. (1984) Urban Political Economy: Emergency, Consolidation and Development, in Smith, P. (ed.), Cities in Transformation: Class, Capital, State, Beverly Hills, Ca: Sage.

Hobbs, H. (1985) The Transnationalization of City Hall: Local Governments in Foreign Affairs, International Studies Association convention paper.

Jacobs, J. (1984) Cities and the Wealth of Nations, Principles of Economic Life.

Kothari, R. (1983) Party and State in Our Times: The Rise of Non-Party Political Formation, Alternatives, Vol. IX.

Kussendrager, N. (1988) Towns and Development: NGO and Local Authority Joint Action for North-South Cooperation, 2nd ed., The Hague, Towns and Development Secretariat.

Lissner, J. (1977) The Politics of Altruism: A Study of the Political Behavior of Voluntary Development Agencies, Geneva, Lutheran World Federation.

Lofland, J. (1987) Consensus Movements: City Twinning and Derailed Dissent in the American Eighties, Davis, California, University of California, Department of Sociology.

Love, J. (1985) The U.S. Anti-Apartheid Movement, New York, Praeger.

McComas, M., Forbes, G., Tancher, G. and Worsnop, R. (1985) "The Dilemma of Third World Nutrition: Nestle and the Role of Infant Formula", Washington, D.C., Nestle Coordination Center for Nutrition, Inc.

Murphy, C. (1982) Understanding the World Economy in Order to Change It: A Plea for Including Studies of social Mobilization in the World System Research Program, International Studies Association Convention.

Nash, J. (1985) Segmentation of the Work Process in the International Division of Labor, in Sanderson.

Nash, J. (1979) We Eat the Mines and The Mines Eat Us: Dependency and Exploitation in Bolivian tin Mines, New York, Columbia University Press.

Newcombe, H. (1983) Peace Actions at the Municipal Level, paper presented to 10th General Conference of the International Peace Research Association, Gyor, Hungary, August.

Portes, A. and Walton J. (1976) Urban Latin America: The Political Condition from Above and Below, Austin, University of Texas Press.

Pradervand, P. (1982) Development Education: The Twentieth Century Survival and Fulfillment Skill, Berne, Swiss Federal Department of Foreign Affairs.

Ross, R. and Trachte, K. (1983) Global Cities and Global Classes: The Peripheralization of Labor in New York City, Review, Vol. VI, No. 3, Winter.

Sanderson, S. (1985) The 'New' Agriculture, The Americas in the New International Division of Labor, New York, Holmes and Meier.

Shuman, M. (1986-87) Dateline Main Street: Local Foreign Policies, Foreign Policy, No. 64, Winter.

Shuman, M. (1987) Building Municipal Foreign Policies: An Action Handbook for Citizens and Elected Local Officials, Irvine, Center for Innovative Diplomacy.

Sikkink, K. (1986) Codes of Conduct for Transnational Corporations: The Case of the WHO/UNICEF Code, International Organization, Vol. 40, No. 4, Autumn.

Snow, D. and Marshall, S.E. (1984) Cultural Imperialism, Social Movements, and the Islamic Revival, in Kriesberg, L. (ed.), Research in Social Movements, Conflicts and Change, A Research Annual. Vol. 7. Greenwich, Ct., JAI Press.

Stavrianos, L.(1981) Global Rift, New York, Morrow.

Takahara, T. (1987) Local Initiatives to Promote Peace, Peace and Change, Vol. 12, No. 3/4.

Takayanagi, S. and Shioya, T. (1983), Peace Policies of Local governments, Peace Research in Japan, 1981-84. Tokyo, Japan Peace Research Group.

Taussig, M. (1980) The Devil and Commodity Fetishism in South America, Chapel Hill, N.C., University of North Carolina Press.

Timberlake, M. and Kentor, J. (1983) Economic Dependence, overurbanization, and Economic Growth: A Study of Less Developed Countries, The Sociological Quarterly, Vol. 24, Autumn 3.

Traitler, R. (1984) Leaping Over the Wall: An Assessment of Ten Years of Development Education, Geneva, World Council of Churches.

Wainright, H. and Elliott, D. (1982) The Lucas Plan: A New Trade Unionism in the Making, London, Allison and Busby.

Wallerstein, I. (1984) Household Structures and Labor-force Formation in the Capitalist World-Economy, in Smith, J, Wallerstein, I. and Evers, H.D. (eds.).

Wolf, E. (1982) Europe and the People without History, Berkeley, University of California Press.

Young, C. (1976) The Politics of Cultural Pluralism, Madison, University of Wisconsin Press.

6 Multiple group loyalties and the security of political communities

Henry Teune

Can emergencing overlapping political entities, now increasing in numbers, attract individual loyalties without diminishing those to previous ones or dividing them? Individual attachment is assumed to be a necessary condition for the legitimacy and the viability of any political system.

Europe, Northern Europe; North America, the Northeast; Asia, South Asia; Africa, South Africa; Latin America, North or South along with the re-emergence of old nationalities. These are some examples of the world now dividing and integrating into new political and economic niches.

Since the enlightenment, the main forces for changing the polities with which people identify, were the nation-state and city. They no longer have the strength they had in the 19th and the first half of the 20th centuries to overcome the identities of blood and locality. And yet the world has become a total system with trappings of institutions of a global political economy - international banking, the group of seven, and transnational professional associations. In the last part of the 20th century the world is being transformed in ways yet to be described (Boulding, 1985). Indeed, the nationalisms of states may have turned out to have been weak and transitional (Snyder, 1982).

After 1945 perceptions of the threat of war and the need for strong nation-states for economic prosperity were the theoretically dominant questions in the social sciences. What happened was the encapsulation and division of the world partially described as the first, second, and third worlds, categories based on a mixture of economic and political concepts.

One lens for addressing questions about a changing world order is that of the political integration research of the 1960's. It was based on ideas of modern social integration with interdepence supplanting exclusive group identities based on birth and place. Political integration was focused on the newly independent states with their multi-ethnic, tribal societies, as well as the world as a whole and within geographic regions. In the 1950s the integration problems for older states were class, center-periphery, and urban and rural conflicts. Internationally, studies of political integration received substantial impetus from the "cold war" stimulating mutual defense arrangements and the re-building of post-war Europe along with their fledgling regional institutions that may become again the foundation of an economic union. As older ethnic group claims to political autonomy came to the fore in Europe and North America in the 1960's, despite strong national political institutions, theories of political integration were proclaimed dead by one of its founders (Haas 1975) and research on national political development faded. But with few exceptions, Pakistan being the most notable, the political boundaries of the world states stabilized in the 1970s, despite some long standing boundary disputes, such as those between China and India, and between Israel and its neighbors. As the post-World War II world order came apart in the late 1980s, both new and old units of human political identity and allegiance were asserted, and new states gained recognition.

The main thesis of what follows is that a new world order will be based on newly emerging world cities with relationships bypassing national capitals, an ascendant world system with transnational institutions, a new localism with political identities, and small political organizations - neighborhoods and residential associations - within both metropolitan areas and large cities (Teune, 1987). This does not mean the demise of large cities and the nation-state, which might stabilize processes of rapid political change. It does mean, however, a change in fundamental relationships between city and state, a political alliance that eroded the influence of the old rural localities in favor of national centers, important first for capitalistic commerce and, later, industrial production (Poggi, 1978). World cities will be linked directly to other cities, countries, and world institutions. Indeed, these new relationships were one of the conditions of the rise of new and smaller political entities.

International relations will be transformed by these new complexities from those of diplomacy, trade-exchange, threat and war. Relations among countries may move from zero-sum to positive sum ones. Any political entity that gets better off, except militarily, will make the world better off and, hence, most, even perhaps all, also better off. This process, however, will - as with all human change - be lumpy, not linear, and certain events, such as regional wars, might end up in substantial set-backs for globalization and localized autonomies.

1. A global system

There are many ways to define a world system, depending on whether its dynamics of change are seen as re-occurring patterns of successions of dominant power centers or system breaks followed by a new type of system historically unprecedented (Modelski, 1987). Scholarly views in the United States run from an anarchic system of independent states to an interdependent world (Holsti, 1989). The debate is in part a consequence of the fact that the world and the nation-state are now changing without obvious anchors in historical precedent. Human systems that are social systems are not merely constituted by members of the human race but are marked by continuous change in the nature of their components and the relationships among them. A sub-set of them are political systems, including an emerging global system. They have the following defining characteristics. First, institutions with influence through hierarchy, consciously acting to control, including making claims to authority. Second, processes that promise and deliver rewards and punishments. Third, commitments of individuals and groups to a collectivity. Fourth, some shared values among their components. All of these are now, albeit weakly, manifest globally.

A system must by definition be integrated, based at the very least on values of what and who is included, although there are many competing claims, such as today among international institutions, nation state, and localities. Measured against these defining properties, the world has a global political economy, although feebly and contradictorily integrated.

2. Regions

Regions are defined as encompassing constituted local units, where some dimensions of their activities are determined by their membership or grouping within the region. The political analogy is the province within national political system, with a center dominating the local in some specifiable ways and with radical discontinuities at the national boundaries, defining the major players in an international system of states, which until now has been dominated by competition and conflict.

Suggested earlier is what long has been obvious. Regions spill over national political boundaries, for example, southern California and Texas with northern Mexico. In such regions certain advantages accrue to proximity and intermingling of peoples, leading to common identities. There are also regions that transcend national boundaries for economic exchanges and cultural sharing, in some cases stimulating the growth of incipient political institutions, if only regularized meetings of political leaders, such as might be developing among recently re-defined areas of central Europe.

Then there are regions with defined institutions, encompassing entire nations, such as the European Economic Community, the North American economic accords, including Mexico unofficially, and the Association of Southeast Asian Nations.

The future of these regions, sometimes free trade zones, is barely understood. What is known is largely descriptive, but they meet the defining criteria of systems mentioned earlier, including that of perceptions and attitudes. They too lay claim to awareness and loyalty by individuals; indeed, they lay the groundwork for weakening national identities and opening opportunities for local ones. The ideas of a Europe or North America appear to compete with those of ethnicity and place. They need not, if multiple group loyalties evolve.

3. New localism

A driving force of modern social development during the last half of the 20th century in developing countries is urbanization for production and bureaucratization; in developing ones, for the provision of amenities and delivery of services. Large cities in the west had the task of managing social and economic diversity resulting from urban migration and, following different patterns, did so by developing an encompassing political organization of municipal government and national standards of welfare to buttress a sense of community. Group indentities were often secured and potential conflicts contained by various kinds of residential and local segregation. Suburbanization created population dispersion and different kinds of economic and group conflicts that were shifted to higher levels of government for resolution, such as national civil rights legislation in the United States.

New forms of urban association for collective action have appeared in many parts of wealthy countries. They are just now being mapped by researchers. It is estimated in the United States, for example, that about 60 percent of privately owned residences are somehow organized into residential associations, yet only one limited report on them is available (ACIR, 1989). In many countries there are neighborhood associations (not cross-national terms) that address problems of near-ecology, such as cleanliness and safety. There are associations that share residential spaces, even internationally, such as time limited occupancy. Industrial parks create political entities that provide services on a semi-volunteer basis. In Poland, in part as a consequence of reduced national governmental control, civic associations have been formed for education and other services. New kinds of political fragmentation are emerging, partly in response to limits of traditional units of governance - the city, province, and nation-state.

This new localism is being reinforced by new technologies of communication. The costs of producing local television news stories have gone down. One report is that over a seven week period in a major midwest television market in the United States, a local network affiliate carried about 400 local news stories (Berkowitz, 1989). Cable television is local, sub-dividing metropolitan areas. A challenging logistical problem in the United States at the 1988 Democratic Party's national convention in Atlanta was parking for nearly 300 television trucks from local stations so that local newscasters could beam a local slant on the proceedings. Local area networks (LAN) can cheaply broadcast across an area of about eleven square kilometers. Computer-based printing has expanded the number of community newspapers that now can be produced quickly and cheaply by part-time people.

The new localism, however, must be seen as more than simply based on physical space. Individuals set up special communications networks that can include like-minded people or those with similar skills from around the world. They can, in addition to economic or recreational functions, engage in activities of political movements as well as build social solidarity. Political parties, contained by the nation-state now can become global. Joint ventures, such as those between the Science Centers in Philadelphia and Kyoto, have led not only to friendships but also to common political outlooks.

The new localism divides, and yet can be tied together through global communications by satellite, ship, and plane. The nation state no longer is the gate-keeper it once was.

4. Loyalty and multiple group loyalties

Not much has been written about loyalty in the United States since the 1960s when scholarly discourse about the concepts of nationalism and national character waned. The concern about loyalty after 1945 with the re-construction of Europe was whether national identities would be overtaken by international socialism or class consciousness, a rival to nationalism in certain parts of the world since the late 19th century. One of the first systematic quantitative cross-national studies was launched by UNESCO to assess attitudes in nine European Countries with nearly 9.000 respondents. That report was published as How Nations See Each Other (Buchanan and Cantril, 1953). The findings were that national identities prevailed over alternatives, such as the same class in other countries. Nonetheless, concern persisted over how French was the French Communist party. Another issue at that time was whether people could be loyal to the United Nations and other international institutions and yet remain loyal citizens of their countries.

Loyalty (allegiance) refers to both a perception and an attitude - a perception that some entity is both relevant and positive. It refers to commitments to persons, places, institutions, and ideals (Guetzkow, 1955). How are loyalties formed? That the entity one is loyal to is rewarding, provides vicarious satisfactions through collective achievements, is inculcated from birth, and assures security from threats by others as well as punishments for disloyalty. How does loyalty to groups move from that of delivering goods and other satisfactions to become a habit? Loyalty without getting something directly in return - contingent commitment - is probably best explained by group habituation over time (Teune, 1964).

Individuals can have multiple loyalties and these loyalties are continuously re-shaping. It is controversial whether loyalty is part of human nature, but this appears to be the case. Another issue is whether there are limits as to how much loyalty an individual has to give. There appears to be no known limit (Guetzkow, 1955).

Must loyalties be hierarchically arranged so that country is number one, for example, family number two, and so on? This is not evident. Indeed, most people living today have experienced radical discontinuities in their political systems - the post 1945 "revolutions", decolonization, and the regime changes of the 1980's. Individuals in fact do not face up to the potential clash of multiple loyalties and therefore assume fluctuating ones. Specific circumstances can bring loyalties into conflict and, when they do, the following responses are possible. First, there is denial of any conflict: "My government would not persecute me". Second, there is compartmentalization: "Render unto Caesar what is Caesar's, and to God what is God's". Third, there is a narrowing of focus: "Housing is not the fault of the national government". Fourth, there is re-definition: "By being loyal to Ireland, I am serving the interests of the United States". Of course, when conflicts cannot be avoided or otherwise resolved, individuals choose, as is the case when governments set out to harm minorities who are citizens of their state.

Loyalties are fluid. Under certain circumstances they can be shaped relatively quickly. At present, new loyalties are forming in Europe with potential divisions into western, central, eastern, southeastern parts. Indeed, older regional identities might emerge from parts of the former Hapsburg Empire.

Loyalty is a necessary condition for political systems. This was among the conclusions of those dealing with question of political integration in the 1950s and 60s. One of the underlying dimensions of viable political entitities was psychological, both individual and collective, and shared identities and symbols (Deutsch, 1953; Jacob and Toscano (eds.), 1964). The reason that loyalty is necessary for a political system is straightforward: politics involves both divisions over collective values and differences in perceptions of how to achieve them. Hence, the political process necessarily involves winners and losers and requires that most of the losers accept the winners, and that the winners will not harm the losers. In secular, stable constitutional states political parties are an integral part of political processes of winning and losing with loyalty to the state undiminished.

5. Localism regionalism and the global system

One of the first great tests of multiple and sustainable loyalties in the modern world system of states was whether it was possible to be loyal to a state without being loyal to the offical religion? The consequence of the European Reformation was that if religious identities were divisive, then only one religion could be tolerated in a single political system. The general outcome of the religious wars in Europe and their settlement in the Treaty of Westphalia was that any alternative to accepting religious diversity was worse, much as the contemporary conclusion that nuclear war is worse than almost any other imaginable condition. A second test was whether loyalty to locality, both area and province (states, in the US), was compatible in nation-states based on the principles of federalism, and on a separation of religion and citizenship. The guestion was not resolved in the United States until the very early 20th century, when all state militia were subordinated to the President as Commander - in - Chief. Nonetheless, local political cultures remain threatened and their options remain those of corruption, sabotage, and other forms of resistance. The Supreme Court in the United States, designed to resolve local and national conflicts, long avoided the issue by deciding that individuals had "dual citizenship" - state and national. There is now only one.

A new global political economy has opened up a variety of aspiring and competing political centers: Europe, Western Europe, Scandinavia. What has been learned is that claims for loyalty do not have to be exclusive; limited claims may be a sufficient base to build and maintain the components and legalized relationship of a viable political entity. In the 1970s, as many times before, material scarcity was seen as a limit to growth and a threat to political loyalties. That fear, of course, will re-occur. But what has also been learned is that there are nearly no limits to social growth, creating new social human organizations and arrangements among them (Teune, 1988). As of yet, limits to individual capacity to give allegiances have not been reached. There may be such limits.

The main way of creating more political entities and integrating them is to increase the scale of the global system, its integrated diversity. Allegiances to those units need not detract from others. A citizen of a city is part of the world system because the city has global relations; the same should hold for somebody living in a region and having loyalty to both it and the country.

A major challenge is maintaining similarities in the values of local groups to preserve their cultural diversity. The ideal of citizen rights, preceded by group rights coming from the development of secular constitutional states, spread rapidly in the 19th century. They were the foundation of liberation movements and de-colonialization. Today the notion of human rights based on being simply a human has taken hold since the 1940s and especially in the 1970s and 80s. Individual human rights concepts, of course, are resisted in certain countries, often at some cost to their involvement with regional groupings and international institutions. Just as claims to national civil liberties clashed with those of local authorities in the 19th and 20th centuries, so will ideas of individual human rights conflict with local and nationally based cultures and politics today. The issue will turn on cultural preservation versus world society, similar to those of species and genes, purity versus mixtures of reproductive matters. In the face of global communication and other intrusions into local cultural niches, erosions of local identities may be difficult to accept, prompting some to resist.

6. The ascendence hypothesis

One general hypothesis confirmed by studies of political integration in the 1950s and 60s is the growth-ascendence-loyalty relationship. Growth, of course, refers to more than simple economic increases in per capita output; it includes enhanced administrative and political capacities (Deutsch, et al., 1957). For loyalty to fix on a center, its ascendence must promise reward and have the capacity to coerce. The critical question in linking ascendence and loyalty is perception of positive change; a new Europe, for example. What will be the trajectory of its increased capabilities and the probability of its failure? The difference between expectations and perceptions of "real" improvement - again concepts from the 1950s and 60s in research on integration - can be mediated by politics, but now that is a politics conducted through global media. Is Western Europe doing better than Eastern? Pictures, voice, and fax have diminished the exclusivity of national governments' control over information and resulting perceptions.

Three dimensions of media, in addition to their penetration of localities, have augmented the potential political control capacities of regional and global institutions. First is the speed of images and messages that communicate regionally and internationally. Second is the intrusion of reporters (observers) without the identities and values of the nations and localities being known. Information from elected representatives and governments will increasingly diverge from media reports of what is going on. Third is the previously discussed local capacity to communicate to others about what is happening locally. Official national data on employment for example will be contrasted, with local experiences.

More than ever before people living in localities, associated with others professionally or politically through networks, grouped into regions and tied to the fate of a global political economy, will seek communities larger than the family or locality, and identities reaching beyond those defined by the quilts of geographic boundaries of, within, and among countries.

The ascendence of multiple world and regional centers, along with changing patterns of economic growth, both regionally as well as in ensembles of innovative sectors, such as bioengineering, will make the world less stable in the short run. The processes of political integration of cities and national regions, buttressed by authority of the state, will be challenged. Some areas will find it easier to bypass the nation-state by direct linkages to world cities, transnational regions, and the global system. Some cities and regions may declare themselves open to the world.

7. Relative decline

Loyalty is part of the foundation of political communities that can provide a variety of collective rewards, including psychological ones of identifying with group achievements. The question is: achievements in what values? Certainly since 1945, and with economic growth, more and more national governments have cast their fortunes with material well being and individual security. But political systems have in the past prospered with the values of art, religion, state craft, and military prowess system (Nef, 1950). Today material values appear to have the upper hand in defining a new world. Economic prosperity is the accepted standard of achievement of most of the world's political communities, indeed, it is associated with democratic governance.

Since the remarkable recent economic growth from 1945-1970, and with several areas of the world moving away from subsistence existence, a few areas in the 1980's - notably Eastern Europe and almost all of Africa - have experienced a real decline in economic consumption, leading some countries to reform their political ways and others to transform their political systems. The promise now is that living standards will improve in the long run in a global political economy. The challenge to legitimacy from loyalty is that of economic improvement compared to one's past and to the progress of others, which with electronic communications makes it ever easier for individuals and groups to do so.

One response to relative decline is withdrawal and the closure of the primordial niches of family, ethnicity, and religion, relying on what is closest and most familiar. That, however, is the antithesis of what is required for the development of new regions and the global system. With decline, external intrusions are responded to as threatening. The consequence might be the breakup of larger, more encompassing political communities that have based their legitimacy on real growth and asserted capacities for betterment (Teune, 1986).

How the world system is shaped depends significantly on world economic growth and how it is distributed. Clearly there are growth centers, and sectors which spill over national boundaries. The problem will be areas of relative decline - the new perpheries - and the consequent withdrawal of their population's commitments to transnational regions and participation in a global system. This depends on whether the world will experience long term growth into the next century. If it does, as some believe, (Ross, 1989) then the loyalties of peoples can be partialed out to new entities without loss, indeed, with the strengthening, of older ones.

8. A concluding statement

The world is in a process of transition. Since 1945 professional scholars of the international system have fragmented, using various concepts to understand change, often retrospectively: the cold war and containment; the economic centers and the peripheries; interdependence; strategic projections of military and other types of national political capacities; the "haves and have-nots": the rise and decline of great powers; the stability of hegemons. This list could be lengthened, and the uncertainties overwhelm the responsibilities to understand. In part this is the consequence of week theories of change and massive impacts of often fickle political decisions.

A few directions of change have been suggested: a new localism, the emergence of new kinds of regions, and the strengthening of a global system, all laced into the older forms of nation-states and cities. Increasing the number and varieties of collectivities with political trappings is compatible with what is known about multiple and partial individual and group loyalties up to some unknown limit. The pace of change may increase, its shape becoming more fluid, and setbacks more frequent. All will be influenced by political leadership, but in what ways is at the moment unclear as new arrangements are being made among those contending for world leadership, including an increasing number who are neither heads of nations nor governments.

References

Advisory Commission on Intergovernmental Relations (ACIR) (1989) Residential Community Associations: Private Governments in the Intergovernment System, Washington, D.C.

Berkoweitz, D. (1989) Creating the News of Local TV, Paper presented to the Annual Meeting of the International Communications Association, San Francisco.

Boulding, K. (1985) The World As a Total System, Beverely Hills, CA, Sage Publications.

Buchanan, W. and H. Cantril (1953) How Nations See Each Other, Urbana, Il., University of Illinois Press.

Deutsch, K. (1972) Nationalism and Social Communication: An Inquiry into the Foundations of Nationalism, Cambridge, The Massachusetts Institute of Technology Press.

Deutsch, K. et al. (1957) Political Community and the North Atlantic Area, Princeton, NJ, Princeton University Press.

Guetzkow, H. (1955) Multiple Loyalties, Princeton, NJ, Woodrow Wilson School of Public and International Affairs.

Haas, E. (1970) The Obsolescence of Regional Integration Theory, Berkeley, CA, Institute of International Studies.

Holsti, K. (1989) Mirror on the Wall, Which Are the Fairest Theories of All?, International Studies quarterly, No. 33.

Jacob, P. and Toscano, J. (eds.), (1964) The Integration of Political Communities, Philadelphia, PA, J.B. Lippincott.

Modelski, G. (1987) Long Cycles in World Politics, Seattle, WA, University of Washington Press.

Nef, J. (1950) War and Human Progress, Cambridge, MA, Harvard University Press.

Poggi, G. (1978) The Development of the Modern State, Stanford, CA, Stanford University Press.

Ross, M. (1989) A Gale of Creative Destruction, New York, Praeger.

Snyder, L. (1982) Mini-Nationalisms: Autonomy or Independence. Westport, CN, Greenwood Press.

Teune, H. (1964) The Learning of Integrative Habits, in Jacob, P. and Toscano J. (eds.), The Integration of Political Communities, Philadelphia, PA, J. B. Lippincott.

Teune, H. (1986) Growth, Development, and Ecology: Crises of Economic Decline, Paper presented to the XI World Congress of the International Sociological Association, New Delhi.

Teune, H. (1988) Growth and Pathologies of Giant Cities, in Dogan, M. and Kasarda, J. (eds.), The Metropolis Era, vol. 1, Newbury Park CA, Sage Publications.

Teune, H. (1988) Growth, Newbury Park, CA, Sage Publications.

7 Identity, autonomy and the ambiguity of technological development

Colin N. Williams

1. Introduction

Conventionally analysts of threatened languages and weakened ethnic groups have identified the modern state, public education and technological change as the chief agencies of cultural assimilation. Currently territorially-rooted group identities are facing extreme pressures which serve to devalue place at many levels in the spatial hierarchy. In this chapter I want to investigate some of the current paradoxes facing threatened minorities and also examine some of the more positive reactions to such pressures within the lesser-used language regions of the European Community.

The central question I want to examine is to what extent recent technological advances can assist in the strengthening of threatened languages. An extension of this concern is the analysis of ethno- territorial identity in an increasingly 'open' and fluid environment, leading one to ask the following questions: What is the relationship between land, language and social context within advanced industrial societies? Do the recent transition procedures which induce social mobility and the erosion of cultural heartlands accelerate language and cultural loss? If the territorial base of Europe's lesser-used language communities is being eroded does this necessarily presage their death?

Further if territory is considered to be less significant as a social variable can we assume that the devaluation of place is a permanent feature of critical social theory? Or is this a temporary aberration to be compensated either through a new re-formulation of territory and social relationships or by an equally temporary over-emphasis on the significance of place and locale in critical social theory?

Globalization and the prominence of post-modernist thought has revitalised the myriad connections between time and space. The devaluation of place, so characteristic of late modernity, is critical to our enquiry and has received much attention of late, leading Soja (1989) to call for a revised ontology for Geography, comprising space, time and being. This new ontology derives from the fruitful cross-fertilization of ideas and trends in Western Marxism and radical geography (Dear, 1990). Space had been marginalized as a key element in social theory by both positivism and Marxism. But Geography had also contributed to this drift because it had neglected to integrate into its thought several key elements of critical social theory. Now that modernism had given way to a postmodernist epistemology, space would be resuscitated as a key factor in social thought. Of crucial import was the manner in which leading theorists from other disciplines were scrutinizing space and reformulating old spatial relationships as new theoretical problems. Thus Wallerstein (1990) and Robertson (1987, 1990a, 1990b) were analysing space hierarchies in terms of globalization and the structuration of the world. Giddens (1981, 1985) was laying the foundations for a critical social theory which paid due recognition to the centrality of space, alongside time, as a key element of both knowledge and practice. Globalization, regionalization, localization, however unattractive as terms, were being reintroduced as significant phenomena for social enquiry, and the tensions both between and within individual levels and the whole hierarchical order were being represented in terms of new languages, new discourses, in short a new social science.

Fragmentation and globalization are intimately connected in the new post-modern order. Of course, to a certain extent they always had been. Consider the impact which Martin Luther's very localised act of pinning his 95 theses on to the door of the Hofkirche at Wittenberg had on the 'globalization' of the Reformation's principles. What is different now is the speed and intensity of the diffusion of knowledge and the simultaneity of its impact in many parts of the world.

What are the fundamental elements of modernity? Giddens (1991) asserts that the two principal characteristics are: (1) the disembedding of social institutions, that is the lifting of social relationships out of time and space and into an indefinite time-distance, and (2) institutional reflexivity, whereby the more institutions mature, the more information is routinely defined, and is not conceived as an independent set of knowledge.

One response both to the devaluation of place and to the rise of a global culture has been a re-examination of locality. In Britain this has largely focussed on a re-invigoration of urban and regional studies by both geographers and sociologists engaged in the locality debates (Duncan and Savage, 1991). Two implications for lesser-used language speakers may be derived from the wider debate. Firstly, that late modernity poses a problem of identity for the self; it increases doubt because of the contingent nature of history and geography. The plural and multi-layered nature of identity offers new possibilities but it simultaneously destroys old cosmologies and habits of routinised obedience which so often pass as the conventional substance of conformist identities in local societies.

Secondly, that the response of lesser-used language speakers to these globalizing trends as experienced in the locality cannot be simply assessed. It clearly is not a dialectical response to globalising trends, it is not a reversion to primordialism or parochialism (despite what majoritarian critics might assert). Neither is it a cultural defence against primarily economic threats to the changing social order. However, it may have much to do with the deinstitutionalisation of territory (Giddens, 1991). The erratic and non-deterministic nature of change does not allow such speakers (nor ourselves as analysts) to predict the future course of events with any great accuracy and this increases the sense of anxiety and of anomie in many cases. It can also limit an ability to influence the political and economic system so as to allow for a greater representation of 'minority' culture.

Spatially this can lead to a de-coupling of land and language and a re-coupling of the majority culture to the state apparatus through the diffusion of new agencies for hegemonic control, eg. the mass media and 'popular press' in some societies, the imposition of a national curriculum in the official language of the state, the acceleration of external control of a region's resources thus tying it closer than ever before to the new world order through the mediation of the central state.

2. The problem illustrated

In common with many other ethno-linguistic minorities, the Celtic heartlands, (Y Fro Gymraeg, the Scottish Gailhealtachd and the Irish Gaeltacht) have been steadily eroded as a result of anglicizing influences and of modernisation writ large. The inexorable trend of language decline and territorial fragmentation has been extensively documented and need not be repeated here (see Aitchison and Carter, 1985; Hindley, 1990; Williams, 1980; Pryce and Williams, 1988, Withers, 1988). This fragmentation and drift reduces the cogency of territorial identity as conventionally interpreted, and militates against the adoption of a uniformly designated territorial language region, within which citizen rights and the primacy of Welsh or Gaelic may be specified and sanctioned (Williams, 1982). At root the territorial basis of the Celtic cultures has been severely eroded during the present century, but in response to the diminution of one of the principal constituents of their identity there has arisen a vigorous social defence movement. This movement has provided a new significance for the land, a new self-consciousness which has been utilized both by the agencies of central government and by the leadership of those communities who feel threatened by the developments of a centralised bureaucracy and the ever-voracious economic imperative of resource extraction and exploitation by commercial interests. In short, as I have detailed elsewhere, the land has become a new battle-ground wherein the conflict between the local and the universal, the indigenous and the exogenous interest groups becomes mediated (Williams, 1987). But territory, as we shall see, is not merely contextual, it is not only a scene for the playing out of socio-economic factors, it is itself a significant source of symbolic and resource power. Its possession and control is often deemed vital to the very survival of specific cultural groups. This is why territorial loss of ownership of culture space, or the perceived 'invasion' of homelands by 'outsiders' evokes such passion, as we have seen so tragically and so very often in Europe generally.

Today the Celtic-speaking communities are in crisis, for the western heartland, its mainstay over the centuries, can no longer be taken for granted. It is daily threatened by a plethora of changes which are largely outside the control of the minority population. Let me illustrate by reference to one case study, Wales.

3. Wales

The territorial redistribution of the Welsh-speaking population, following broader socio-economic trends, is shaping a new geographic reality for stable bilingualism and cultural reproduction. For, whilst in proportional terms the language is still dominant in the north and west, in absolute terms the majority of Welsh speakers inhabit urban areas in industrial South Wales and along the North Wales coastline (Figure 1). The freasons for both population redistribution and the growth of a significant sector of Welsh-speakers in angilicized areas is well understood.

Processes, common to many multilingual contexts, such as the in-migration of non-native speakers, language displacement and cultural shift, the revolution in telecommunications, and access to the media, have all reduced the probability of inhabiting settled Welsh-speaking communities as a local majority.

As a consequence of these factors we can no longer define the internal linguistic divisions of Wales with such confidence as did previous generations of scholars. Today, there are many gradations of Welshness in the community. Instead of talking of a 'Welsh-speaking community', it is far more realistic to talk of 'Welsh-speakers in the community', even within many parts of the heartland areas (Williams, 1989). Thus many individuals are now more autonomous, seeking language contiguity without necessarily expecting that interaction to take place within geographic contiguity.

Further, the cultural influence of a social mass of Welsh speakers predisposing a new generation to reproduce the "langue" and the culture can no longer be taken for granted. The old domains for language reproduction no longer apply in as comprehensive a fashion. A crisis mentality has characterised this complex situation since at least the mid 'sixties when a number of social movements were established with the express aim of politicising and radicalising the Welsh population. To a certain extent, groups such as Cymdeithas yr Iaith Gymraeg, Adfer and Plaid Cymru have been singularly successful, both in placing the future of the language on the political agenda, and in being instrumental in changing attitudes and the social conditions for the reproduction of the language. In fields such as bilingual education, the media, planning and the law, new domains and agencies have been constructed which have served to institutionalise Welsh within a partial bilingual society. Fundamentally, of course, such new agencies by their very nature change the relationship both between the autonomous individual and the state, at both central and local levels (Williams, 1982; 1987; 1989).

Central to this transformation is an intriguing paradox. Whether coincidental or causal, there is a real irony that at a time when the extension of Welsh into new and promising domains has been achieved there is a corresponding territorial retreat of Welsh in former heartland areas, threatening even the possibility of there being any large scale regional or urban-based majorities in the next century. Does the diminution of a territorial identity chime the death knell of Welsh culture, or could one envisage community without propinquity and with what consequence for the survival of the culture?

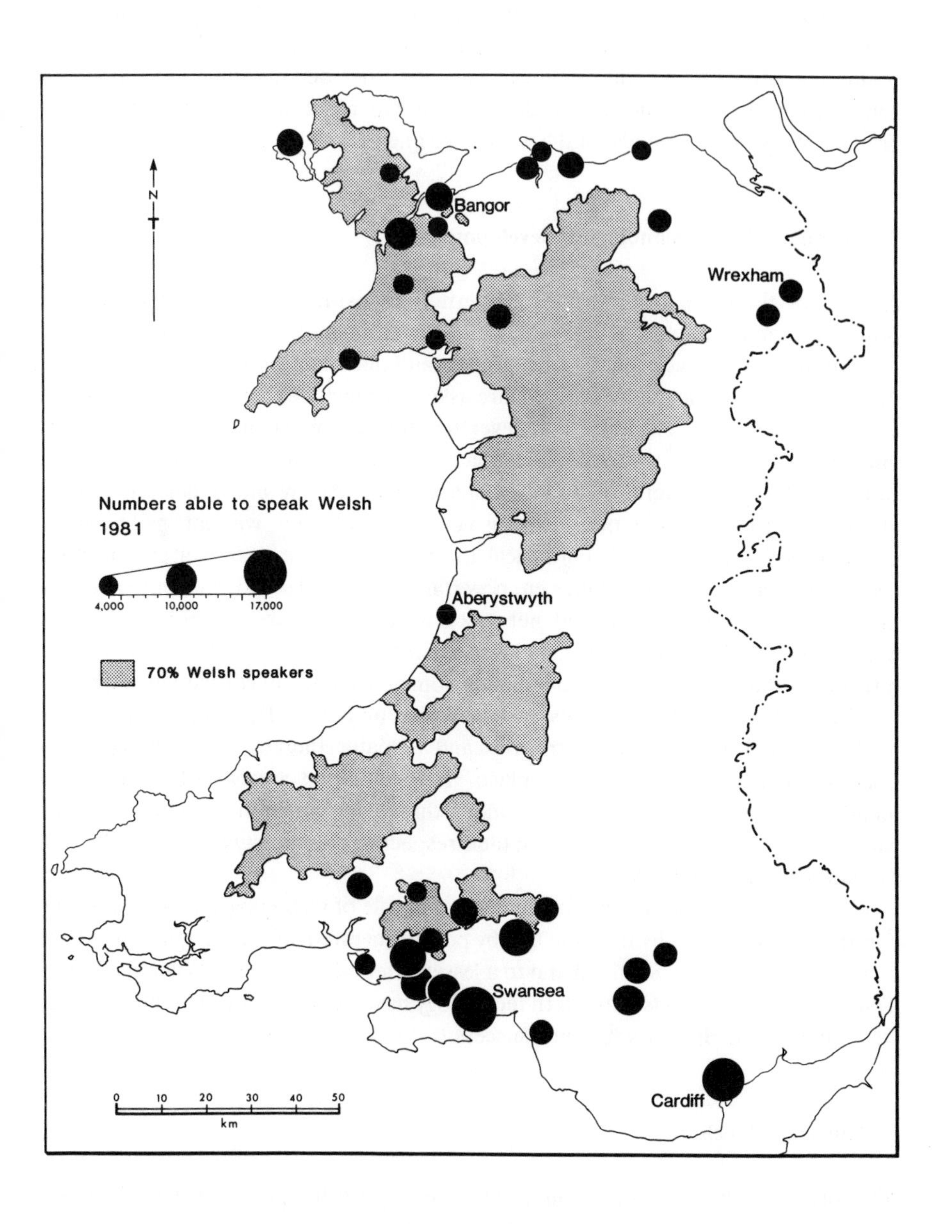

Figure 1 Absolute and proportional distribution to Welsh speakers in 1981
Source: Williams, C. 1989, p. 43

Let me elaborate upon the paradox. Despite a partial language revival in the past thirty years, there is a real danger that without language planning, technological assistance and political support, the opportunities for speaking Welsh, even in traditional core areas will diminish daily, as the demographic and linguistic composition changes, and as the demands of the modern economy threaten to displace Welsh as a language of the workplace and of wider social interaction.

4. The ambiguity of technological development

As part of the move toward what some term "the post-modern society" with all its principled implications of globalization, the transformation of place-centred geography to a transactional flow geography, and that most cumbersome of phrases, the 'deterritorialization' of society, we are asked to conclude that territorial identities are no longer so relevant. I believe that this is an error of judgment and interpretation. True the scale of human activity is changing apace as are the conventional parameters of bounded space. Increasingly individuals are more atomised, more autonomous, seeking cultural contiguity without geographical propinquity as a result of technological advances. Thus the surface areas of many lesser-used language communities are now fragmented and sub-divided into a host of more discreet, interest-oriented networks, which may have different threshold populations, scales of operation, and range of attraction. This, however, refashions territory, rather than makes it redundant as some conclude. In consequence we need to analyse how revived languages, such as Welsh, and other European tongues are likely to penetrate into new territories and domains thereby constructing a new relationship between identity and place. It follows that a new critical aspect of language survival is how languages under threat are mounting a counter-spread campaign to engage new speakers in their respective community (for examples see Dorian, 1989; and Williams 1989).

Critical to this response has been the pivotal role of technology. In the past the control of technology by the state and by powerful vested interests, guaranteed the anglicization of Wales, Scotland and to a lesser extent, Ireland also (Williams, 1988). Today, however, aspects of modern technology have been employed in the language struggle of Celtic Britain, with some success.

5. Educational technology

"One dramatic change in society in the last twenty years has provided an acid test for a minority language. When information technology, micro- computers, home and school computer based learning software, satellites and interactive video discs have begun to transform society, a minority language and culture is under threat" (Baker, 1987, p.5). Roberts has recently asked several critical questions about the role of mass technology in threatening cultural survival in general and Welsh-medium education in particular. For example, "does the arrival of advanced technology, overwhelmingly backed by English language software, in a predominantly Welsh medium classroom influence the linguistic ethos of the class? ... Do children associate high technology with English culture and equate Welsh culture exclusively with "eisteddfodic gamboling in cerdd dant and cynghanedd? ..."

Will children, armed to the teeth with keyboards and modems and technological knowhow switch out of the local 'parochial' culture?" (Roberts, 1987, p.55).

Of course, this is a repetition of the fears engendered by the intrusion of English a century earlier when the then technologically-advanced process of print capitalism flooded Welsh homes and schools with pamphlets, newspapers and textbooks. The reaction then was to adopt the principles of mass technology and construct a parallel Welsh-medium popular press, denominational literature, and eventually educational texts and materials. I am not underestimating the difficulties involved in this parallelling process merely alerting attention to the fact that the abiding threat of the technology of a mass culture can also be used as a spur to action by activists within the minority culture. Research by Baker (1984, 1985) found that the microcomputer was being used almost entirely in English within the formally designated Welsh-medium schools. (Secondary Schools reported 97% usage in English; Primary Schools 86%). In an attempt to reverse this process a Welsh Panel of the Micro-electronics Education Programme was formed in April 1984, three years after the establishment of the DES funded national body, charged with disseminating information, promoting curriculum development, serving as a link within the Welsh computer network, and advising MEP (Wales) on future activities and in- service training (Roberts, 1987, p.57). Despite meagre funding and limited backing, the panel achieved a great deal in its three-year limited life viz it provided a Welsh version of the MRP Primary Software package, it rationalised the translation of INSET packages on mathematics, languages, infants, problem-solving, published a software catalogue, produced a range of technical terms, later adopted by the Welsh Joint Education Committee for the use of examination candidates, and provided a national focus for computer education (Roberts, 1987, pp.57-8).

However, such initiatives, which are so characteristic of the dynamism of bilingual education in Wales are also ephemeral and partial because of the absence of a permanent, national educational body.

In recognition of the growing need to provide just such a national forum, the Pwyllgor Datblygu Addysg Gymraeg (Welsh Language Educational Development Committee) was established in 1987 (Williams, 1989). It was given a five-fold task, namely:

1) to provide a forum to discuss Welsh language education policies;
2) to identify needs for development, priorities among those needs and means of meeting them;
3) to co-ordinate developments in Welsh language education in order to ensure the optimum use of available resources;

4) to provide information and publicity;
5) to designate areas of research and development (PDAG, 1988; Jeffreys, 1989).

It quickly recognised that if Welsh medium education was to prosper three requirements had to be met urgently. Firstly, the establishment of a large data bank which would contain comprehensive listings of key research findings in bilingual education and evidence of various educational practices and systems in bi- and multilingual societies. Secondly, it determined the need to undertake an audit of all Welsh-medium teaching in respect of staffing levels and curriculum development. Thirdly, it sought to collate analytical evidence of good teaching practice and patterns, representative models of Welsh-medium instruction and significant materials which could be distributed nationally using new video and computer-based technology.

The Welsh office provided an interim grant to develop three centres located at the Language Studies Centre, Bangor, the Aberystwyth Resources Centre at the University College of Wales, and the National Language Unit, Treforest. An extension of these and other centres was envisaged in the PDAG final report, for they were each deemed to provide specific services in one of the following areas: teacher training; textbook and educational publishing for schools, including computer software; fundamental and applied research on education, bilingualism and language development.

In essence then, we have the promise of a rudimentary national educational plan for the Welsh-medium sector. Central to this plan is educational technology, with each participating school using its computer links to obtain Welsh-medium materials, hard copies, and interactive teaching programmes provided by the national educational centres. The speed, economics of scale, and quality of materials thus obtained will ensure a vast improvement on the former, rather fragmented and ad hoc system of education. In addition, national standards of competence in spoken, written and read Welsh, in various subject areas, may be enhanced by such technology. Were these provisions to be extended into the significant sector of further and higher education, then this central agency of language reproduction would be a very effective user of distance-learning technology, as has been proven by the Open University, the Open College, and BTEC.

There is also the whole question as to whether computer facilities will increase the chances of survival for Europe's lesser-used languages. Of course, it depends upon the human capital involved, but just as print capitalism democratised many discriminated languages in the last century by allowing popular and relatively cheap periodicals, pamphlets and books to be published, so may computer software herald the democratisation of many fragile and lesser-used languages. Computer translations, super-computers a thousand times more powerful than today's machines and the growth of a computer-literate generation in Europe all presage a more hopeful survival rate for many ethno-regional identities. Localism is compatible with globalism and need not lead to parochialism. Indeed one of the more encouraging features of many ethnic situations in Europe is precisely this awareness that new opportunities are opening up because of socio-technical advances and the general shift towards more open, accountable and democratic social institutions. True there will be contradictory messages, conflicting aims, ill-suited political initiatives and reforms, which constitute the ever present tension between nation, state and citizenship. However, the new pluralism we are witnessing is eroding the old certainties of the European state system. It is in this twilight niche that many see the non-contiguous, computer-based social networks of lesser-used language speakers developing. At times this can have an Orwellian doom and gloom hue, leading to over-centralisation of power and manipulative control via both fiscal and technological means. But at other times such networks can have a truly liberating and democratising effect, especially if they are grounded in the popular aspirations of the minorities struggling for equality and survival.

Nowhere is this ambiguity of control and effect more evident than in the media, as we have witnessed with very diverse results in contexts as varied as Tienaman Square, Bucharest, Estonia and Albania, of late.

6. The media

For decades, members of Europe's linguistic minorities have been calling for greater access to, and control over, the mass media for they long recognised that the media, together with education, public sector administration and the law, were the institutional bases for cultural reproduction. The Arfe Report adopted by the European Parliament in 1981, and the Kuijpers Resolution of 1987 have reinforced this perspective, leading to a more formal emphasis on the provision of the requisite infra-structure for lesser-used languages to be represented within the mass media. However, as we are all too painfully aware, guaranteeing access to the media is often a sensitive and politically volatile move. In a recent visit to Greece, on behalf of the European Bureau for Lesser-Used Languages, I witnessed the depth of vitriolic chauvinism ranged against the introduction of Albanese or Vlach communications on the radio, let alone within local newspapers. Such variance from a norm of national congruence is highly suspect to the controlling majority, for as Sartre reminds us 'To speak Basque is a revolutionary act'. The values, ideas and messages imparted through a lesser-used language circulation network are often (though not necessarily so) at variance with those of the state's majority, hence the intransigence to establish communication systems in the lesser-used languages.

Yet, without access to the media, which overarches space and distance, and re-combines and re-unites disparate speakers, it is doubtful if relatively weak and embattled linguistic communities can survive well into the next century.

The role of the media in reproducing mass culture at all scales is very well reported in the literature, and even better appreciated by the consumer. Witness the recent reports that the 1990 World Cup Finals have been watched by a global television audience of 20 billion in 147 countries - the month-long 52 match tournament culminating in a single final on July 8th watched by one-and-a-half billion viewers simultaneously. This is real power in a highly competitive world.

However, the role of the media within lesser-used languages is less well understood. Ned Thomas (1989) has recently reported to the European Community on several features of the development of mass communication systems with lesser-used language communities. I quote the more salient characteristics of his report below for they point to a number of anomalies.

> Media in a given language provide the forum within which shared experience and shared problems are discussed, often from very different standpoints. Outsiders in the majority group often perceive a minority as having a single, monolithic, highly politicized stance and many resist the establishment of media in the minority language, fearing that the air-waves will be dominated by a single point of view. Media are an essential part of democracy in whatever language or size of language they operate. Indeed in those areas of the EC where literacy in the lesser-used language is poor because of past discrimination in the education system, radio and television in their own language can have the special function of admitting to the spoken democratic debate people who are neither very fluent in the state language nor very literate in their own (p.4).

This is an important justification for the role of the media, especially in multilingual societies generally, as within Central, Eastern and South-Eastern Europe. The transition to democracy is a fragile enough phenomenon for strong cultures, for the weaker it could pose a further threat as I have alerted elsewhere, for

> If the new cultural order of 'unity in diversity' is to become a reality in the future Europe, then much greater attention to the implications of 'development from below'...(including mass technology and access to the media)...needs to be stimulated; otherwise participatory democracy in the new Europe will be yielded to the tyranny of the majority in the name of progress and development, the watchwords of the centralising state and of its dominant elite (Williams, 1990, p.244).

Thomas also argues that "the long-established traditions of music, song and poetry can be perpetuated and find a large audience through the media. But they rarely survive media treatment in their untouched original form. Culture is not being 'preserved' but 'transformed' when it is carried into the electronic media" (p.4).

Herein lies another ambiguity inherent in modern technology. When set aside the professional products of an international telecommunications industry, the home grown productions of a regional or national system are apt to appear dated, parochial and unsuitable for mass consumption. This is even more acute when such productions are originated by the majority culture, either as a sop to minority interests, or to highlight the idiosyncratic and peculiar nature of a minority culture.

"The folklorization and museumization of a minority culture are much more likely to occur when highly traditional cultural products of the minority are embedded in programmes made within majority languages, and presented as changeless objects for the study and curiosity of others" (p.5). An excellent example of this is the treatment of Old Order Amish communities within the contemporary United States.

A further feature is the economic aspect of the development of the mass media, both in terms of job creation in a diverse set of related occupations and in the export potential of televisual material. This is a vital feature if members of the minority community are to be employed in the private, commercial sector where too often the language is excluded. This clearly has important social psychological, language status planning and behavioural implications for a specialized division of labour within the lesser-used language community. The media not only transmit material, they also help establish new norms, new domains and new perceptions which seek to extend the hitherto restrictive domains of most languages (Thomas, 1989, p.6; Williams, 1989, p.46-48).

This question of legitimization of new domains and identity reformulation is crucial, but can so often be perceived as being of parochial interest only. Hence the globalization issues discussed in this volume are of profound consequence. Thomas makes a telling point when he argues that if the media in lesser-used languages are able to provide a mix of local, regional, national and international material then they can be an "important means of internationalizing the consciousness of their own group. That is an important function, for just as no culture can survive without institutions of its own, so no culture can survive as an autarchy, impervious to outside influence. If cultures are unique, they are so because each culture stands at a unique cultural crossroads, not on a unique cultural island" (p.6). This platform is the means both to launch and to receive contributions from the wider world and thus becomes a pivotal agency for (ethno-regional) national minorities.

Such considerations suggest an ever increasing role for technology in identity formation and cultural reproduction. Specific examples of the success achieved by determined minorities would include radio and broadcasting in Catalonia, Euskadi and Wales, and the cross-fertilization of ideas and practice which these nations enjoy through membership of the European Broadcasting Union. Control of the media in this manner is a major boost to cultural development and political representation for it allows direct access to major and local events through the mediating role of the former lesser-used language, thus legitimizing its use still further within new domains.

Let me conclude by stressing some of the implications of the discussion on place and territorial identity. The trends and issues discussed above lead to a clear conclusion. If the Welsh language, for example, is to resist marginalization it will have to break out of fairly restrictive domains and become a fully institutionalized language of society (Williams, 1989). But in order to achieve such language domain spread there needs to be a political recognition of the value of Welsh culture throughout Wales, for the guaranteeing of minority group rights in such spheres as the law, public administration and education is an expensive exercise of freedom. However, there is an acute irony that at the very time that such domain spread appears to be realized, the territorial retreat of Welsh is reaching a crisis point in the western heartland. A simple illustration of the influence of demography on language maintenance will suffice.

Twenty years ago many schools in the western heartland had predominantly Welsh-speaking children, today with the influx of English-speakers most schools are coping with an unbalanced linguistic situation, creating additional conflict. Even where the total numbers of Welsh-speakers has increased in recent decades, they are still telling examples of where the proportion speaking Welsh in the community has fallen by 10-20%, indicating the pervasiveness of in-migrants in the rural heartland.

7. Some key questions unanswered

In the absence of supportive language planning legislation we may ask whether or not an autochthonous culture can survive indefinitely without a clearly identified territorial resource base within which it is dominant? Does it risk instant paralysis because it is unable to command a place within its own national space?

Do the recent advances of technology liberate minority cultures from the confines of tradition, habit, routine behaviour and localism? Or should we more properly see technology as an adjunct to, rather than a substitute for, place-specific forms of social interaction? If so, with what implications for domain construction, for resource deployment and for the development of computer-aided 'artificial realities'?

Are there measurable thresholds beyond which it is both uneconomic and untenable to advance the scope and scale of technological developments for minority cultures, if the necessary infra-structure is lacking? If so, what are they and to which forms of technology do they apply? For example, would it be advisable for a minority to press for its own television channel, if the majority of its potential audience were still functionally illiterate in the minority language? Need radio and television always follow, rather than precede, comprehensive educational reform where the lesser-used language is recognised within the local system? Can a bilingual television service remain stable or is there an inevitable tendency towards functional unilingualism in the majority tongue with the second language becoming replaced by a transnational medium such as English, French or Russian.

Should language rights be predicated primarily on the territorial or the personality principle of language planning? Does territorialization, as evidenced by Belgium and Canada, serve to aggravate or neutralize language-related group conflict?

What are the class implications of developing a bureaucratic-technical intelligentsia within the minority culture? How do they manipulate the new opportunities afforded by mass technology to further their own, and their group's interests?

Are elitism, a new professional/technocratic intelligentsia and a burgeoning bureaucracy, the necessary progeny of the recent marriage between language activists and the local/central power brokers? We are used to treating minority languages as languages of resistance to an often uncaring or hostile state government, but we are not yet fully equipped to deal with the minority language as the language of power, of establishment positions, in short, of governance.

What role does the European Community, the Council of Europe, and agencies such as the European Bureau for Lesser-Used Languages have in facilitating inter-group networking on the media, technology and cultural reproduction?

These are a few of the questions we need to address before we rush too quickly to announce the death of several European Lesser-Used Languages. I am not unmindful either of the context within which all these aspects of social change are mediated, namely the larger question of global inter-dependence and state-regulated behaviour on the one hand, and the much wider view of the influence of technology itself in shaping most aspects of our daily lives.

I have taken such features as infra-structural developments, transport and communication for granted in this argument, but a quite legitimate analysis of their role in assisting cultural displacement can be made, as I have elsewhere in relation to globalization as a phenomenon.

My central conviction has been to highlight the ambiguity of technology on the one hand and the critical necessity of mobilizing political power to release resources to utilize such technology in the service of the minority culture on the other. Allied to this is a fear that we are abandoning the role of place and territory too readily in our analyses, rather than seeking to reformulate their influence, not as a determining, but as a contextual factor in the cultural reproduction of minorities in that most difficult of struggles, the struggle for identity and relative autonomy in an inherently unequal world.

References

Aitchison, J. and Carter (1985) The Welsh Language 1961-1981: An Interpretive Atlas, Cardiff, The University of Wales Press.

Aitchison, J, and Carter, (1985) The Welsh Language at the 1981 Census. Williams, C H 1985 Area, 17.

Baker, C. (1984) A Survey of Microcomputer Usage in Primary and Secondary Welsh-Speaking Schools, London, ESRC.

Baker, C. (1985) Aspects of Bilingualism in Wales, Clevedon, Multilingual Matters.

Baker, C. (1987) Editorial Introduction, in Bilingualism and Bilingual Education. Education for Development, Vol. 10, No. 3.

Carter, H. (1988) Culture, Language and Territory, BBC Wales Annual Radio Lecture, Cardiff.

Dear, M. (1990) Review of E.W. Soja, 'Postmodern Geographies' Annals of the Association of American Geographers, Vol. 80, No 4.

Dorian, N. (ed.), (1989) Investigating Obsolescence: Studies in Language Contraction and Death, Cambridge, Cambridge University Press.

Duncan, S. and Savage, M. (1991) Commentary: New Perspectives on the Locality Debate, Environment and Planning A, Vol. 23.

Featherstone, M. (ed.), (1990) Global Culture: Nationalism, Globalization and Modernity, London, Sage Publications.

Fishman, J. (1989) Language and Ethnicity in Minority Sociolinguistic Perspective. Clevedon, Multilingual Matters.

Giddens, A. (1981) Power, Property and the State, London, Macmillan.

Giddens, A. (1985) The Nation-State and Violence, Cambridge, Polity Press.

Giddens, A. (1991) Contribution to conference on Nationalism in a Post-Marxist World, London, L.S.E., 1st March.

Hall, S. and Jacques, M. (eds.) New Times: The Changing Face of Politics in 1989 the 1990s, London, Lawrence and Wishart.

Hindley, R. (1990) The Death of the Irish Language, London, Routledge.

Jeffreys, H. (1989) Applying the Principle of Equal Opportunity to Present the Case for Welsh-medium Provision for TVE1 Extension in Wales, Cardiff, PDAG.

Kofman, E. and Williams, C.H. (1989) Culture, Community and Conflict, in Williams, C.H. and Kofman, E. (eds), Community Conflict, Partition and Nationalism, London, Routledge.

Pryce, W.T.R. et al. (1988) Sources and Methods in the Study of Language, Williams, C.H. 1988 Areas, in Williams, C.H. (ed), Language in Geographic Context, Clevedon: Multilingual Matters, PDAG 1988 Interim Report of the Secondary Working Committee, Cardiff, PDAG.

Roberts, H.G. (1987) Microelectronics - The Welsh Connection, Education for Development, Vol. 10, No. 3.

Robertson, (1987) Globalization Theory and Civilization Analysis, Comparative Civilizations Review, No. 17.

Robertson, (1990a) After Nostalgia? Wilful Nostalgia and the Phases of Globalization, in Turner, B.S. (ed.), Theories of Modernity and Postmodernity, London, Sage Publication.

Robertson, (1990b) Mapping the Global Condition: Globalization as the Central Concept, in Featherstone, M. op. cit.

Soja, E.W. (1989) Postmodern Geographies: The Reassertion of Space in Critical Social Theory, New York, Verso.

Thomas, E.M. (1989) News and Information Networks for the Lesser-Used Language Communities, Aberystwyth, Mercator Project.

Wallerstein, I. (1990) Culture as the Ideological Battleground of the Modern World System, in Featherstone, M., op. cit.

Williams, C.H. (1980) Language Contact and Language Change 1901-1971: A Study in Historical Geolinguistics, The Welsh History Review, Vol. 10, No. 2.

Williams, C. H. (1982) Language Planning and Minority Group Rights, Cambria, 9, (Reprinted in an expanded version), in Hume, I. and Price, W.T.R. (Eds), (1986) The Welsh and their Country, Llandysul, Gomer.

Williams, C.H. (1987a) The Land in Linguistic Consciousness: Evidence from the British Isles, Sociolinguistica, Vol. 1.

Williams, C.H. (1987b) Location and Context in Welsh Language Reproduction, in Williams, G. (ed.), The Sociology of Welsh, International Journal of the Sociology of Language, Vol. 66.

Williams, C.H. (ed.), (1988) Language in Geographic Context, Clevedon, Multilingual Matters.

Williams, C.H. (1989) New Domains of the Welsh Language: Education, Planning and the Law, in Day G. and Rees, G. (eds.), Contemporary Wales, Vol.3.

Williams, C.H. (1990) Political Expressions of Underdevelopment in the West European Perhiphery, in Buller, H. and Wright, S. (Eds), Rural Development: Problems and Practices, Aldershot, Avebury.

Withers, C.W.J. (1988) Gaelic Scotland, London, Routledge.

8 Identification as a process: Territories as an organizational or a symbolic area

Bernard Poche

In the last few decades it has become common to consider that spatial awareness has shifted significantly, in line with what is assumed to be a tendency towards integration into larger reference units than those current up to now (in other words, states). This tendency is referred to as globalization or internationalization, and it is equally common to establish a link with the risk of a corresponding reduction in phenomena of territorial attachment. The logical and necessary correlate to the globalisation of the world, whose archetypal models are generally borrowed from phenomena connected with technology, communication and world markets, is the unification of cultural phenomena, and in consequence (if we take the process a step further) the supremacy of attachment models which are not necessarily territorial. An illustration of this is provided by those who refer to a system of values (democracy, rights of man, environmental protection) which is assumed to be universal in application and which could constitute *the cultural accompaniment* to the technological and organizational globalization phenomena referred to above.

This approach is not always expressed so bluntly, but it does correspond to what underlies a large number of contemporary attitudes, including those in the field of social sciences. In the following pages our aim is to show, first that the implicit reasoning to which we refer is not as strict as it might at first appear, and secondly that certain phenomena related to spatial awareness actually run contrary to this and do not support the transfer between territorial identities and delocalized cultural schemes.

The movement referred to at the beginning of this text is not the only one which may be detected. Concurrent with it is another tendency - which it would be mistaken to take as running parallel to it - which involves a reassessment of local and regional idiosyncracies. This reassessment takes various forms, but it should be noted that it is not restricted to straightforward localism and neighbourhood movements and that it has been emphasized in the last few years by the dislocation of the empires and federations of the socialist world, which has often been characterized, and wrongly so, as an expression of nationalism. In fact the socialist world really founded its spatial awareness on an homogenizing effect, linked to the will to eliminate both "exploitation" and social and "cultural" archaisms.

Two types of phenomena can therefore be observed simultaneously. They seem to correspond to a crisis in our ability to apprehend the various forms, whether united or federal, of the nation state. (It is important to note this, for we shall see later that the problem is far from being limited to the institutional or organizational form of a society). On the one hand, as has often been remarked, states are involved in networks of alliances which reduce their sovereignty, rendering it almost obsolete, and are overwhelmed by economic and relational phenomena which appear to render their political frontiers pointless. On the other hand, states attempted to monopolise the processes of symbolic identification and belonging by reducing territorial culture to the realm of private life (often even in federal states). They are losing this monopoly now; perhaps it was only an illusion...

The question of the relation between globalization and territorial identity is clearly a complex one. If a relation is made between the latter's supposed crisis and the appearance of transnational phenomena (European, global, etc.) it is possible to consider that the revival of micro-local particularities is not a territorial problem, because it is limited to the neighbourhood and in no way relates to any spatial symbolism of any importance. On the other hand it might also be taken to be a straightforward expression of sociability, corresponding to an increase in individualism. This would mean that localism in its narrowest sense and cosmopolitanism were converging over the "ruins" of the territory considered to be the basis of societal identification. To prove this it is sometimes suggested that micro-local sociability coincides in time with a whole series of other movements (ecology, the defence of ethnic minorities in large towns, womens' rights) which have nothing in common with the major regional cultures whose defence characterized the years between 1960 and 1980 in Europe.

Although we cannot deal with this question here, it should nevertheless be noted that the movement defending regional cultures was not without its ambiguities. It was accompanied in particular by a tendency to "folklorise", which is a subtle form of "neo-functionalization" designed for a changing world: frequently originating with intellectuals, the defence of local languages - like the defence of regional architecture - tended to integrate the languages into a consumer system, based on tourism, resulting in endless arguments about the "Indian reserves" which this approach tended to create. It is clear that claims to local identity, of the sort that one may encounter at present, call into question, on the contrary, the role of a cultural alibi attributed to distinctive awarenesses in the "modern" nation states, or, in other words, the status of protected minority in which it was thought they could be contained. The sociological problem of territory thus appears more relevant than would be the case in the straightforward treatment of an ethno-historical residue.

1. The ambiguities of globalization

There is no question of denying the empiric reality of the phenomena on which the notion of globalization is founded. It should nevertheless be pointed out that current analysis links globalization and the intensification of exchange, a point which merits discussion. Neither of these phenomena is as immanent today, nor as absolute as one might imagine. The multiplication and acceleration in the exchange of information and the movement of personnel is beyond doubt: but it is not sufficient to change the nature of a phenomenon - the relative knowledge of the various parts of the inhabited world - noted by historians to be much older and above all much less restricted to an "elite" than has sometimes been claimed.

Without returning to specific events such as the Crusades or the Napoleonic wars, it is clear that, from the 17th century onwards "economic" migrations, whether lasting or temporary, brought different populations into contact with one another: the population of the Alps emigrated in winter towards Lyon or Turin (B. Poche, 1987a); pilgrimages also took village people to distant destinations, as Joan of Arc's mother who travelled to Rome, without anyone expressing the slightest surprise (G. Lévi-Pinard, 1974). E. Weber is surely a little naive to suggest that it was only with the appearance of the railways that French peasants were able to go and sell their products in neighbouring towns, and thus escape from relative isolation (E. Weber, 1983: 300-303). After all we know that cheese from the Tarentaise massif (Savoy) was appreciated in Rome... in Antiquity.

It is true that these journeys and the associated knowledge do not involve the loss of any of the characteristics particular to a given group. The peasants of the Savoy Alps who spent part of their active life in Turin were necessarily tri-lingual (dialect, French commonly used as a vehicular language on the western flanks of the mountains, and Piedmontese); my own research has shown that this continued to be the case almost up to the present day, and we know that the idea of border controls was completely unheard of in those days: territories and their inhabitants were subject to rules of allegiance to feudal lords and monarchs, to their jurisdiction and taxation, but individual movement was unhindered. And on returning home they reintegrated their initial frame of reference.

1.1. The naturalization of progress

Apparently it was not until the start of the process of political unification - and above all, the wars that marked the last century and a half - that the idealistic vision of world citizenship first appeared. However this imaginary construction would undoubtedly not have developed at the same speed without the parallel development of two associated phenomena: the development of audio-visual information; the concentration of the means of production and the techniques used for conquering markets and distribution networks.

Here again, the phenomena are beyond question. But their "transfer" to the field of social construction is founded on analogies which may be contested. To cite the most glaring example: we are all conscious of the risk involved in deducing from communication theory that the actual content of the messages conveyed is necessarily uniform. The problem of "translation" will be touched on subsequently, but we can address, without further ado, the prospect of an impoverishment of the cultural habits of the various peoples which would result from the progressive adoption - even if it were to be spread over several generations - of "international English" as the unique means of expressing scientific ideas not to mention the fruit of other intellectual or cultural domains.

The problem of technology and the economy, which is not central to our analysis, cannot be ignored. It would be naive to be surprised that its analysis is marked by traces of scientism. But the general impression is that, in passing from the 19th to the 20th century, this very scientism has changed from being a somewhat demiurgic and humanist awareness (the domination of the *anthropos* over nature) to the construction of a techno-economical calibration system for historical time.

In a context which appears to be closer to hyper-modernity than to post-modernism, progress appears to have been "naturalised", losing all relevance to any social debate and even more so to any form of conflict, with the exception of the most marginal concerns ("green movements"). Is the time scale of discoveries and what is generally referred to as development to replace an astronomical and physiological clock? This point of view is supported by an endless succession of examples taken from human and ecological crises in the course of the last few decades: populations and cultures have been annihilated; irreversible damage has been done to the animal and vegetable components of the biosphere; artificial environments have been created, in particular in the holiday and so-called leisure business; cast off products and waste material accumulate uncontrollably and micro-climates change (perhaps even the climate as a whole). As a counterpart to these phenomena, which are nevertheless social phenomena, the global-modern approach has been joined by an hyper-ideology which reduces all our attitudes to a simplistic relationship opposing "natural evolution" and "outdated nostalgia". As if by magic this ideology removes any factual evidence from the realm of social conflict, assigning it to some sort of planning logic and "adjusting our aims", to a large extent depriving social agents of the ability to decide personally how to order their own lives.

1.2. Political globalization, a historical archetype

Social time is not the only victim of this process. Due to political control, social space is also being "naturalised". The formation and subsequent crisis of the nation state play a major role in our conception of the relationship between integration and territorial identity.

Initially the nation state appeared to be a federative body. Independently from particular institutional systems, it fulfilled a specific, political and military function, rising above ethnic or cultural considerations. But in addition to this role, which was borrowed from the monarchies of the Ancien Regime, a whole series of state systems developed, reaching further and further into the fabric of society. The development of nation state ideologies led states to monopolise social control to an ever-increasing degree. Culture and standards were imposed by a dominant group, based on a specific ethnic identity or a political power base (cf. Max Weber, 1959, part. : 137-142, 149-158). Attempts at levelling were commonplace: the Flemish part of Belgium "adopted" French as the language of culture and the vehicular language of the élite; disregarding any historical or cultural logic, Italy was subjected to a highly centralised system of government and an appropriate ideology ("Adesso l'Italia è fatta; bisogna fare gli Italiani", said Massimo D'Azeglio); Prussia and then, after 1870, the German Empire methodically reduced the independence and specificity of the various components of the Germanic world, if nothing else in institutional terms (cf. the liquidation of Bavaria so vividly portrayed by L. Visconti in his film "Ludwig").

The assimilation between the social form and the state tended to make the former one-dimensional and entrust the latter with a monopoly, not just of legitimate physical violence as Max Weber pointed out (ibid. p. 113) but also of the management of social relations (and even relationships). This was the first means of integrating groups, which for want of a better word we shall refer to as ethno-cultural, into political constructions whose contingent character cannot, in most cases, be denied. Constructions were supported by ideological efforts - in particular in education - which have already been dealt with thoroughly by historians. But if the idea of the Nation, in the form of a nation state, was nurtured by the French revolution as a political weapon and to a certain extent the means to social emancipation - a theme which was borrowed by the "national liberation movements" fighting the Nazi occupation and subsequently colonial domination - there is nothing to prove that this idea actually squared with processes of social integration or the correlative development of a new territorial identity.

An indication of this is to be found in the origins of the crisis which struck the foundations of the structure, imposed from above, in almost all the nation states based on the European model (including those which followed the upheaval of the First World War). Two aspects of this crisis deserve our notice: first the so-called minority claims which correspond to a refusal of the nation's ability and right to take under its wing populations who may reasonably lay claim to another identity, often that of a neighbouring nation (or ethnic group or culture); secondly the so-called regional or nationalist movements which contest the relevance of the unifying character of the nation state when confronted by a host of infra-national, or sub-state identities. These phenomena take several different forms:

- they correspond to the collapse of the symbol status of state, as is the case for instance in France, because of decolonization; in Italy, because of the state's inability to overcome the mafia and organized crime (malavita) and to escape from the discredit associated with abusive clientelism and corruption; in England, because of the gradual decadence of a trade-based economy and the ensuing social crisis; in (ex) socialist block countries because of the crumbling of the founding myths, linked to the inability to maintain a repressive hold on society, and so on;
- they take the form of protests by social groups against an involvement (treated as an unjustified encroachment) in functions which they see as being the responsibility of the so-called "civil society". Depending on the degree of development and the odds involved (material or symbolic), protests may concern emblematic, linguistic or cultural questions, claims relating to economic

management or even the detachment of some of the administrative functions of the state. In previously federal states or centralised states subjected to severe crises the limits are blurred, on the one hand between states - whether unified federal or confederate - and on the other hand between the state (political control) and society (social control supposedly based on a consensus);

- consequently they aim to disassociate the monopoly constituted around a link between state and society; they reduce nation state identification to what is at best one of many representative processes; above all they oppose the process of integration claiming that the state is not in a position to take exclusive charge of what can be referred to in general terms as the status of the people. It is because of this that the claim is often under-estimated: integration into the state as a whole has been encouraged so much over the last century and a half that it has become a "natural" phenomenon, even in areas which *at first sight* have no need of this type of reference (ethics, artistic creation, religion, etc.). Society, deprived of any means of viewing its own image, except via politics, is bound to realize that, in numerous serious crises[1], its awareness (in both senses of the term, as creation of image and as recognition of intermediate groups) by the state is no longer sufficient unless it is accompanied by profound identification, which integrates the individual with society at an intermediary level. Consequently we must recognize the duality of the two processes, social attachment and political control, and admit that the state is perhaps not, in the terms of the definition it has inherited from its military past, the system best suited to operating this elementary phenomenon of identification that we call *sociality*.

This detour into the problem of the nation state serves two purposes, with regard to the overall problem of integration and territorial identity:

1) it situates the problem in an historical context and movement; and above all
2) it shows that earlier forces, under the cover of contributing to the "formation of a nation" - a concept which is perhaps not significantly different, *mutatis mutandis*, from contemporary "internationalisation" - show signs of ambiguity. These forces suggest a certain *captatio benevolentiae* of social history and awareness, serving a supra-social operator, whether real or virtual (the increasing globalisation) in charge of embodying all the components of society[2], of controlling and redistributing them.

To use a technological and organizational paradigm to characterise this imaginary social process simply accentuates the reference to a possible role of the "public" power. The latter is given the monopoly of the management of the various elements that make up the paradigm. Declarations which are not covered by the "dominant language" rapidly take on the tone of fringe claims or of considerations which are not for the moment the concern of the normative, redistributing power of the state (or international system). The "responsibilities" of the integrating structure gradually extend to include cultural activities (or more exactly managing the production of forms of expression) and consequently aesthetics; to ethical questions, and by extension to religion; to all aspects of the status of a private person, including those which have no relevance to "public order". The widespread introduction of "economic" procedures causes behaviour related to reproduction and death, sexuality, cult movements and art to be subjected to factors which tend to integrate and standardise it.

At a more empiric level, the definition of the nation state as: 1) a unifying factor of absolute law, 2) the historical archetype of the process of integration, makes it impossible to admit the process of *sociality* at any other level, apart from the process of *sociability*, which is necessarily at work at the minimum level of the locality or neighbourhood. Sociability, though carefully organized by the state (cf. the archetypal examples of housing and pre-school care for children used by Z. Mlinar, 1991) remains a private affair, on condition that it only results in formal, or perhaps even emotional structures, in the narrowest sense of the word, and does not in any way intrude on the social sense.

It is clear that long before the question of international, technological or economical networks was raised, and quite separately[3], policies of integration into larger units had begun to push any development of a sense of public, but non-institutional and non-state[4] awareness, back into private life, controlling and reducing it as much as possible. "Territorial identities" were, at this stage, dismissed implicitly to an archaic level, and certainly excluded from the realm of modernity. In the context of the latter there is no longer a standard, didactic language to describe them, excepting for historians and museum curators: this is how ethnology started. From being a science devoted to the description of "elementary" (cf. Durkheim, 1979: 4-5), primitive, social forms it has come to be concerned with minor, rural, "regional" forms which have no present historical destiny. Henceforward ethnology, which studies man as a private agent, in situations which do not affect the overall course of society, and sociology, which generalises and rationalises to a large extent on a functional basis, will remain separate as scientific processes.

2. Territorial identity: permanence and redefinitions

We shall devote the following pages to showing that territorial identity, following its own logic, develops along other lines from those concerned by globalisation. However, in order not to appear to be advancing another form of supra-social construction, it is necessary to return to the foundations of non-functional sociology, which render possible this analysis. With this in mind, we shall treat the social group and its operation, not as passive products in a techno-economic movement, independent from human society, but as the result of a continuous, endogenous process of social representation (self-representation or self-reference). This process combines, as Cooley said, individuals and society, symbolic forms and the "account" of the world (to use the language of H. Garfinkel, which is inspired by a similar logic).

Indeed it is necessary to trace back to William James and his successors the statements concerning the fundamental unicity between what Ch. H. Cooley calls "material knowledge" and "social knowledge" (Cooley, 1926: 60), their convergence occurring in the midst of what he calls the "mental-social-complex" thanks to a permanent relationship between the symbolic system and the system of meaning: "We must not forget (...) that the symbol is nothing in itself, but only a convenient mean for developing, imparting and recording a meaning, and that meanings are a product of the mental-social complex and known to us only through consciousness" (op. cit. 68). We can set alongside this text, the famous quote from William. I. Thomas: "Preliminary to any self-determined act of behaviour there is always a stage of examination and deliberation which we may call the definition of the situation" (quoted by L. Pierrot, 1983: 17).

These quotations are the basis of what we shall call the notion of "auto-referential" identity. They can be complemented by the thesis of the structuring of a group on the basis of the world of objects, as it is reconstructed by the group as a series of social constructs, an idea which was developed formally by H. Blumer on the basis of the ideas of G.H. Mead (H. Blumer, 1986: 68-70).

The group, in whose midst the symbolic language is constructed, develops its intelligibility of the world not in terms of a series of abstractions, but by using what it achieves: the process which makes the relationship between individual and society pertinent. This may equally well concern the physical environment, the linguistic resource constituted by the history of the group's myths and their verbal expression, or the reintegration, in attainable space, of immaterial objects conveyed by the communication network.

These analyses do not explicitly define the notion of territory, but they do nevertheless make possible an approach to our relation to the *physical world* which is significantly more precise - and sociologically speaking more operational - than the theories of functionalist inspiration. We should recall briefly the position adopted by Schütz in his article "*Phenomenology and the social sciences*" with regard to the notion of proximity: "*The categories of familiarity and strangeness, like that of accessibility, which is essential, come into play here. The latter one refers back to the fact that my "loci" are grouped as a function of: 1) what is really within my reach or has been; 2) what is accessible to others and would therefore be potentially accessible to myself were I not here (hic) but there (ilhic); 3) that which, varying freely within open horizons, is unattainable*" (based on the French translation, A. Schütz, 1987: 187) which goes along with what the author says about the world of work: "*It is the world of physical things, including my body; it is the field for my movements and my bodily operations, etc.*" (op. cit.: p.125 and also pp. 104-109).

Finally, by his progressive approach to a relative definition of oneself and others, followed by the construction of a system of symbols, and then of a global definition of the situation, the group creates itself in a process one may consider as being identificatory, rather than identitary, but which is an application of the social structure on space, the term *identification* only serving to connote a meaningful content.

To complete this theoretical detour by the analysis of the complex process, which may be termed as such, the identification mechanism affects three social fields or domains:

a) The first is what we may call recognition: it is based on the awareness that society (in other words, individuals as well) has an awareness of itself in a given space, which in addition serves to define that space, using a process of self-reference. It is the image that society gives itself, for itself and for the outside world; this is an identification problem, which in addition is often implicit.
b) But, in second place, in order to be able to last and to enter into an exchange, a reflexive exchange with oneself and exchange with others, this recognition needs ways of expression through which it can be formulated. In the front line we find language, in its spoken form and all that is part of the symbolic language, in other words a series of conventions and codes, metaphors and personal experiences.
c) Finally, the third field is made up by the construction of a social world of objects, in the sense used by Mead and Blumer. These objects are not only "physical" objects belonging to the morphology, climate and biosphere, to which denominations and "usage values" are attached, but also specifically appropriated technological products and the organic forms, perhaps even institutional, through which this awareness, once expressed, is sanctioned by standards and, if appropriate, given a collective instrument of action.

It is this ability to enable the individual to recognize, express and standardize which is characteristic of what we may refer to, with the help of Simmel, as the concept of territorial *social form* (G. Simmel, 1981: 171-206; B. Poche, 1987a: 603-604). This is neither an archetype in the Weberian sense of the term, which is a reconstruction with heuristic aims, nor is it a structure as the structuralists understand it, a timeless, abstract and reproducible element. It is an empiric scheme, which enables society to identify itself, constantly feeding on new elements, until finally, it disappears, only to be replaced by another one; but it is always an element of the *Lebenswelt*[5], and not an exogenous imposition.

Consequently, the problem we are confronted with in dealing with the phenomenon of globalisation is not that of a disappearance of identificatory signs and contents. We think that we have shown that the material/functional processes of globalization, and the interpretive processes by which individuals and groups appropriate the former, are of a different order, and that the formation of society (Simmel's *Vergesellschaftung*) does not adhere to techno-organisational processes by using - as it were - a carbon copy, in the way that certain contemporary political ideologies would have us believe, but by processes of awareness and interaction involving the material world as it is lived. A brief look at the most accessible form of symbolisation, in other words language, will enable us to measure the fragmentation/translation principle which is at the heart of our sense awareness of the world.

2.1. *The situation of "local languages"*

Strangely enough, this problem, which is widely exploited for purposes of militancy or protest, seems to have been the subject of relatively few analyses in interpretative sociology, perhaps because it is heavily charged with affectivity. A sociological analysis readily reveals the continuum constituted by the notion of oral language between the different social groups (contact between languages) and in temporality (constant re-use of linguistic resources). It also constitutes a continuum between the group, its material environment and its system of thought. Consequently it is a *forming form*, whereas the categories used to describe a language scientifically as an object which can be rendered autonomous, developed on the basis of a paradigm of the written language and the supposed "deformations" due to usage, constitute *formal forms* on the basis of technical criteria (language, dialect, patois, creole, pidgin, etc.). The spoken language participates in a (symbolic) system nominating the world, which "makes the latter exist" according to a social intelligibility, which corresponds to what ethnomethodologists call "natural language".

Consequently, each group possesses its "oral dictionary", in accordance with the formula used by, amongst others, Cicourel (A.V. Cicourel, 1979: 57-58), and what linguists call a "vehicular language", in line with the demands inherent to their approach, is in fact in the position of a *koiné* or middle language.

In consequence the social problem of language is not a problem of "a standard and variety", which would suggest that - in a functional construction - variety, developed from what is standard by the changes wrought by common usage, be reduced to the rank of a vernacular language. In fact, if we look at history, variety generally precedes a standard: we know that the latter is almost always produced by a standardising process starting from a particular variety and affected by contingent circumstances. We know, for instance, that French was constructed using Francian, an Ile de France dialect at the end of the Middle Ages, while Italian was developed by Dante from the Tuscan dialect, and Luther did the same for German in order to translate the Bible; more recently, the Catalan linguist, Pompéu Fabra "normalised" Catalan at the end of the nineteenth century. Efforts to create a written language are not necessarily connected to the appearance of a centralising political power: even when a literature exists, the symbolic affirmation may very well only refer to the ambition of a social group to mark a social territory, that of the preeminent position it wishes to assign itself: indeed this is encountered more frequently than cases of political centrality. On the other hand, this sort of "normalisation" may succeed at a linguistic level and yet fail in social terms: this is the case with the Provençal of the famous writer, Mistral, in the 19th century; one might even add, with a touch of black humour, that the "normalisation" of the partisans of Occitania, almost a century after that of Mistral, which they violently reject, met with no greater success.

The fact that a language has been standardised does not invest it, as if by right, with a specific sociological status, on the contrary, its sociological position is fairly insensitive to whether or not it has been standardised, to whether standardisation has been attempted, has been successful or not, or even not undertaken at all. In fact, it does seem that there are - sociologically speaking of course - three levels of language. For each level there are one or more corresponding speech registers involving an exchange between the standard (real or virtual) and practice:

1) The language of the central state or, in the case of a federal state, the language of the "ethnic" group which, for a certain period of time, assumes a dominant role: this is the case with French, Castillian ("Spanish"), literary German (*Hochdeutsch*), Russian, standard Dutch (ABN), etc.
2) Regional languages or non-state based *koiné*, whose status may be completely official, may (or may not) have their own literature, press, public usage, etc. but are nevertheless forced to coexist with a language, which, though perhaps not dominant, is certainly spoken by a majority, imposing on the inhabitants of the corresponding zones (or federal republics) *de facto* bilingualism, not practised by the central population as a general rule: this is the case with Welsh, Piedmontese, Friulan, Ukrainian, etc; it is also valid for Catalan, Slovene, and in reality the languages of the former Yugoslav federation for the purposes of practical coexistence with Serbo-Croatian. This second level can to a large extent be assimilated to the more or less virtual *koiné* constituted by the large regional systems which have not been standardised and/or unified, such as the linguistic families of the "political territories" of Germany (Schwäbisch, Niederdeutsch, etc.), France (Breton, Occitan, Francoprovençal, etc.), Italy (Venetian, Emilian, etc.).
3) Dialects in the strict sense of the term, in other words local variations of linguistic families: quite independently from the notion of "patois", which is micro-local, Piedmontese can be sub-divided into about ten dialectical families (turinèis, lansèis, etc.), while Occitan ranges from Gascon to Nissard, etc.

This brings us to a series of remarks which will gradually take us to the notion of a *regional economy of awareness*.

In the preceding pages, the notion of territory is predominant over the notion of linguistic link or absolute criteria of "family". This is a sociological analysis, but it does have the advantage, on the one hand, that it takes account of the fact that - in terms of a meaningful time scale - languages are not deduced from a mother language, and on the other hand it puts the gaps in awareness on a higher level than "formal", phonetic or morphological breaks. As the break which separates Piedmontese from the Lombard dialects, or Venetian from the Emilian dialects, is felt very keenly in social terms, it is of little importance to a sociologist of languages that the "technical difference" may be, for the linguist, of a more or less absolute order.

In addition, the evolution in time of the relation between the various languages is *a priori* fairly unpredictable. We have mentioned the case of Flemish in Belgium, but the relation between Czech and German in Bohemia arose historically in the same conditions. At present, the fundamental difference between configurations such as: 1) the re-emergence of Catalan, whose horizon is in any case difficult to fix (all Catalans understand Castillian, and a minority is in the habit of writing Catalan - still? - in Catalonia); 2) the establishment of Allemanic in Switzerland, in relation to literary German (*Schwyzerdütsch* is moving into primary education, the media, etc.); the stability in the use of Tyrolean dialect in Alto-Adige; 4) the perpetuation of languages like Lithuanian, Slovene and the languages of the Yugoslav federation - does not seem clearly evident from a sociological point of view.

Introducing *international English* (in the Netherlands, in Scandinavia, in the Slav areas of Europe, and further afield, as for instance in India) actually only introduces yet another diglot system. In fact, in the role of a *lingua franca*, and no longer that of a *koiné*, English - as often as not - simply replaces another language (German in eastern and central Europe, French in the parts of western Europe covered by the Romance languages) or displaces understanding: that a Swede and a Dane may either converse in English or may use their respective languages, disregarding the slight differences, does not change a great deal in the social process of cross-border interaction, and hardly implies that the border be abolished. Diglot or polyglot systems along the lines of English-Slovene-Serbocroatian or English-Russian-Lithuanian are not necessarily any more complex than systems involving French-Francoprovençal-Piedmontese, French-Alsatian-Hochdeutsch or Castillan-Catalan-French which have been used for centuries. To forget this is to draw a parallel between language and an algorithm, which it obviously is not. This implies that language does not translate - or no longer translates - the relation between the individual, the "reality of the world of his daily life" (A. Schulz) and the material world. To support the idea that this relationship has been rendered obsolete by the modernist revolution involves admitting that internationalization has achieved what the nation state never succeeded in obtaining: the elimination of the link between speech and a system of meaning. But this would be based on the assumption that the symbolic system is no longer produced by groups in response to their communication requirements or their need for inter-subjectivity. This approach would be the precise opposite of inter-actionism.

Instead of this a supra-social artefact has appeared, an apparatus, exogenous by definition, constantly producing symbols intended to be consumed by society. Society is thus deprived of any freedom of choice as to how it builds the means to express its processes of sociality, its *Vergesellshaftung*, as G. Simmel puts it. For this last hypothesis, the spoken language is based on *newspeak*[6], a rationalised communication system and no longer an inter-subjective combination of impulses and awareness. The fantasy exists, and sociology is powerless to act as umpire in a debate between the two postulates; the most we can do is point out that one is dealing with neo-scientism and no longer just functionalism.

Our aim has been to show that it is not by necessity that breaks and extensions of linguistic groupings occur, and that a language undoubtedly does more to *translate* the operation of a group than it does to maintain or stimulate it. The link between group and territory is mainly a question of the social operation of awareness. In certain cases this operation will be embodied in a specific language: in other cases the same "regional" language may be reused and enriched by several different groups. The differences, apparently minimal, which separate the three or four[7] official Scandinavian languages are closely related to the awareness of breaks running through a whole, which is both real and deeply fragmented - nothing appears to suggest that those differences are in the process of disappearing[8]. There is no reason why the same should not be true of the various Romance languages (including Catalan), German (including Swiss Allemanic and perhaps even Alsatian) or Slav languages. The problem emerges as *a regional economy of awareness: a priori* it is a question neither of linguistics nor of technological inter-exchange or globalisation.

2.2 The problem of territorial identification

The regional economy of awareness is, of course, a very complex problem: it necessarily draws on elements which we have suggested as being "identification components", recognition, expression and constructed coding. But it can only draw on these elements in the context of a dynamic process: on the one hand nothing suggests that a division which is founded in history is destined to last for ever, and on the other the "aggregations of sociality" depend on multiple, labile factors.

It is, for instance, quite licit to plead for recognition of the disappearance of elementary locality as the basic level of identification[9], but on condition that one remembers that this locality was always part of one, and often several, mini-regional identification spaces (cf. B. Poche, 1989). But it would be somewhat strange, in a perspective of awareness, to deny the permanent anthropological operation (and not persistent or remanent) of identification phenomena in our daily lives; the only problem is of a topological order: aggregations whose extension is more or less vast, or sliding on the edge, of certain frontiers. But it is not enough just to assert it. Let us look into the problem in greater detail.

If we base our approach on the theoretical foundations mentioned above, then we can say that the territory is the area in which four types of investment are at work simultaneously:

- the investment of familiarity by which the individual recognizes a space as the actual and present (we do not say: natural!) framework for the exercise of the various acts, which make up the evolving combination of desire and what is possible, and constitute his life as an individual and as a member of society in all its compartments[10];
- the sensitive investment by which an individual projects himself emotionally on a bio-morpho-climatic environment and acquires systems of habits which socialise his primary instincts. We define these instincts as the reacting system to the interface between his body and the "environment", cf., for example, John Dewey: a habit is a "form of successive associations where one element reintegrates the next, and so on", or indeed "Habit means special sensitiveness or accessibility to a certain class of stimuli, standing predilections and aversions" (quoted by Meltzer, Petras and Reynolds, 1980: 17)[11];
- the retrospective investment through which one takes possession of a whole range of semantic and symbolic equipment, which, as in the mythical story, *names* (standardises) all the visible equipment, turning it into a social construct and

explains its presence using a history or several cross-referenced histories (cf. B. Poche, 1988b, 1990). This "symbolic language" which is reread, revisited, deformed, travestied, etc. is one of the components of the intelligibility of the world;

- finally, the speech-linguistic construction. By this expression we mean the process by which the socialised individual superimposes three different levels of consciousness: a) the "vehicular language", a social abstraction composed by the accumulation of objects, knowledge and techno-organizational procedures socially proposed as taken for granted. This proposal has no regard for their actual genesis, their connections and their aims[12]; b) his effective appropriation and internalization of these elements as given to him from outside; and c) the combining he has to operate in his everyday life between this internalization and the three systems of projective investments just mentioned (recognition of surrounding space, sensitiveness towards the physical environment, elaboration of standards concerning the history and categories of the social context).

We shall restrict ourselves to suggesting, without further demonstration or more detailed reference to phenomenological sociology, that the individual constantly transforms the data taken from the various globalizations[13] into a *hic et nunc*. It is this constant transposition between "standard" and "variety", to use the linguistic terminology, which constitutes the real process of the construction of the senses: it is at this level that *sociality* takes shape. One does not put into practice a technological or organizational standard as such, without readaptions, hybrid systems and local "bricolages", any more than one speaks a "linguistic standard".

The problem is far more a question of establishing a categorization, which takes account of problems of scale, and a conceptualization, which makes it possible to escape from spatial formalism and the functionalism of globalization phenomena[14].

Scale categorization too is a process, which is more delicate than it might appear, for the first three types of investment studied do not operate in the same direction. To make systematic use of the communicational process as a substitute for material relation or as the construction of "an imaginary environment" would lead to multiplying the contradictions about the nature of interaction. Apart from a few rare exceptions, individuals do not live on motorways or high-speed trains: only *apparatchiks* do. Systems of interpretation are generally made up within the meshes of the planetary networks. The threads and the knots of these networks constitute social artefacts which do not interconnect blank, totally receptive individuals, but rather link up with preorganized milieus. These milieus elaborate themselves, partly for reasons of internal arrangement, partly according to strategies developed precisely to keep themselves clear of these global systems.

Consequently the sociological question is to uncover the balances which are born, not so much from the planetary circulation of information, as from the manner in which this modifies local systems of meaning. To take an example, countries like Belgium or Italy (particularly the north) - which are generally considered to be very permeable, in terms of their scientific or managerial approach, to influences from the United States - nevertheless continue to develop, in the midst of their own fragmentation, autonomous systems of senses, even if, for certain specific activities, they do "absorb" the English language[15].

We must also identify the limits of these territorial analogies. If we start from the assumption (cf. above) that the relationship between long distance and local travel has not substantially changed in comparison with the past, the notion of proximity has undoubtedly become a little broader, but not necessarily by a great deal and not in all directions: taken in isolation, it may well contain more than one single social content, and it is here that we shall find the forms of investment quoted above as so many forms of what we have referred to as *recognition* and *expression*.

On the basis of the detailed analysis of isolated cases and as yet fragmentary analyses of other situations, it seems that this broadening which acts on the mobilisation of certain similarities between situations relevant to human ecology, in its most general aspect, combines several factors, all based on the balances between antagonistic pushes and pulls. Let us list some of these factors:

- the use of historic or ethno-cultural antecedents when constituting a process of recognition between Us and the Others. This modality, often supported by a language and which has a significant influence on the notions of people and nation, is extremely widespread, despite the impassioned controversies that it arouses. This is the dominant tendency to be found, for example, in situations as in Corsica[16], Slovenia, Alto-Adige (South Tyrol), Belgian Flanders, etc;
- the use of similarities between socio-economic-ecological configurations, based partly on their historical permanence, partly on analogous attitudes when confronted with the image of sensitive components of everyday life. The difference between Us and Others refers less in that case to the notion of people than to that of spatial frontier, which though vague is clearly felt, in the "cultural" coding of daily practice. This is the case for instance with the French Alps (essentially Savoy) and its continuation towards the Swiss part of the Lake Geneva basin; it is doubtless equally true for many regions whose ethnic character is either very diffuse or has been blunted by the imposition of central power (the north of France, Puglia in Italy, certain areas of southern Spain);
- the use of a powerful residue of a feeling of auto-organization, never completely interrupted, in particular in economic life and certain customs, and the consciousness of a clear limit which separates - or which should separate - the "controlling" state interventions from the internal management of questions confronting "civil society", with its own localized control processes[17]. The difference between Us and the Others is based on the high value attached to the latter as a criterion of autonomy, and on the wish to keep the interventions of central power and de-territorialised standards to a minimum. This approach is largely responsible for what were called, mainly in France, the regionalist movements of the sixties and seventies (the archetypes are the Breton and Occitan movement, but the same principle could be observed elsewhere, for instance in Savoy[18]). But the claims and proclamations to be heard at present in Lombardy, and to a lesser extent in Piedmont, or the peripheral areas of the United Kingdom (Wales and

Scotland), and the deep sense of difference and relative autonomy of management in the regions constituting the ex-GDR and which is expressed to a large extent by the organization in the Länder, seem to fit into this category[19]. It does occur, as we have already stated, that this awareness is reawakened by a crisis in central government, but it is not a general rule.

These various forms of "balance under tension" between pure locality and all the larger aggregations (whatever they may be) are neither clear cut, nor exclusive; as we have stressed, they constitute particular *factors*, which may be combined. The examples we have quoted are at best cases which can, if handled with precaution, serve as slightly more pronounced archetypes. It will be noted that we have not relied, in an absolutely demonstrative manner, in the preceding pages, on the notions of minority or nation, nor on the *founding* role played by a language. We have simply shown, allusively, the notions in the midst of vaster categories in an attempt to show the operational combination of the "investments" described above.

The defence of a language may be a powerful instrument for mobilizing people, and an effective argument for supporting the notion of autonomous production of a social awareness. Language, in itself, is only one of the possible ways of marking the limit, of *saying* the prime irreducibility of these various productions. This irreducibility which is societal (and not cultural, as is claimed by those who reduce sociology to culturalism) is obviously not driven by the difference between languages. To suppose that, would be to believe that the various codes involved can be *switched* without any particular problem, and that our mythical horizon is constituted by a universal language. On the basis of our assumption, they can be *translated*, with the inevitable uncertainties which that involves; it is an entirely different approach.

3. The return to ambivalences: organizational level and societal level

It is clear that extremely detailed research would be required to confirm these notions of identification. But the procedures we have described and the examples that we have drawn upon are sufficiently clear to free us from the monopoly of a somewhat mechanistic conception of globality and from a "millenarian" fear of the end of territorial identities. Certainly the social link cannot be the object of imprudent anticipations, whether they be of a global or micro-local order; what is difficult is to find a way of observing how it is created, drawing on "progress" data (and conflicts) from everyday life.

This is what our concept of sociality means: the place where, *existentially*, the members of a society are conscious of the *perceptible* presence of the society in question, in all its dimensions and not only those which emerge from the abstract organization, and where they *express* that consciousness. On account of the misappropriation of this notion of society, the question has become almost inaudible in the rational language used by a person answering an opinion poll, for example, which is itself expressed in a rationalized language and context. But it is sufficient to observe the speed with which our sociologist colleagues "relocalize" their attitude and language, as soon as what is concerned is the question of themselves as private persons, or merely the choice of an example, and no longer their scientific ability as analysts or generally valid model builders: a frequent experience which remains difficult to treat scientifically.

This is the nub of the ambivalence: the contamination of the language used in the permanent recomposition of what is social, of the "maintenance of social forms" discussed by Simmel (1981), by the abstract organizational language, whether it be that of the state-equivalent (or power), of the technology-equivalent or the modelling-equivalent. There is no shortage of functional categorizations of space, in media language (or so it is called, the natural language for a group which scarcely extends beyond its adepts, its promoters and its profiteers): under-developed countries, socialist countries, natural areas, "North" and "South", market areas, leisure areas, and so on, not to mention the "rich" vocabulary of urban and regional planning. It is not surprising that in this language, whose genetic property is to be switchable, the problem of limits seems to dissolve. We shall simply quote one example, without dwelling on the history behind it: the term "province", which in the last few years, with its various correlates (provincial, provincialism, etc.) is in the process of submerging France. This debate strikes us as being very instructive in that, far from continuing Balzac's debate (*Scènes de la vie de province*), it transposes and surpasses it. In fact, it creates two functional categories of space. On the one hand we have Paris alone, and it is neither necessary nor opportune to characterize it as "the capital". On the other hand we have "la province" as a whole. In our opinion this dichotomy of language and ideology covers three connotations. It opposes:

- a space which can be defined in all possible dimensions, generalized and transformed into an archetype, versus a space whose peculiar absence of differentiation is caused by it being uniformly one-dimensional, reducing/reduced: it is its sole characterization in this dual analysis, and it prevents a parallel comparison from even being considered. Paris is everything; "la province" is definitively nothing but itself;
- a self-generating space capable of producing meaning and contents, versus a space lit by an outside light: meaning produced in the provinces can only be naive or utilitarian, meaning produced in Paris is both endogenous and absolute, the only standard which is both licit and indisputable;
- a space enjoying the ability to reach all places and to define/denominate all things, versus a space destined by nature to be the repository of traditions, of roots and of the world, past and present, of "protected" biological events, all this justified not by considerations of balance or alternative, but to bear witness to the old days, to non-competitive life (in both senses of the word), to "recharge our batteries"[20].

If we touch on this debate, it is in order to reveal the root of the problem of absorption completely: absorption substitutes an abstract walk-on, moving through schematic spaces, a "judgmental dope" to use H. Garfinkel's expression[21], for the complexity and depth of the social fabric and the beings with limits and sensitivity which build that fabric, and subsidiarily! inhabit it.

4. Conclusion: political control and social regulation

The principal aim of this incursion into the theory of social awareness in the context of modernity was to reveal, as two distinct categories, the territory of politico-economic integration and the territory of social identification. The first is the space of the exogenous management of the social world; the second is the territory, not only of the world of everyday life (cf. Schütz, op. cit.: 105-106), but also of the world of the construction of sense and/of through language. As such, there is no reason why the two territories should coincide. We have considered their fluctuations: they are not of the same order. Fluctuations in the spatial organization of political control are not recent: ancient China and the Roman Empire represent attempts at globalisation, supported in both cases by their own technology. We have examined in greater detail certain recent fluctuations, in particular those which concern the nation state, and we could stress the fact that they conceal attempts to unify the paradigms. So we have attempted to demonstrate that, as long as the sociological approach did not abandon its conceptual instruments, it could only reveal the uncertainties of this unification. On the other hand, the fluctuations in territorial identification appear fairly ancient too, but much slower in their drift, satisfying quite different anthropological laws, in which the endless reconstruction of the tangible world plays a major part.

There is clearly no question of granting some form of absolute privilege to social spaces in the light of this sub-division. But we should observe that: 1) the question of spatio-political integration, once it is complicated by the technological postulates we have mentioned, conceals an implicit finalism, or even "moralism", which is undisputed, and which corresponds to a perfectly explicit finalism in a majority of the "cultivated" media, in particular in western Europe (cf. the debate during the autumn of 1990 in Great Britain and the fall of the Prime Minister, Mrs. Thatcher, who was not sufficiently "European"); 2) that to concern ourselves with social awareness, integrating its affective side, involves finding the necessary means to record the languages of identification and their conflicts, without being discouraged by the anathema, also quite explicit, applied to "nationalisms" and "separatisms"[22]. Many of the crises that are stigmatised in this way, and the corresponding vocabulary, seem to arise from the confusion between social control and political regulation.

Our analysis of the awareness of territory is designed to caution the reader against this confusion. It is always possible to debate the "end" of ethnographic idiosyncrasies, but it is perhaps more important to note that these have been constituted in the collective imagination at the cost of a contradiction, which is undoubtedly not the result of chance; the old identification systems, the ones which go back, in the words of the chronicles, to "time immemorial", cared little for tradition and the conservation of memory. The theory of social progress has introduced a division into social work between "enlightened" worlds, by definition unlimited, and "savage" worlds, devoted to well-earned rest. But surely this enterprise of globalizing social sense has already shown, in the totalitarian utopias of the thirties, its equivalents in practical terms and its consequences? Territorial identity exists; one only needs to look at it. With the proviso, of course, that one does not decide, rather shamefully, that it is not compatible with the latest "standard" designed, predictably, to precipitate transmutations and permutations. This is not a fatality; the major novels, which appeared at the time of the utopias referred to above (Zamiatine, Huxley, Orwell) set themselves the task of saying this. To elevate society's relentless drift to a transcendent position is equivalent to emptying the sociological approach - our glance turned upon ourselves - of all meaning.

Notes

1 For example the techno-economic upheavals and their consequences on the distribution of individuals in areas of personal activity - "employment" - and training, and the protection of the environment - cf. the decisive role of the Chernobyl catastrophe in the USSR - and to an even greater degree those that break down the consensus foundation of social order - cf. the impact of terrorism, of state totalitarianism, of crime already mentioned for Italy, but which it is far from monopolising, to cite just a few examples.

2 It is not relevant to discuss religion here, but the interlocking of religion and politics *in the modern sense of these two notions* (and not in the medieval sense) is glaring, whether we look at the Christian religion in Poland or the rebirth of various fundamentalist movements or other configurations.

3 For example, the problems of free trade and the rapid growth of maritime transport in the 19th century, driven mainly by the English, did not give rise to the slightest sign of integration between them and their commercial partners - quite the contrary; on the other hand they were homologous with the destruction of the awareness of rural England and its system of farming, in order to make way for high-pressure industrialisation which owed everything to the constitution of the British nation state along lines which would subsequently come to be referred to as militaro-economic.

4 The Le Chatelier law which abolished corporations, and indeed the linguistic policies at the same period of the French revolution (cf. M. de Certeau et al., 1975) went in this direction.

5 To use the terminology of philosophy may seem risky. We should recall the definition given by J.F. Lyotard, "the *Lebenswelt*, a world in which the constituting subject receives objects as passive syntheses previous to any precise knowledge (...), the transcendental *ego* constituting the sense of these objects implicitly refers to a passive intake of the object, to a primordial complicity with the object (...). The world dealt with here is clearly not the world of natural science, it is the whole (...) of all of which there is and of which possibly can exist" (J.F. Lyotard, 1986: 39-40). The reader will note the links with G.H. Mead.

6 The expression is obviously borrowed from George Orwell.

7 Norwegian exists in two parallel forms.

8 No more, of course, than those which separate the various Slav languages of the south.

9 Unless it is brought back to the surface thanks to neighbourhood sociability, as we stated earlier.

10 Here we say social life - we are one step below sociality (see below) and above neighbourhood sociability, social life amalgamating several systems of sociability. One can recognise here what several forms of functionalism have almost reduced to the level of a caricature: the "four functions" of planners (Le Corbusier, 1957, article 77) as the "simple reproduction" of purist Marxist theory.

11 J. Dewey returns to and develops the tradition of W. James, op. cit., p.5.

12 "Concealing the circumstances of (their) generation" as was once said of ideology.

13 *"The actor uses his knowledge like social structures to treat, one after the other, as they occur, the situations lived as so many "here and now's"*. from H. Garfinkel quoted as an epigraph to *Arguments ethnométhodologiques*, 1984.
14 Thanks, for example, to excessive use of the politico-organisational paradigm, which we have criticised before in relation to the nation state.
15 As far as the problems specific to Belgium are concerned, one may consult H. Dumont et al., 1989. Regarding the linguistic evolution of Italy under Anglo-Saxon influence cf. G. Sanga, 1981.
16 Cf. the debates during the autumn of 1990 concerning the modification of its status within the French republic and the legal use of the notion of a Corsican people, widely discussed in the French press.
17 We shall quote one example, which though minor is powerfully expressed; hunting rights confronted with "delocalised" claims by nature protection groups and at the other end of the chain, the relation with work and the social organization of economic life (for instance the regions of northern Italy faced with the procedures of the central state, and to an even greater extent with the problems of the regions of southern Italy). The fact that these awarenesses sometimes appeal to fantasy in no way reduces their symbolic effectiveness.
18 The bibliography concerning these movements is considerable: we shall simply quote, without necessarily adopting the conclusions of the authors, for France, Dulong, 1975; Quéré, 1978; Touraine, 1981; for Switzerland, Bassand and Guindoni, 1982; and our article, Poche, 1979.
19 Regarding the last point the reader will note the extreme disparity in size of the **Länder**, ranging from the *Staatsstädte* in Hanse and Saar to Bavaria, which constitutes an interesting contrast with the obsession in France for "(administrative) regions on a European scale". What does this mean? It is true that almost no-one in France has considered the question of identification, and that when the question arises (Corsica) it raises an uproar.
20 This dichotomy seems so clear-cut and irreducible that we recently heard someone say, referring to an area located about 60 km from Paris: "it's the provinces, in a way", with a discreet qualifying phrase to avoid appearing to qualify the place irremediably as part of the outcast fringes of the conurbation (the programme *Challenge* on France Inter radio, November 26 1990).
21 Quotation cf. note 13.
22 Cf. the debates in international public opinion regarding the need not to "destabilise" the leader of the Soviet Union, Mr. Gorbachov, by encouraging separatist movements in the Baltic republics or the Caucasus.

References

Arguments ethnométhodologiques (1984) Paris, Cahiers du CEMS n° 3, Ecole des Hautes Etudes en Sciences Sociales.

Bassand, M. and Guindani, S. (1982) Maldéveloppement régional et identité, Lausanne, Presses Polytechniques Romandes.

Blumer, H. (1986) Sociological implication of the thought of George Herbert Mead, in Symbolic Interactionism - Perspective and Method, Berkeley, University of California Press.

de Certeau, M. et al. (1975) Une politique de la langue, la Révolution française et les patois : l'enquête de Grégoire, Paris, Gallimard.

Cicourel, A.V. (1979) La sociologie cognitive, Paris, Presses Universitaires de France.

Conein, B. (1984) L'enquête sociologique et l'analyse du langage : les formes linguistiques de la connaissance sociale, in Arguments ethnométhodologiques, Paris, Centre d'Etude des Mouvements Sociaux, EHESS.

Cooley, C.H. (1926) The roots of social knowledge, American Journal of Sociology, Vol. 32.

Cuisenier, J. (1990) Ethnologie de l'Europe, Paris, Presses Universitaires de France.

Dulong, R. (1975) La question bretonne, Paris, A. Colin.

Dumont, H. (ed.), (1989) Belgitude et crise de l'Etat belge, Actes du colloque organisé aux Facultés Universitaires Saint-Louis, Bruxelles, Publications des FUSL.

Durkheim, E. (1979) Les formes élémentaires de la vie religieuse, Paris, Presses Universitaires de France (1ère éd. 1912).

Egger, K. (1978) Bilinguismo in Alto Adige, Bolzano, Athesia.

Garfinkel, H. (1967) Studies in ethnomethodology, Englewood Cliffs, N.J., Prentice Hall.

Goffman, E. (1987) Façons de parler, éd. française, Paris, Ed. de Minuit.
Grafmeyer, Y. and Joseph,I. (1979) L'Ecole de Chicago, naissance de l'écologie urbaine, Paris, Champ Urbain.
Huxley, A. (1975) Le meilleur des mondes, French translat. of Brave new world, Paris, Plon, (1st English edition 1929).
Lapierre, J.W. (1988) Le pouvoir politique et les langues: Babel et Léviathan, Paris, Presses Universitaires de France.
Le Corbusier (1957) La Charte d'Athènes, Paris, Ed. de Minuit.
Levi-Pinard, G. (1974) La vie quotidienne à Vallorcine au XVIIIe siècle, Annecy, Mémoires de l'Académie Salésienne.
Lyotard, J.F. (1986) La phénoménologie, Paris, Presses Universitaires de France.
Meltzer, B.N., Petras, J.W. and Reynolds, L.T. (1980) Symbolic interactionism. Genesis, varieties and criticism, Boston, London, Routledge and Kegan Paul.
Mlinar, Z. (1991) "Individuation et socialisation dans l'espace : qu'avons-nous appris ? Expériences yougoslaves" in Espaces et Sociétés, n° 64. Paris.
Orwell, G.(1972) 1984, trad. française, Paris, Gallimard, 1972 (1st English edition 1949).
Pierrot, L. (1983) Interactions sociales et procédures cognitives de production du sens. Le cas des femmes immigrées, Thèse de 3e cycle, Université de Provence, Aix en Provence.
Poche, B. (1979) "Mouvement régional et fondements territoriaux de l'identité sociale : le mouvement régionaliste savoyard" in Cahiers internationaux de Sociologie, vol. LXVI, Paris.
Poche, B. (1987a) Localité et construction langagière du sens - Pour une sociologie cognitive des groupes sociaux, Thèse de doctorat d'Etat, Paris, Université de Paris V-Sorbonne.
Poche, B. (1987b) "La construction sociale de la langue" in France, pays multilingue, ouvr. coll. G. Vermès et J. Boutet, éd., Paris, L'Harmattan.
Poche, B (1988a) "Un modèle sociologique du contact de langues: les coupures du sens social" in Langage et société, n° 43, Paris.
Poche, B. (1988b) "Histoire de la localité, histoire des mythes" in Sociologie du Sud-Est, n° 55-58, Aix-en-Provence.
Poche, B. (1989) "La représentation sociale des coupures territoriales sur la crête des Alpes. Formulations langagières et racines historiques" in La frontière: nécessité ou artifice ? Actes du XIIIe Colloque franco-italien d'études alpines, Grenoble, Université des Sciences Sociales.
Poche, B. (1990) Lyon tel qu'il s'écrit, romanciers et essayistes lyonnais, 1860-1940, Lyon, Presses Universitaires de Lyon.
Quere, L. (1978) Jeux interdits à la frontière, Paris, Anthropos.
Sanga, G. (1981) "Les dynamismes linguistiques de la société italienne (1861-1960) : de la naissance de l'italien populaire à la diffusion des ethnicismes linguistiques" in Langages, n° 61, Paris.
Schutz, A. (1987) Le chercheur et le quotidien (part French translation of Collected Papers), Paris, Méridiens-Klincksieck.
Searle, J.R. (1972) Les actes de langage, essai de philosophie du langage, éd. fr. Paris, Hermann.
Simmel, G. (1981) "Comment les formes sociales se maintiennent", 1897, republished in Sociologie et épistémologie, Paris, Presses Universitaires de France.
Tönnies, F. (1957) Community and Society, (American edtion of Gemeinschaft und Gesellschaft), New York, Harper Torchbook.
Touraine, A. et al.(1981) Le pays contre l'Etat, Paris, Seuil, 1981.
Weber, E. (1983) La fin des terroirs. La modernisation de la France rurale (1870-1914), Paris, Gallimard.
Weber, M. (1959) Le savant et le politique, Paris, Plon, 1959 (originally published as Politik als Beruf, 1919).
Zamiatine, E. (1971) Nous autres, Paris, Gallimard, 1971 (written in 1920; 1st French edition in 1929).

9 Interdependence, globalization and fragmentation

Gilbert Larochelle

The concept of interdependence was thrust to the foreground in the theoretical literature of international relations in the 1970s. The well known debates pertaining to interdependence opposed, on the one hand, Richard Cooper, Ed Morse, Oran Young, Robert O. Keohane and Joseph Nye - who saw it as a proper category for the description of contemporary reality - and, on the other hand, Kenneth Waltz, Karl Deutsch and Alexander Eckstein, who were more inclined to subscribe to the theory of the resurgence of political nationalism and economic protectionism. These schools of thought argued over the course of global evolution, trying to prove to each other that either the integration or the constantly increasing differentiation of its components were the consequences of interdependence. The recent cooling of this debate is attributed less to the victory of one camp over the other than to their mutual inability to simultaneously consider contradictory tendencies which coexist concurrently, and indeed develop, in symbiosis.

The principal objective of this study is to show that what is commonly described as "globalization" escapes both of the above-mentioned effects of interdependence. This is because globalization absorbs them in a union that is certainly less unusual than particular in the form (Robertson 1990:18) it assumes today. In fact, the antagonism between the global and the local, for a time crystalized around the concept of interdependence, conceals convergences. It would be recognized that the theme of globalization simultaneously describes concrete dynamics and the study of a world order in mutation, and it therefore includes the two processes of integration and differentiation which are themselves characterized by the concurrent establishment of remarkably dense networks of interactions (technological, institutional, communicative, etc.) and the demand for the recognition of identity (local, ethnic, symbolic, etc.). The present species of globalization creates rather than abolishes situations of conflict, or at least creates resistance to the threat to individuals' territorial attachments. This reinforces the natural tendency of groups to defend that which distinguishes them from other groups. Unity and division mutually presuppose each other (Dupuy, 1989), as the present European situation indicates, where political integration of the continent coexists with rising nationalism (Estonia, Latvia, Georgia, Armenia, Kosovo, Corsica, etc.).

It is therefore clear that the idea of interdependence must be reconsidered from the conceptual and empirical points of view by questioning the dichotomous mental schemes (homogeneity/heterogeneity, integration/disintegration, unity/diversity) which supported a vindictive academic debate. Following this necessary redefinition it must be shown how the new definition can account for the dialogue between interrelated complementary processes, which are already active at the transnational level, and in a limited way, at the local level.

Current usages of the notion of interdependence presuppose the iron-clad duality between the national and the international spheres. However, this notion does not survive any critical examination. Two images are usually associated with such a traditional interpretation: that of a civil society, evoking the authenticity of a social link in which universality is in a certain manner guaranteed, although contained in a nation state, and that of an anarchy in which a plurality of states are reduced, like the individuals in the works of Hobbes, to a generalized state of homo homini lupus. Indeed modernity, is sometimes thought of as the dualism between a culture acquired by virtue of the social contract, and a natural state which is a symbol of disorder. Modern societies function primarily on the basis of territorial unification and of attempts to shape national identities, notably by the homogenization of the social fabric in its linguistic, cultural and, particularly, ideological aspects. The appearance of the nation state at the dawn of the Renaissance is linked to a new protocol for the demarcation of the border between the one and the many; most importantly, to the role of the state as the historical producer and structural mediator of identity and difference (Blumenberg, 1983; Walker, 1984).

Furthermore, in this line of thought we can describe the following process. The medieval unity of Christendom was shattered by the nation state system. Nevertheless this system implied a certain principle of latent unity and an international order consisting of minimal tolerance and the balance of power (Bull, 1977; Kratochwill, 1981; Cohen, 1981; Walker, 1984). Several authors (Bull, 1977; Vincent, 1981; Navari, 1982), question the application of Hobbes' schema to relations between states. These authors emphasize the danger of transposing individual behavior to the interaction between societies and argue that this English philosopher was a theorist of coexistence between states. Therefore, through a sort of mixing of paradigms, pluralism in the international sphere may appear as a particular and novel form of universal integration, (Walker, 1984; Caporaso, 1989; Nardin, 1983). Thus diversity reveals itself as a phase in the process of unity.

Nevertheless, merely reducing this dualism seems insufficient since it still preserves the unity of analysis that characterizes modernity, i.e. the notion of society symbolized and defined by national borders. Clearly this Rubicon must be crossed. This can be accomplished by recognizing, on one hand, the legitimacy of a sociology of globalization whose purpose would be the study on a global scale of new dynamics which occur outside the classical framework of nation states.[1] Furthermore, a sociology of globalization would require categories different from those of modernity (Featherstone, 1990; Robertson, 1990; Wallerstein, 1987), because globalization is not simply internationalization, or the increase of bilateral exchanges between societies. Yet, globalization can not be reduced to the hegemonic extension of a culture in the process of gaining recognition of some kind of universality. Such an interpretation would only revive the theories of imperialism while heralding the establishment of a world Empire.

The theoretical dichotomies and inflexibilities of these schools of thought can be removed by demonstrating that globalization does not preclude the resurgence of local concerns, or of what Smith (1981) calls The Ethnic Revival. The idea of post-modernity can serve to describe this process of rediscovery and promotion of minority cultures which modern imperialists reject in favor of the homogeneity that they seek. This idea presupposes, above all, the observation of the irrepressible territorial pluralism of cultures in the world, the rejection of society as the base of analysis and, by correlation, the disappearance of the traditional borders between national territorial cultures.

All these aspects of postmodernity will be discussed here only in relation to their presumed connection with interdependence. Furthermore, this theme does not claim to exhaust all the possible and significant expressions of globalization, but rather seeks to express a dissident perspective with respect to conventional wisdom, which sees in globalization the triumph of unity over multiplicity. Finally, an equation emerges, in the form of a paradox: the universalization of objects creates an increase in the differentiation of subjects. Hence, the theories of postmodernity provide a preliminary explanation of this polarization because they question the historical credibility of social universality by showing the permanence, if not the revival, of local territorial identifications.

1. The idea of interdependence and its territorial dimension

In its most general sense, the idea of interdependence does not necessarily imply the notion of territory. Rather, it indicates the bilateral constraints, positive or negative, that individuals exercise over one another in these social interactions. All collective social interaction carries traces of such influence, since it is implied by society-making in itself, as philosophers from Cicero to Durkheim have abundantly demonstrated.

In the field of international relations, one must consider the territorial aspects of interdependence to fully understand its implications. A concept considered ambiguous by some (Caporaso, 1978), useless by others (Lall, 1975) and, bitterly debated by all, with little consensus as to its meaning. Interdependence can nevertheless be defined strictly for the purpose of this demonstration as: the set of mutually influencing interactions that exist between politically organized and geographically circumscribed groups of human beings.[2] This principle of mutual conditioning of societies implies that changes occurring in one society are bound to affect the others in some way. War remains one of the most absolute and constraining forms of interdependence. So too do situations of unlimited cooperation among nations, though their effects are less harshly felt. Two diametrically opposed aspects of this phenomenon account for two commonly accepted definitions of interdependence, a) that of a sensitivity to external forces by which a society is influenced or conditioned, b) that of a vulnerability which, through a dissymetrical relationship of power, subordinates one society to the politics of the other which has become dominant.[3] However, regardless of which definition is relevant, the geographic proximity of the societies in question constitutes the causa prima from which multilateral ties have historically emerged in the intervals between human communities.

The preliminary marking of space is, in a certain sense, postulated by the very notion of interdependence. In effect, interdependence has existed *lato sensu* since the birth of primitive societies (Stojanovic, 1978). When a group claims and settles a territory, this creates the favorable conditions which find, in the marking of its territory, the very symbol of its justification (Duchacek, 1986). The territorialization of human groups is synchronous with the establishment of relations with other groups. That which unites also contains that which excludes. The statement "I'm from here, you're from there" suggests the existence of a barrier which simultaneously proclaims the interdependence of identity and difference. This implies *de facto* the assertion "that which I am requires that I account for what you are, so that I can be differentiated from you." The recognition of a common territory functions as a semantic support for social identifications. Maintained by coercion or by consent, this consists of vested interests which are defined by internal and external authorities. The boundary between these is the beginning and the end of international relations. The truth of this statement is clearly evident, both in sedentary barbarian tribes and in modern societies. From the dawn of civilization, men have partitioned the world into geographic entities that today cover the whole surface of the globe, and they claim to be superior to others on the basis of their self-declared characteristics. Duchacek (1986) remarks "All territorial authorities engage in verbal, visual and symbolic propaganda to make their identity with the territory separate from that of the rest of the world" (p. 17). The modern idea of sovereignty - in the theories of Jean Bodin, in the sixteenth century - strengthens rather than detract from the dominance of territorial envy that characterizes western societies (Boulding, 1959), without turning the historical record into an anthropological necessity as does Friedrich Ratzel (1987). One must remember that interdependence has always existed because of the relationship between space and human political entities.

The territorial differentiation of social groups constitutes a factor of distinction of their respective economic power. This not only supports the localization of a system of order, but also encompasses potential resources necessary for material production. These effects generates a dissymetry of "primitive inequality" (Stojanovic, 1978). Diversity of natural conditions concerning raw materials, energy availability, and the means of communication leads to the development of complementary trade between societies, which creates interdependence (Laurent, 1980). Nevertheless, according to the period, territorial distinction serves as either the justification for autarcic introspection or the indicator of openness and multiplication of various exchanges.

2. Modern interdependence: the hegemony of the global over the local

During its industrialization phase in the nineteenth and twentieth centuries, modernity progressively reduced, if only by colonization, the system whereby the local was expressed only in the framework of nations. This modern type of interdependence can only occur in the framework of the expansion of a dominant culture, ideology or economy where the eclipse of the local in favor of the international appears as their natural destiny because of their antagonism. That this nationalism (political) and protectionism (economical) should surface sporadically confirms *a contrario* interdependence, and the complex and unexpected interaction to which both are constrained (Nye, 1976). The concept of markets, the economic equivalent of territory, is redefined by the unprecedented growth of transnational actors (Wolfers, 1962) and multinational corporations (Vernon, 1971) since the Second World War. This concept's explosion on the global scene initiates the erosion of the state's exclusive role in international relations and causes the birth of new centers of power (Brown, 1973). Although the demise of the state is not yet a "fait accompli" (Krasner, 1989; Haskel, 1980; Bull, 1979; Haass, 1979) this diversification of centers of power and the resulting complexification of their operations generates an informal and often involuntary system of permeable sovereignties (Duchacek, 1986) due to extra-national influences.

The characteristics of the coexisting contradictory tendencies in the international arena are derived as much from the realist paradigm as from the transnational school. These are: a) states and non-state actors fight for control of the society; b) both force and cooperation function as instruments of change; c) the hegemony of the political sphere is somewhat challenged by the increased importance of economic aspects. It is fitting to note that the spread of these processes coincides with a progressive semantic sliding of the notion of interdependence, which *a priori* was linked to the geographic division of space and then came to describe the disappearance of territorial identifications, forgetting the local aspect of the exercise of power, and its expansion.

Modernity has always proclaimed universalism as the destiny of human communities. Most contemporary authors in international relations have tried to express this idea, while some have presented it as a simple description of a social reality. Rosecrance at al. (1977), for example, postulate this in a very explicit fashion. Refusing to accept interdependence defined as the simple relations between societies, they perceive it as a positive determination which they place in opposition to "a mere connectedness" (p. 441).[4] The purpose of the definition of interdependence is not to characterize the word but to describe its social effects: "we mean the direct and positive linkage of the interests of states such that when the position of one state changes, the position of the other is affected and in the same direction" (p. 427).[5] The phenomenon exists only here, if it is qualitatively oriented by a symbol: a futurist narrative in which the multiple progresses toward unity, difference toward identity. The empirical proof comes from economic indicators of the movement of goods and leads to the conclusion that trade brings societies closer together by the convergence of interests as is expressed by Smithian thought. In conclusion to their analysis, the authors write that interdependence is likely to be determined by the structure of political cooperation among states (p. 443). The causality of interdependence is thus changed to confusion between that which is real and that which is desirable, between objects and people, concluding with a suggestion of rational reconciliation between both reality and desire. This analysis climaxes with a pathetic appeal: "greater cooperation is manifestly needed" (p. 444). In "Interdependence: Myth or Reality?" (1973). Rosecrance and Stein had questioned the validity of the indicators of interdependence as well as its status. On the basis of statistical evidence, they viewed it as a reality, but also elevated it into a myth of universal brotherhood: "the failure to meet the challenge of higher, necessary cooperation could mean higher possibility of conflict" (p. 23). Laurent (1980) echoes this: "the conscience of a co-responsability is essential in order to .manage interdependence/ in a spirit of loyal cooperation" (p. 672). The discourse of the Trilateral Commission, founded in 1973 and inspired by Zbigniew Brzezinski, who had formulated its grand intellectual orientations in Between Two Ages (1969), is presented as the political response to the expansion of the phenomenon of interdependence.[6]

The resurgence of the myth that the earth is but one single nation, presents nothing new, since it borrows its principal characteristics from stocism, medieval Christianity, sixteenth and seventeenth century jusnaturalism, eighteenth century cosmopolitism and twentieth century universalism. However, the contemporary linkage of this myth with the concept of interdependence comes from four specific confusions:

a) A unilateral definition of the concept of benefit as a result of interdependence.
b) A permutation of the facts by their desired social effects as the limitation of the area of influence of interdependence (Baldwin, 1980).
c) A subordination to the values of modernity as a required end product of interdependence.
d) A tendencious eclipsing of the local in favor of the global as the condition for the advancement of interdependence.

The positive definition elevates the phenomenon of interdependence to a relationship without dissymetry, beneficial to all and distinguished by an element of reciprocity, the obtaining of mutual advantages and, by consequence, of a social consensus. It goes on to suggest that globalization consists only in the universal pursuit of material gains, and that the sole quest of this destiny is enough to motivate human communities "in the same direction". Before it can be held responsible for social interaction, the modern myth of interdependence rests upon the world-wide exchange of objects, which constitutes a necessary condition for the universal gathering of human beings. "The Terrestrial City", notes Dupuy (1989, p. 20), "is organized as an order of things rather than as an order of persons." The accumulation of goods and the increase of trade do not by themselves prove its spread, but the access to economic wealth is indeed often presented not as a substitute, but as a support for democratic institutions, if not a support for a collective project.

The call for a "planetary humanism" by the Trilateral Commission stands as a highly up-to-date example of an intellectual fusion of the technology of interdependence, of human rights and of a political sovereignty extending to the point of universality (Larochelle, 1990). In this context of the expansion of relations which are neither those of time nor place, since communications have abolished the effects of both, the race for economic assets imposes itself as the *ratio dominandi* whose power of seduction is for the most part the result of efficiency. The quest for wealth in the international order and the cries of the less fortunate for a bigger piece of the pie are part of a materialist revision of the concept of equality for which the demand has moved from "I am" to "I Have", from the "quality of persons to the quality of things." (Dupuy, 1989, p. 20)

In other words, the attack of the global on the local, so characteristic of the notion of interdependence, applies most strongly to things and to the techniques for their accumulation. Now, because the concept of what is good is by no means constant - as it does not by itself call upon a specific social conduct in humans - it follows that interdependence depends upon the values preferred by individuals, by societies, and indeed by the cultures within which these values manifest themselves. The idea behind interdependence is not derived from universally accomplished facts but from the universal accomplishment of particular values, notably those of modernity. In this regard, the reductionism which is implied in a positive definition of interdependence must be understood as an expression of the western myth of the transparent communication of goals so dear to the philosopher Juergen Habermas. The image upon which it depends is that of a transparent world in which interdependence proceeds from the universal desire to acquire the benefits created by modernity: "to see higher interdependence as a fundamental force for better relations among nations." (Rosecrance et al., 1977, p. 426). The changes anticipated herein do not reveal themselves exclusively in the quantitative - where they are habitually confined by the theoreticians of interdependence - but also in that of the qualitative, since they suppose a universalization of the definition and a tight linkage to the idea of perfectibility.

However, contemporary social changes seem to be less and less consistent with the perspective of an interdependence described in the exclusive sense of the social integration of human communities.[7] In fact, for approximately the last twenty years, the local has been vehemently resisting the global attempts at levelling. Régis Debray (1986, p. 26), writes: "The end of the universal bursts in the universal explosion of particularisms." The rule of ownership through universalization of local and national economies is undergoing the counter-offensive of groups demanding recognition of their identities and advancing their specific cultures within and without national boundaries. Europe in 1992 constitutes a fine example, where the local is hotly disputing continental integration. Similarly, Canada is presently undergoing a process of explosion not only in the two main linguistic communities (the French and the English), but also in a great variety of claims by ethnic communities, notably the

Amerindians. From this time onwards, the failure of modernist socialization in moving toward the universal, and the explosion of the local D stimulated by technology D inserts the local in the cacophonous conversation of a plurality of cultures, a phenomenon which Featherstone (1990) interprets as globalization.

3. Postmodern interdependence: the return of the local in the global

By its very dynamics, contemporary globalization reassigns the processes of interdependence to new horizons, notably the de-territorialization of international relations, a process which operates through communications technologies and the circulation of information. The idea of proximity, the traditional determinant of the mechanisms of socialization, somehow loses the capacity to explain interdependence (Mlinar, 1990), since technical progress has abolished the effects of distance and isolation. Rather, associations are no longer linked to territory: the contemporary individual, at least in the West, participates through the media in what happens at the other end of the world. The technology contributes decisively to the weakening of sovereignties and the de-territorialization of interdependence. In creating a planetary *agora* where man is contemporary of all events at all times, interdependence overturns the characteristics of modernity, especially the separation between the national and the international fields, as clearly demonstrated in the Gulf War. The superseding of borders entailed by this process is not limited entirely to communications, even if they are more common within political entities than between them (Duchacek, 1986). On the economic level, these repercussions strengthen the following manifestations of interdependence: a) the international division of labour; b) the specialization of functions; c) the increase in the volume of trade; d) the multiplication of informal economic networks outside the framework of nation-states. On the other hand, technology permits us to catch a glimpse of two unique possibilities in human history that testify to its importance as a multiplying factor of interdependence. According to certain authors (Young, 1969; Morse, 1972; Cooper, 1968), its origin must be situated in 1945. These are the possibility of an exhaustion of natural resources and, on the politico-military scene, the annihilation of life on this planet (Rock, 1964; Laloy, 1978). It is without doubt in reference to this dramatic possibility that the French writer Paul Valéry stated precisely in 1945 in Regards sur le monde actuel: "The finite world has begun". We must further note that this present finite nature of the world is concurrent with, if not explained by, the apparently infinite variety of the technical instruments which are available to transform it. It implies that a "world civil society" already exists which, far from being able to present the characteristics of the unit, assumes those of a mosaic whose irreducible fragments are those of local cultures.

Furthermore, the chief characteristic of this return of the local in the movement of globalization passes through co-existence, concurrent at times with heterogeneity and homogeneity in the center of the modern framework of nation-states. Mlinar (1990, p. 57) also saw that this fundamental diversity affects that which he calls "the traditional model of territorial organization". Because of this, we might add in the wake of

Featherstone (1990), globalization introduces paradoxically the universality of difference: "globalization", writes Arnason (1990, p. 224), "is by no means synonymous with homogenization... it should rather be understood as a new framework of differentiation." Régis Debray (1986, p. 27) comments in an enlightened fashion: "... the greater the acceleration of technological renewal, (...) the destruction of community territory and of the frameworks of traditional life, the standardization of tools and of products, etc., the greater the gradual return to founding ideals, to the sources and symbols of the threatened ethnic membership. The more (material) progress, the more (spiritual) regression; the more equalization occurs, the more boundaries are built; the more fragmentation occurs, the more tribalization. Modernity will be archaic or it will not be at all. And when humanity "in progress" is civilized by its own hand, it simultaneously becomes savage in its head and heart (...). This model has, at least, the merit of explaining why the third industrial revolution, "defying all logic" renews the escalation of tribal conflict and the resurrection of religion, not only on the periphery but at the very center of the industrial world."

The idea of postmodernity serves precisely to take into account this return of the local and the predominance of singularity over universality, the individual becoming an agent of globalization (Archer, 1990), since he acts in a context which is itself tightly linked to the global environment.[8] At least in the field of international relations, it rests on four primary characteristics from which, in my opinion, must be taken the theoretical redefinition of the contemporary processes of interdependence: a) pre-modernist neo-traditionalism; b) the eternal return, or the rupture of the linear nature of a universal destiny; c) the mixing of shifting traditional boundaries between social structures; and d) the de-hierarchization of symbolic universes.

The interaction of the local and the global in postmodernity creates new contours in the social field. One of the present aspects of globalization is certainly what one could label the appearance of a sort of "neo-feudalism", in the way in which often ethnicity-based fiefs multiply and become at the same time identity groups in the Merton sense (Lechner, 1984). Even if the distinction between the global and the local appears increasingly problematic (Robertson, 1990), the complexity that ensues proves it is foreign to the discourse legitimizing modernity. The cause of this is the existence of a sort of social mosaic loosely based on those which were found in pre-nation-state Europe, and also, at the same time, the insertion of the local in a global space where there is a constant negotiation of the interaction between cultures.

Régis Debray (1986, pp. 27-28), describes for us the dance of globalized differences: "Let the music begin: Shi'ites against Sunnis or Arabs against Persians, Alawites against Sunnis, Cypriot Turks against Cypriot Greeks, Druzes against Marionites, Jews against Mulsims, Kurds against Arabs and Persians, Moors against Berbers, Sikhs against Hindus, Singhalese against Tamils, Germanics against Slavics and Slavics against Turks, the Catholic against the Orthodox, the believers against the atheists, Hazaras and Pashtuns against Russian occupants, Baluchi against Punjabi, Vietnamese against Khmers Rouges and Chinese against Vietnamese or vice-versa, "canaque" (Polynesian for "man") against "caldoche" (local term for Caucasian inhabitants of New Caledonia)". The conflict is by no means an historical one limited to postmodernity. However, the novelty resides in the unprecedented possibility of bringing about a global recognition of the local, because the representation of the latter is globalized.

The interdependence of the end of this century not only appears to be archaic (Debray), it is also marked by a movement of entropy. It no longer appears possible to uphold, as Karl Marx did, the radical idea that social homogenization is the only and necessary consequence of the universalization of trade: "The national divisions and the antagonisms between people are already disappearing more and more with the development of the bourgeoisie, freedom of commerce, the world market, uniformity of industrial production and the way of life these imply." Ironically, the opposite is actually taking place in the former Soviet Union and precisely for the same reasons, notably those of a globalization in which the interdependence of a plurality rather than of a unity is an effect rather than a cause of globalization. Moreover, the globalization of entropy on the local level is creating territorialities which become more and more ethnico-symbolic[9] and mutually relative. Paradoxically, the increase of intercultural borders diminishes the groups' capacities for exclusion and identification of local differentiations. The rhetorical and the symbolic always remain. When the occasion presents itself, they surface most viciously, but the co-existence of a virtually infinite number of these symbolic territories creates by necessity a greater tolerance which Featherstone (1990, p. 11), calls a sort of ecumenism: "With globalization, the person who was unequivocally outside now becomes a neighbor, with the result that the inside/outside distinction fails. This can lead to responses of ecumenism, tolerance and universalism in which everyone is included, or resistance to globalization in the form of counter movements such as the various non-Western fundamentalisms which react against Westoxication."

If the movement of entropy toward the local manifests itself, among other phenomena, by a de-hierarchization of symbolic universes, it does not follow that the identifications of the individuals have become interchangeable. On the contrary, although the cries for a reconciliation of identities through national sovereignties are diminishing, they continue to make themselves micro-territorially specific, but in a globality that de-territorialized the symbolic universes. The paradox here lies simply in the fact that the local problems are hereafter experienced in the virtual universality of the international arena and, inversely, that this universality no longer has its own substance. Zulus of Africa, Punjabi of Asia, Indians of America, Muslims of Azerbadjan, etc., serve to show that the universal is no more than the theater in which social elements interact, claiming their specific identity in a mutual interdependence.

In democratic or authoritarian societies, in the West as in the Third World, international movements today are experiencing the painful return to the local at the cost of a notable drop in their audience. All of the universal fraternities, whether they be known as Communism, Islamism, or Christianism, have proven incapable of reducing the attachment of man to his piece of the earth, certainly a more and more fragmented but no less effective symbol. Despite certain recent attempts to plead in favor of a world society (Burton, 1972, 1984), these appeals were unable to transcend territorial distinctions and the identifications based on them. This is supported by the comments of Duchacek (1986, p. 31): "A universalistic ideology conquers territorial state and so through its triumph becomes a prisoner." Karl Marx himself underestimated this territorial dimension of politics by postulating that class solidarity would inevitably overtake that of the nation which, in his opinion, were nothing more than illusions, a reflection of the bourgeoisie. "Workers have no nation", he declared in The Communist Manifesto (p. 43), and their political emancipation would bring about territoral emancipation permitting the appearance of the profound interdependence of social solidarities. The irony of history, states Duchacek (1986, p. 36), is that territorial identifications proved themselves stronger than the transnational brotherhood: "instead of nations being socialized into a proletarian international commonwealth (Proletarians of all countries unite!), socialism was nationalized, that is territorialized." The image of the "global village" is therefore only valid insofar as the global does not erase the village! And in this regard, technology can serve the goals of universalization as well as it can serve the claims of the local.

4. Conclusion: postmodernity, globalization and fragmentation

The myth of interdependence constitutes modernity's last effort to bring about the universal transparency and the hegemony of values that it represents. This application of a theory based on the uprooting from a territory finds its ultimate justification in the world market. Modernity has thus sublimated Reason, technology and social ties to the absolute reality of objects. This realism is not, however, the contrary of idealism but its necessary complement, as Walker (1987, p. 67) notes: "... Realism becomes less a hard-headed portrayal of international realities than a systematic evasion of the critical skills necessary for a scholarly analysis of those realities."

The theory of interdependence as defined by Cooper, Young, Rosecrance et al., proceeds from the desire to overcome the diversity of appearances, which would promise unification and a better understanding between nations.[10] Against this liberating vision, the counter-theory of Waltz, Deutsch and Eckstein exhibits the strengthening of defensive barriers and isolationism of all kinds. The analysis proposed herein remains incomplete in many ways. However, it has attempted to demonstrate that neither of these perspectives is totally convincing: beyond that which divides them, the presuppositions even upon which their convergence is founded brings a generalised scepticism.

Europe is presently experiencing the co-existence of globalization and fragmentation, combined with the awakening of political identifications which are by no means subordinated to economic concerns. An entire series of events, not classable within the premises of modernity, are presently appearing: the "aggressive" emergence of minorities, the collapse of large empires, and the processes of continental unification which nineteenth century leaders like Simon Bolivar could only have dreamed about.

Therefore, what is collapsing is not so much the varied process of globalization, but rather its anticipated result: unity. The concept of postmodernity, despite the weakness of its theoretical rigor, maintains the minimal advantage of showing the collapse of the above premises through intellectual lines of thought which can already be perceived: a) a criticism of epistemological realism, b) a refusal of theoretical reductionism, c) the abandonment of the hope to achieve total knowledge as well as universality in the social sphere, d) the acceptance of disorder and complexity, e) the valorization of daily life, f) the substitution of consensus for conflict in view of the unsurmountable difficulties in the discussion of values, g) the re-emergence of the local.

All of these dimensions are less novel than they are newly felt. The territorial variable by no means exhausts all of them, nor does it determine them in the absolute, but it can serve to show the limits of certain uses of the concept of interdependence. Indeed, it can show that interdependence is linked to territory in a certain manner, even though its relationship with the territory has become considerably more complex in the present context, both by implosion of the local and explosion of the global.

Notes

1 "The challenge for sociology, still attempting to come to terms with the interest in culture in the 1980s which has seen a lowering of the boundaries between it and the other social sciences and the humanities, is both to theorize and to work out modes of systematic investigation which can clarify these globalizing processes and distinctive forms of social life which render problematic what has long been regarded as the basic subject matter for sociology: society, conceived almost exclusively as the bounded nation-state" (Featherstone 1990, p.2).

2 The literature on the concept of interdependence is too often based on conventional intellectual positions, which present definitions of interdependence in relation to positive and negative influences. For a positive definition see Rosecrance et al (1977, p. 426-27). For a negative definition see Waltz (1970). It is necessary for our purpose to abandon these two types of interpretations, given their common moralizing.

3 This distinction was originally proposed by Waltz (1970, p. 210) and developed by Keohane and Nye (1973). Duvall argues that it is based on two of the most commonly accepted meanings of the word dependence: 1) a conditioning relationship; 2) a subordination of the relationship. Furthermore in the literature on this subject, the opposition between vertical and horizontal interdependences is also frequently used in a manner consistent with Duvall's two forms of interdependence (see Gasiorowski, 1985)

4 For a similar position, see the article by Alex Inkeles (1975).

5 The text underlined here appears in italics in the original text. Rosecrance et al. (p.426) justify the progression from a natural position to a positive definition in the following terms: "Most students, of course, have wished to use interdependence in a positive sense to see higher interdependence as a fundamental force for better relations among nations."

6 In the Commission's second report, Duchene et al. (1974, p. 35) write: "A world which has reached current levels of interdependence is condemned by technological and economic progress to still more complex relationships in the future, must devise new forms of common management. "For a similar opinion, see Skolnikoff (1972).

7 The Marxist school of thought does not differ considerably from its liberal opponent in the interpretation of interdependence. For example, Marxists criticize the internationalization of exchanges, assimilated to the avatars of capitalism, as it is unable to contain crises in overproduction inherent to its system. Economic interdependence is seen as a subterfuge, if not as

downright exploitation; it is a null-sum-game (see Tollison and Willett, 1982), where one partner's profits are acquired only at the price of dispossessing the other. Conquest is represented by the search for new markets, and its finality is to preserve profit margins. This is a kind of imperialism, "the supreme phase of capitalism" (Lenin). In this perspective, an omnipresent power can only hierarchize the interacting forces. However, to this principle of the classic school, of which Clausewitz remains the most important figure, can be added the hope for a possible end result, which is the idea of revolution. The main assumptions of this school of thought are integrated into the theories of dependence, which systematize the irreducible dissymetry between the centers of exchange and the perverse consequences of the global division of labour. The international sphere, then, merely enlarges the civil society; when it does not replace it, it reproduces all its fundamental contradictions, notably the proletarianization of the Third World and the concentration of wealth in the West. This is no longer a mere juxtaposition of political entities, but a planetary political system (Sfia, 1971). These theories associate the ideas of Lenin, Clausewitz and Samir Amin. Despite their subtle differences on the they refer to a theme of rational reconciliation. Dependence could only become interdependence through partaking in the universal transparency of modern values. These values imply that "having as much as the next man" can be the foundation from which new social solidarities may spring forth. Dependence is a system which converges with interdependence to result in an apotheosis of a new brotherhood which has yet to be built. Among the theories of dependence and interdependence, those of scientism, ethnocentrism and mechanism are all equally appropriate.

8 Zygmunt Bauman (1989, p. 152), writes: "... the models of postmodernity, unlike the models of modernity, cannot be grounded in the realities of the nation-state".

9 Bauman (1990), writes: "There are now, therefore, much fewer centrifugal forces which once weakened ethnic integrity. There is, instead of a powerful demand for pronounced, through symbolic rather than institutionalized, ethnic distinctiveness."

10 See note 9.

References

Alker, H., Bloomfield, L.P., Choucri, N. (1974) Analysing Global Interdependence, 4 Vols, Cambridge, Mass., Center for International Studies, M.I.T., Vol. 1., Analytical Perspectives and Policy Implications.

Archer, M.S. (1990) Theory, Culture and Post-Industrial Society, in Featherstone, M. (ed.), Global Culture: Nationalism, Globalization and Modernity, London, Sage Publications.

Arnason, J.P. (1990) Nationalism, Globalization and Modernity, in Global culture: Nationalism, Globalization and Modernity, London, Sage Publications.

Baldwin, D.A. (1980) Interdependence and Power: A Conceptual Analysis in International Organization, Vol. 34, No. 4.

Bauman, Z.(1990) Modernity and Ambivalence, in Featherstone, M. (ed.), Global culture: Nationalism, Globalization and Modernity, London, Sage Publications.

Bauman, Z. (1989) Sociological Responses to Postmodernity, in Mongardini, C. and Maniscalco, M.L. (ed.), Modernismo e Postmodernismo, Roma, Bulzoni Editore.

Blumenberg, H. (1983) The Legitimacy of the Modern Age, Cambridge, Mass.

Boulding, K.E. (1959) National Images and International Systems, Journal of Conflict Resolution, No. 3.

Brown, S. (1973) The Changing Essence of Power, Foreign Affairs, January 11.

Brzezinski, Z. (1969) Between Two Ages: America's Role in the Technetronic Era, New York, The Viking Press.

Bull, H. (1977) The Anarchical Society: A Study of Order, World Politics, London, Macmillan.

Bull, H. (1981) Hobbes and the International Anarchy, Social Research, Vol.48, No. 4.

Bull, H. (1979) The State's Positive Role in World Affairs, Daedalus, 108.

Burton, J.W. (1972) World Society, Cambridge, Cambridge University Press.

Burton, J.W. (1984) Global Conflict: The Domestic Sources of International Crisis, Brighton, Weatsheaf.

Caporaso, J.A. (1978) Dependence, Dependency, and Power in the Global System: A Structural and Behavioral Analysis, International Organization, Vol. 32, No. 1, Winter.

Caporaso, J.A. (1989) Introduction: The State in Comparative and International Perspectives, in Caporaso, J.A. (ed.), The Elusive State: International and Comparative Perspectives, Newbury Park, Sage Publications.
Cohen, R. (1981) International Politics: The Rules of the Games, London, Longman.
Cooper, R. (1968) The Economics of Interdependence, New York, McGraw-Hill.
Cooper, R. (1972) Economic Interdependence and Foreign Policy in the Seventies, World Politics, No. 24, January.
Debray, R. (1986) Les empires contre l'Europe, Paris, Gallimard.
Delaisi, F. (1925) Political Myths and Economic Realities, London, Noel Douglas.
Deutsch, K.W. and Eckestein, A. (1961) National Industrialization and the Declining Share of the International Economic Sector, 1890-1959, World Politics, No. 13, January.
Deutsch, K. (1953) Nationalism and Social Communications, Cambridge, MIT Press.
Duchacek, I.D. (1986) The Territorial Dimension of Politics: Within, Among, and Across Nations, Boulder, Westview Press.
Duchene, F., Mushakoji, K. and Owen, H.B. (1974) The Crisis of International Cooperation, The Triangle Papers, No. 2.
Dupuy, J.R. (1989) La clôture du systme international: la Cit terrestre, Paris, Presses Universitaires de France.
Duvall, R.D. (1987) Dependence and Dependencia Theory: Notes Toward Precision of Concept and Argument, International Organization, Vol. 32, No. 1.
Feather, F. (1980) Through the '80s: Thinking Globally, Acting Locally, Feather,F.(ed.), Washington, World Future Society.
Featherstone, M. (1990) Global Culture: An Introduction, in Global culture: Nationalism, Globalization and Modernity, London, Sage Publications.
Fery, L. and Renaut,A. (1938) Penser les droits de l'homme, Esprit, March.
Gasiorowski, M. J. (1985) The Structure of Third World Economic Interdependence, International Organization, Vol. 39, No. 2.
Haas, E. (1975) Is There A Hole in the Whole? Knowledge, Technology, Interdependence, and the Construction of International Regimes, International Organization, Vol. 29, No.3.
Haass, R. (1979) The Primacy of the State...or Revising the Revisionnists, Daedalus, 108.
Haksel, B. G. (1980) Access to Society: A Neglected Dimension of Power, International Organization, Vol. 34, No. 1.
Hertz, J. (1968) The Territorial State Revisited: Reflections on the Future of the Nations State, Polity, No. 1, Vol. 1.
Holst, K.J. The Necrologists of International Relations Theory, Mimeo, Van-couver, British Columbia University, (Cited by Caporaso, 1989).
Inkeles, A. (1975) The Emerging Social Structure of the World, World Politics, Vol. 27.
Hoffmann, S. (1975) Notes on the Elusiveness of Power, International Journal, Spring.
Keohane, R.O. and Nye, J.S. (1972) Transnational Relations and World Politics, Cambridge, Harvard University Press.
Keohane, R.O. and Nye, J.S. (1973) World Politics and the International Economic System, in Bergstein, F.C. (ed.), Future of the International Economic Order: An Agenda for Research, Lexington Mass., Lexington Books.
Keohane, R.O. (1977) Power and Interdependence: World Politics in Transition, Boston, Little.
Krasner, S.D. (1989) Sovereignty: An Institutional Perspective, in Caporaso, J.A. (ed.), The Elusive State: International and Comparative Perspectives, Newbury Park, Sage Publication.
Kratochwill, F. (1981) The Human Conception of International Relations, World Order Studies Program, Occasional Paper No. 9, Princeton, Princeton Center of International Studies.
Lall, S. (1975) Is 'Dependence' a Useful Concept in Analysing Underdevelopment?, World Development, No. 3, November.
Lapy, J. (1978) Quand l'interdépendance absolue a fait son temps, Réalités, No. 385.
Larochelle, G. (1990) L'imaginaire technocratique, Montréal, Les éditions du Boréal, 440 pages.
Laurent, P. (1980) Gérer l'interdépendance, Projet, No. 146.
Lechneer, F.J. (1984) Ethnicity and Revitalization in the Modern World System, Sociological Focus, No. 17.
Marx, K. (1966) Le manifeste du parti communiste, Paris, Union générale d'eitions.

Mlinar, Z. (1990) Territorial Identities: Between Individualism and Globalization, in Antoni Kuklinski (ed.) Globality versus Locality, Warsaw, University of Warsaw.
Morse, E. (1972) Transnational Economic Processes, in Keohane R.O. and. Nye J.S. Transnationalism in World Politics, Cambridge, Mass.
Nardin, T. L.(1983) Morality, and the Relations of States, Princeton, NJ, Princeton University Press.
Navari, C. (1982) Hobbes and the 'Hobbesian Tradition' in International Thought, Millenium, Journal of International Studies, Vol. 11, No. 3.
Nye, J. S. (1967) Independence and Interdependence, Foreign Policy, No. 22.
Ratzel, F. (1987) La geographie politique: les concepts fondamentaux, Paris, Fayard, 220 pages.
Robertson, R. (1990) Mapping the Global Condition: Globalization as the Central Concept, in Featherstone, M. (ed.), Nationalism, Globalization and Modernity, London, Sage Publications.
Rock, V. (1964) A Strategy of Interdependence, New York.
Rosecrance, R., Alexandroff, A., Koehler, W., Kroll, J., Laqueur, S., and Stocker J. (1977) Whither Interdependence?, International Organization, Vol. 32, No. 2.
Rosecrance, R. and Stein, A. (1973) Interdependence: Myth or Reality?, World Politics, Vol. 26, No. 1.
Sack, R.D. (1986) Human Territoriality, Cambridge, Cambridge University Press.
Sfia, M. Salah (1971) Notes pour une analyse du système mondial, Sociologie et Sociétés, Vol. 3, No. 2.
Skolnikoff, E. B. (1972) The International Imperatives of Technology, Berkeley, Institute of International Studies, no. 16.
Smith, A.D. (1981) The Ethnic Revival, New York, Cambridge University Press.
Stojanovic, R. (1978) L'interdépendance dans les relations internationales, Revue internationales des sciences sociales, Vol. XXX, No. 2.
Tollison, R.D., and Willett, T. D. (1982) Power, Politics, and Prosperity: Alternative Views of Economic Interdependence, The Annals of the American Academy of Political and Social Science, 460.
Vernon, R. (1971) Sovereignty at Bay: The Multinational Spread of U.S. Enterprises, New York, Basic Books.
Vincent, R.J. (1983) Change and International Relations, Review of International Studies, Vol. 9, No. 1.
Walker, R.B.J. (1984) Culture, Ideology, and World Order, Boulder, Westview Press.
Walker, R.B.J. (1987) Realism, Change, and International Political Theory, International Studies Quarterly, Vol. 31.
Wallerstein, I. (1987) World-System Analysis, in Giddens, A. and Turner, J. (eds), Social Theory Today, Oxford, Polity Press.
Waltz, K.N. (1970) The Myth of National Interdependence, in Kindleberger, C.P. (ed.), The International Corporation, The MIT Press, Cambridge, Mass..
Whitman, M.V. (1979) Reflections of Interdependence: Issues for Economic Theory and U.S. Policy, Pittsburg, University of Pittsburg Press.
Wolfers, A. (1962) The Actors in World Politics in Discord and Collaboration, Baltimore, Maryland.
Young, O.R. (1969) Interdependence in World Politics, International Journal, Vol. 24.

10 Epilogue

This volume was intended to be a contribution towards the very first attempts at inclusive coverage and interpretation of changes at all levels of territorial social organization and towards the interpretation of the cross-level dynamics of its transformation (restructuring) at the threshold of postmodernity.

The contributors to this volume are less oriented towards the conventional cores of some social science disciplines and more towards the crossing of their boundaries and sharing their separately accumulated knowledge and experience. Rather than following the mainstream, they are reaching towards a (re)combination of the findings from the established fields. Thus the chances for what Dogan and Pahre (1990) call "innovation at the intersections of social sciences" should be increased.

The common denominator of all of the contributions is that they do not view the process of globalization on its own, i.e., from a single, linear perspective. Instead, they attempt to expose the dynamics of the interplay of expanding interdependence in space on the one hand and of the strivings towards greater autonomy and the assertion (or preservation) of distinctive identity within the narrower territorial framework, on the other.

The social sciences were unprepared for coping with the complexity of the present changes in territorial social organization, for several reasons:

1) Their concepts, formed at a time of nation building, are not suitable for the present reality of higher individuation and globalization.
2) A unidirectional understanding of trends of change from small to large territorial systems did not provide an adequate starting point for a theoretical interpretation of the contradictory processes of socio-spatial restructuring.
3) The attention focused on merely a single level of territorial organization, and left aside the cross-level dynamics which is crucial in understanding the process of globalization and the transformation of territorial identities.
4) The separation of structuralist and behaviouralist approaches was not conducive to focusing on the changing relationships between the actors and their expanding social context.

5) The inertia of the sectorial conceptualization of social life in territorial communities - related to issue areas such as economy, culture, politics - was another inhibitive factor restraining sensitivity towards increasing autonomy (differentiation) and global integration.

Since globalization implies the increasing inclusiveness of diversity, it thus at the same time imposes a higher level of generalization and a need for the formulation of viable, testable and more encompassing theories. This is hard to achieve in an area - see Smith et al. (1989) for world politics - "in which there is considerable *achievement* to produce an *ordered and coherent description of events* .." (italics by Z.M.). Still it is hoped that by the paradigm of the unity of opposites of individuation and globalization (or by other similar conceptualizations found in this book) we make a step forward beyond such a state of affairs.

By rejecting the unidirectional and unilinear interpretation of development we extend the *sensitivity* both toward increasing diversification (subsystems' autonomy) within the territorial units and for the extension of interdependencies across these units. Thus, at the same time we move beyond the inertia of the hardened perceptual screen which was formed at the time of "nation-formation". This inertia still conditions a certain *cognitive time lag* which can be seen e.g. as a discrepancy between the globalization of society and the globalization (or fragmentation) of social science.

One of the outstanding questions we addressed was: When does the assertion of an identity at one level imply the erosion of identity at another (higher or lower) level of territorial social organization? Two (extreme) positions are quite common, i.e.:
a) that one does not interfere with the other, they co-exist in a complementary way;
b) they are related in the sense of a zero-sum game.

While our interpretation indicates that they are interrelated, this does not imply a constant relationship; rather it is changing from a zero-sum type of exclusivity to one of permeation.

The present (inherited) territorial identities were established on the basis of more restricted accessibility in space (higher time-cost distances) and thus it cannot be assumed that they could be preserved without a thorough transformation in the context of "global flows". Even when they are protected by (newly established) nation-states - as in the case of several small nations in Europe - this represents more a form of short-term "solution" rather than a long-term assurance of their preservation in the presently known form.

While on the one hand territorial (and particularly national) identities, e.g. in Western Europe, are *more than ever protected* against territorial expansionism, they are at the same time *more than ever threatened* in terms of transnational economic, political and cultural permeation. The chances are therefore declining that they could survive as relatively closed territorial systems (identities as "islands" or "billiard balls"). Rather it can be expected that (considering both their population as well as the natural and constructed environment) they will become internally increasingly heterogeneous. On the basis of the wider accessibility of the components of the variety of the world, it can be expected that both individuals as well as their flexible associations and their environments will become increasingly diversified.

Both individuation and globalization are changing the role of the three general categories of human association, i.e. territoriality, consanguinity and interest. Since the first two assume the role of ascribed characteristics of a particularist nature, they tend to collide both with the tendency toward the uniqueness of actors as well as with the universality of world standards.

The increasing flexibility which is one of the main features of postmodernity provides the new context within which the convergence between the *actors* and *structures* takes place. With the process of individuation, individuals and groups acquire the possibility to choose among the alternatives and selectively to associate with others, each of them thus creating their unique network in the global context. Instead of automatic acceptance of the predefined structure, the actors are the ones who choose from the increasing diversity in time (the elements of the cultural heritage) and space (from various territorially distinctive cultures). A higher level of individuation implies both that the actors are less predetermined by their immediate environment, and that their actions are also less predictable on the basis of the knowledge of such an environment.

In approaching our subject - at the threshold of post-modernity - we observe both the tendency toward world homogenization of increasingly diversified segments as well as resegregation of diversified "minority" cultures. With the time-space compression there is increasing competition among the particularities for the status of universality. Globality (universality) is achieved either: a) on the basis of the expanding domination of a given particularity at the expense of others, or b) on the basis of the consensus and common acceptance of the global standards.

We do not assume some constant *basic unit* of society (be it the family, local community, region, nation-state or individual); rather we observe the processes of socio-spatial restructuring which provides the broader context of understanding of the changing role of territorial and non-territorial actors.

The long-term perspective could be traced as a *convergence* of locality and globality. This is congruent with the shift from the "space of places" to the "space of flows" as well as with the concept of "time-space compression". In these terms the vision of the future appears as approaching the stage when all the diversity of the world could be found or be accessible in each of the "territorial" units and when the components of a given unit are dispersed all over the world. While this is still primarily a model, it does at the same time help to understand many empirical observations in the context of the emerging "information society".

Distinctive territorial cultural heritage can either: a) become much more widely shared (globalized), b) represent one of the components in the (re)construction of a particular environment, c) be preserved as an item of folklorization and museumization, or d) completely wither away.

Instead of assuming *a priori* that preservation of the given territorial identities is a question of will , of policy and of the protective mechanisms, it seems more adequate to *study to what extent* a certain commitment (such as that of the European

Community to protect the diversity of national and regional cultures in Europe) can be implemented within the context of long-term developmental logic which may not be congruent with such a commitment.

The interpretation of the subject of this book touches upon many important social values and policy issues. These values may even prevent the unrestrained and unbiased interpretation of reality. There seems to be a kind of ungrounded optimism in the important international fora nominally committed to the preservation of territorial cultural diversity. There is a tendency to avoid the recognition of the problem of incongruence between global integration and preservation of territorial diversity. A declaration of values ("we must preserve diversity", "diversity as a richness of Europe" etc.) often acts as a substitute for the analysis of the actual changes.

The claims towards possessing the right to be different (e.g. France in relationship to the encroaching Americanization of Europe) tend to be directed toward a "higher level" of territorial organization, while the opposite tendencies tend to prevail in the relationship toward the subsystems at the (first) lower level.

Protective mechanisms, particularly at the level of the nation-state, tend to be established (instituted) in many issue areas: they are part of the economic protectionism, of immigration policy, of communication policy, language policy, defence policy, cultural policy, environmental protection etc. However their common characteristic is that they can be effective more as short-term measures rather than as providers of any long-term solution. In terms of the prospect of a "Europe without borders" their restrictive role will be increasingly limited (e.g. the legal restrictions preventing foreigners to own land - as they exist in some European countries - are incompatible with their aspiration to become or to remain members of the European Community).

The strategy of dissociation (de-linking) - as the main policy outcome of the dependency theory - was not realizable in terms of the relationships of the Third World countries (periphery) to the world core. Analogously, it is hard to expect that dissociation could represent an effective defence-mechanism which might provide long-term protection for the inherited territorial identities (diversity) in the context of a higher level of global integration, e.g. in Europe or North America.

It is very common to hear of the commitment to the principle of "unity in diversity". However such a formulation does not specify the unit of observation. Thus it can be understood as the incorporation (in the sense of preservation) of different territorial (cultural) systems in their integrity or it may only concern particular components of these systems.

We cannot expect to have only one of the mutually interdependent processes: global integration or socio-spatial differentiation (individuation). Thus it is not realistic to pretend to promote integration (as in Europe) without differentiation of previously relatively closed "territorial communities". Territorial dissociation could not provide long-term protective mechanisms for ethnic, cultural and political identities to survive in the context of "global civilization" without a radical transformation.

Although territorial dissociation may provide short-term protective mechanisms for the survival of ethnic, cultural and political identities, in the long-term perspective a radical transformation (including de-territorialization) will be unavoidable.

References

Dogan, M. and Pahre, R. (1990) Creative Marginality: Innovation at the Intersections of Social Sciences, Boulder, Westview Press.

Smith, M., Little, R. and Shackleton, M. (eds.), (1989) Perspectives on World Politics, London, Routledge.

Notes on contributors

Chadwick F. Alger is Mershon Professor of Political Science and Public Policy, Ohio State University. He has published widely on decision-making, communication and socialization in The United Nations and on the participation of local people in world affairs. He is co-editor of A Just Peace through Transformation: Cultural, Economic and Political Foundations for Change, 1988 and of Conflict and Crisis of International Order: New Tasks for Peace Research, 1985. He is past president of the International Studies Association (1978-79) and former Secretary General of the International Peace Research Association (1982-86).

R.B.A. DiMuccio is a Ph. D. candidate in the School of International Relations of the University of Southern California. He specialises in international relations theory and the political philosophy of international relations. His dissertation focuses on "The Structure of Conflict: Interdependence and Great Power War in the Modern States System".

Gilbert Larochelle is associate professor of political science at the University of Quebec at Chicoutimi in Canada. He has published many articles which focus on the concurrent trends of technological globalization and emerging regional identities against the backdrop of apparently withering national boundaries. He has also published in French a book entitled L'imaginaire technocratique (Montréal, 1990).

Zdravko Mlinar is professor of sociology at the University of Ljubljana, Slovenia. He was previously Dean of the Faculty for Sociology, Political Science and Journalism. Since 1981, a member of the Slovene Academy of Sciences and Arts. Served as President of the Research Committee for Social Ecology of the International Sociological Association. Publications include : "Contradictions of Social Development", 1986, "Humanization of the City", 1983, both of which won awards, "Developmental Logic of Social Systems (co-author with H. Teune), 1978, Social Ecology of Change (co-author), 1978, "Sociology of the Local Communities", 1974.

Bernard Poche, Docteur-és-Lettres, is a researcher at the French National Centre for Scientific Research (C.N.R.S.), section of Sociology, and senior lecturer at the University of Grenoble (France). Since 1985 has been a member of the editorial committee of the review "Espaces et Sociétés". Among his publications are "France, a multilingual country" (co-author), 1987; "Lyon, a self-description" (Lyon tel qu'il s'écrit), 1990; "Public authorities and Arts" (Pouvoirs publics et création, co-author), 1991.

James N. Rosenau is the Director of the Institute for Transnational Studies at the University of Southern California as well as Professor of Political Science and International Relations. He is a past President of the International Studies Association and has also been a member of the faculties of Rutgers - the State University of New Jersey and Ohio State University. His research has focused on the analysis of foreign policy, global interdependence, and political adaptation. His most recent publications include Turbulence in World Politics: A Theory of Change and Continuity (1990), co-authorship of American Leadership in World Affairs: Vietnam and the Breakdown of Consensus (1984), and co-editorship of Journeys Through World Politics: Autobiographical Reflections of Thirty-four Academic Travellers (1989), Global Changes and Theoretical Challenges: Approaches to World Politics for the 1990s (1989), and New Directions in the Study of Foreign Policy (1987).

Raimondo Strassoldo graduated in political science at the university of Trieste, 1967, and studied urban and rural sociology at the University of Trento. He has taught this discipline at the Universities of Trieste, Milan, Udine and presently Palermo. He has also been director of the Institute of International Sociology, Gorizia, 1972-1978. His research interests have included human ecology, regional planning, the sociology of disasters, and the sociology of international and inter-ethnic relations. His books include: "Sviluppo regionale e difesa nazionale", 1972, "Sistema e ambiente", 1977, "Temi di sociologia delle relazioni internazionali", 1979.

Henry Teune has been a professor of political science at the University of Pennsylvania since 1961. His co-authored books include The Integration of Political Communities, The Logic of Comparative Social Inquiry, Values and the Active Community and Developmental Logic of Social Systems. For the past five years he has chaired a faculty seminar on human nature. Currently he is directing a research programme on "The New Democracy and Local Governance", a comparative study of democratic values and change in countries of western and eastern Europe, Asia and the United States.

Colin H. Williams is Professor of Geography at University of Staffordshire, Stoke on Trent, U.K. He has held visiting appointments as a Fulbright Scholar at Pennsylvania State University and as a Swedish Institute Scholar at the University of Lund. He is a committee member of the Research Committee for Social Ecology of the International Sociological Association. Among his edited or authored publications are: "National Separatism" 1981, "Language in Geographic Context" 1988, "Community Conflict, Partition and Nationalism" 1989 (co-edited with E. Kofman), "Linguistic Minorities, Society and Territory" 1991. His latest book "Called Unto Liberty" is scheduled for publication in 1992.